Company Financial Reporting

An Introduction for Non-accountants

JOHN STITTLE

First published 1997

2 4 6 8 10 9 7 5 3 1

Blackwell Publishers Ltd
108 Cowley Road
Oxford OX4 1JF
UK

Blackwell Publishers Inc.
350 Main Street
Malden, Massachusetts 02148
USA

British Library Cataloguing in Publication Data

A CIP catalogue record for this book is available from the British Library.

Library of Congress Cataloging in Publication Data

Stittle, John.
    Company financial reporting: an introduction for non-accountants / John Stittle.
      p.   cm.
    Includes index.
    ISBN 0-631-20166-1 (alk. paper)
    1. Financial statements. 2. Corporation reports. 3. Financial statements – United States.
I. Title.
    HF5681.B2S69 1997
    658.15'12 – dc21

                                   97–10148
                                   CIP

ISBN 0-631-201661

Commissioning Editor: Tim Goodfellow
Desk Editor: Linda Auld
Production Controller: Lisa Parker

Typeset in 10 on 12 pt Optima by Best-set Typesetter Ltd., Hong Kong
Printed in Great Britain by TJ International, Padstow, Cornwall

This book is printed on acid-free paper

99

Contents

Preface

In recent years, there have been many books written on the topic of company financial reporting. Unfortunately, most of these books have tended to be written and orientated towards the specific needs of accountants and students aiming to qualify as accountants. Many of these books are highly technical, concentrate too heavily on detailed technical matters, and are generally incomprehensible to those students who are not intending to become accountants.

This book, Company Financial Reporting: an introduction for non-accountants, examines company financial reporting from the perspective of the 'generalist'. There are many students of company financial reporting who wish to study accounting courses and modules as a component part of their overall course. These interested parties include students of business studies, management, social science, humanities, science, engineering, technology and law. Managers, instructors and other professionals wishing to obtain an introductory understanding will also find the text useful.

The book concentrates on a conceptual understanding of the crucial aspects of company reporting. Whilst gradually leading the reader through the key aspects of company reporting, the book explores developments in the subject from both a UK and international perspective. Particular emphasis is placed upon interpretation and analysis of financial statements.

The reader is encouraged not to accept the financial statements at face value, but to make a critical examination of the accounts and to draw appropriate inferences and conclusions. The book makes no apology for not exploring many of the mechanics of company accounts production – there is no need – accountants will perform most of the detailed mechanistic preparations. But the non-accountant does need to be able to interpret and comment upon the results. The major purpose of this book is to assist the reader to understand company reporting in a concise, user-friendly and professional way. Although the size of the book necessarily means that not all the aspects of company reporting can be covered in detail, it nevertheless provides a solid foundation on which students can success-fully build and enhance their studies.

The book is particularly aimed at students approaching this topic for the first time. It will be especially useful for students on introductory degree level courses, HND, DMS, general introductory company reporting courses and anyone inter-ested in pursuing this topic.

Acknowledgements

The following companies have kindly agreed to the use of extracts from their Annual Report and Accounts:

Bass plc
BOC Group plc
British Telecommunications plc
Burton Group plc
Cable and Wireless plc
Whitbread plc

Additionally, grateful acknowledgement is made to the Accounting Standards Board for allowing the use of extracts of FRS 1 (revised), *Cash Flow Statements*.

APPRECIATION

Many thanks to Marian Belkaid, Laura Kyffin and Gill Maggs for their unfailing efforts in bringing a degree of order to my mountains of paper.

Also thanks to my colleagues who suggested constructive changes and improvements to the drafts and to Tim Goodfellow and Lisa Parker of Blackwell Publishers for their assistance.

Lastly, and by no means least, grateful appreciation is expressed to Linda Auld who so patiently and thoroughly checked my manuscripts.

Any errors are, of course, entirely mine.

John Stittle
Anglia University
Chelmsford
1997

1 | Introduction

This chapter examines:

- the nature of corporate financial reporting;
- regulatory framework accounting concepts.

Company financial reporting is largely concerned with communication and accountability. Over the last few decades there has been an enormous growth in the perceived needs of groups that have an interest (in varying degrees) in the content of company reports. This growing interest has been exceeded only by the growth and the complexity of business activities and, in particular, developments in the nature and diversity of business organizations.

To reflect and report upon the activities of these business organizations, the accounting requirements and reporting responsibilities have grown enormously. In other words, there is a need to develop the communicative purpose of limited companies. There is a need to report periodically, not only to the owners of the business, (the shareholders) but also to other interested parties. Furthermore, this process of communication is an integral part of achieving and enhancing the process of accountability. The managers of business enterprises must account to the owners for the performance of the assets that they hold on behalf of (and in stewardship for) the shareholders.

The principle means by which this communication and accountability process is achieved in most companies is by the publication of an annual report and accounts – (the so-called 'financial statements').

FORMS OF BUSINESS ENTITIES

Under English legislation, there are essentially three fundamental forms by which a business can be conducted: as a sole trader, a partnership or as a limited company. A sole trader is an individual who is conducting a business in his/her own name. In the eyes of the law, a distinction is drawn between the individual as a business person and the individual as a private member of society. If a sole trader incurs debts in his/her business capacity that cannot be satisfied, the creditors can seek legal redress against the sole trader as a private individual. In other words, the law regards unpaid debts of the business as being debts of the individual.

A partnership consists of two or more individuals who join together in a business sense and agree to share the profits and losses of their business. In many ways, a partnership has a similar legal position to that of a sole trader. If a partnership cannot meet its business legal obligations and debts, then the partners (in a similar manner to that of a sole trader) will be liable to meet the partnership debts in a personal capacity. If one particular partner cannot meet his/her own share of the losses then the other remaining partners may become liable for the defaulting partner's share of the debts.

In the UK, the process of forming a limited company will radically alter the legal position. In the UK, a common method of conducting business is through the medium of a limited company.

A number of limited companies are designated as *public limited companies* and show the designation *plc* after their title. Whereas a (private) limited company usually has only a few shareholders, a public limited company may have massive numbers comprising of individual shareholders and financial institutions. Any limited company that is not designated as a plc is deemed to be a private company.

In a private limited company the shareholders may often be actively involved in the management of the company. In a public limited company (by virtue of the size of its shareholding base) involvement (at management level) by individual shareholders is usually non-existent.

As far as the share capital of a private limited company is concerned, there is normally no active market in the shares. These companies are not allowed to issue shares to the public and shares can only be bought or sold on a personal basis. On the other hand, shares in a public company can be freely offered for sale to the general public.

A company that is designated as a public limited company must have at least a minimum issued share capital of £50,000. The company's Memorandum of Association must also specify that it is a public limited company and the company must have at least 25 per cent of its share capital paid-up (Companies Act 1985, sec 1, 11 and 25). It must be appreciated that although a company is a public company, its shares may not necessarily be listed (or quoted) on a Stock Exchange. (However, to be listed on the London Stock Exchange, a company must be a public limited company.) To be classified as a 'listed company', for example on the London Stock Exchange, companies must fulfil additional disclosure and accounting requirements over and above the legal and accounting regulations.

Because the status of a limited company allows considerable legal privileges, the reporting requirements have become heavily regulated by the legal and accounting processes. In the eyes of the law, a limited company has a completely separate identity from that of its owners. The business can trade, incur debts, buy and sell assets, and employ workers in its own legal name. If the company cannot pay its debts, the principle of incorporation (i.e. the formation of a legally constituted limited company) means, that in most circumstances, the investors (shareholders) in the company cannot be held personally responsible for their business's debts and liabilities. If a company cannot meet its liabilities then the maximum amount an investor can forfeit is the amount of their original investment in the firm's share capital. The formation of a limited company will bring down 'a veil of incorporation' that completely separates the responsibilities of the investors from that of the company itself.

Since shareholders in limited companies can gain legal protection from the business debts and responsibilities, the benefits derived from incorporation are regarded as a considerable privilege in English Law. Accordingly, in return for being granted these legal advantages and privileges, limited companies must grant a major concession in return. Unless a business meets the exemption criteria by being classified small or medium, all limited companies must file their own financial statements with the Registrar of Companies at Companies House. The filing of accounts with the Registrar allows any creditor, supplier, potential investor or indeed, any member of the public, to access the information contained in the financial statements.

This public disclosure process contrasts with sole traders and partnerships, who merely have to produce accounts to satisfy the requirements of Governmental taxation authorities. Whereas information concerning a sole trader's and partnership accounts will remain totally confidential to the business's owners and the taxation authorities, the accounts of a limited company will be open to public inspection and scrutiny.

STEWARDSHIP AND ACCOUNTABILITY

In public limited companies especially, there is a clear distinction between the owners (shareholders) and the control (the management) of the entity. Shareholders delegate the operations and management of their company to their elected representatives – the directors. These directors are deemed to hold and utilize the company's assets in stewardship for or on behalf of the shareholders. In many large companies – perhaps with many hundreds of thousands of shareholders – the management of the company may be conducted by only 12–15 directors. In effect the directors are holding the assets in trust or on behalf of the many shareholders. At the year-end, the directors need to account for the handling of the assets, in other words – to explain their stewardship.

This formal process of explaining this stewardship is fundamental in ensuring the accountability of the directors. The major means by which this process is achieved is by the publication of the company's annual report and accounts. Legally, every shareholder and debenture holder must be sent a copy of the financial statements every year. In addition, a copy must be placed annually on record at Companies House. In theory, these financial statements contain significant financial information and also form a important line of communication between directors and shareholders. As a result, the financial statements must comply with very strict and detailed legal and accounting rules. To ensure that the directors actually conform to these comprehensive provisions, the financial statements will need to be audited by independent accountants. But it is not just the legal categories of shareholders and debenture holders that are interested in the financial statements. There are a number of other interested parties – termed *user-groups* – who may wish to have access to all or some of the information contained within the financial statements.

USER-GROUPS

One of the first investigations into who were the user-groups of corporate reports was initiated by the accountancy bodies in 1975. Although it was several decades ago, the *Corporate Report* identified the major user-groups and their respective needs, and the groupings it identified are still valid and form a useful classification.

The *Corporate Report* viewed the fundamental objective of corporate reports as being 'to communicate economic information about the resources and performance of the reporting entity to those having reasonable rights to such information' (para 3.2). The user-groups are identified as:

1   Equity investor group – which includes existing and potential shareholders.
2   Loan creditor group – includes existing and potential holders of debentures and loan stock.
3   Employee group – including existing, potential and past employees.
4   Analyst-adviser group – including financial analysts and journalists, economists, researchers, stockbrokers and other providers of advisory services.
5   Business contact group – including customers, trade creditors and suppliers, competitors and those interested in acquisitions and mergers.
6   The government – including the tax authorities, governmental supervisory agencies and local authorities.
7   The public – including tax payers, consumers, community and special interest and pressure groups.

STATEMENT OF PRINCIPLES

A recently issued exposure draft from the Accounting Standards Board, the *Statement of Principles*, extends the objectives of financial statements to include the assessment of the stewardship of the management. This conceptual exposition of accounting defines the objective of financial statements as:

to provide information about the financial position, performance and financial adaptability of an enterprises that is useful to a wide range of users for assessing the stewardship of management and for making economic decisions. (Ch 1, para 1.1.)

The Statement notes that financial statements 'that meet the needs of providers of risk capital to the enterprise will also meet most of the needs of other users that financial statements can satisfy'.

The Statement identifies the users to be:

1   employees;
2   lenders;
3   suppliers and other creditors;
4   customers;
5   government and their agencies;
6   the Public.

The Statement also expounds the qualitative characteristics of financial statements. It identifies the primary qualitative characteristics that relate to content (relevance and reliability) and those characteristics that relate to presentation (comparability and understandably).

The qualitative characteristics are defined as the characteristics that 'make the information provided in financial statements useful to users for assessing the financial position, performance and financial adaptability of an enterprise'.

In defining relevance the Statement requires information to have 'the ability to influence users by helping them evaluate past, present or future events or confirming or correcting their past evaluations'.

Additionally, to be useful, information must also be reliable. The Statement defines information as being reliable 'when it is free from material error and bias and can be depended upon by users to represent faithfully what it either purports to represent or could reasonably be expected to represent'.

The Statement stresses that financial statements should be 'readily understandable by users' (para 2.30). The Statement notes that 'an important factor in the understanding of financial information is the manner in which the information is presented.' Although financial statements cannot meet all the needs of all users, the Statement notes that financial information is prepared on the assumption that users have 'a reasonable knowledge of business and economic activities and accounting and a willingness to study the information with reasonable diligence'. Information about complex matters should be included 'because of its relevance to the economic decision making needs of users'.

ACCOUNTING CONCEPTS

A company's financial statements are drafted in accordance with four basic accounting concepts. SSAP 2, *Disclosure of Accounting Policies*, identifies these four key concepts as:

Going concern

The going concern concept is defined in SSAP 2 as the assumption that the company 'will continue in operational existence for the foreseeable future, ... there is no intention or necessity to liquidate or curtail significantly the scale of operations' (SSAP 2, para 14a). In practice, this assumption would mean, for example that the assets in the balance sheet would not be shown at a 'forced sale' value which might be considerably less than the assets' current value.

Accruals (or matching)

The accruals concept implies that 'revenue and costs are accrued (that is, recognised as they are earned or incurred, not as the money is received or paid), matched with one another ... and dealt with in the profit and loss account of the period to which they relate' (para 14b).

Consistency

The consistency concept means that there should be 'consistency of accounting treatment of like items within each accounting period and from one period to the next' (para 14c).

Conservatism

The concept of prudence (or conservatism) means that 'revenue and profits are not anticipated, but are recognised by inclusion in the profit and loss account only when realised ... and provision is made for all known liabilities (expenses and losses) whether the amount of these is known with certainty or is a best estimate in the light of the information available' (para 14d).

If accounts are prepared on the basis of assumptions which differ in material aspects from any of those listed above, the facts should be explained. In the absence of a clear statement to the contrary, there is a presumption that the four fundamental concepts have been observed.

SSAP 2 also requires that the accounting policies adopted for dealing with items which are judged material or critical in determining the profit or loss for the year and in stating the financial position should be disclosed by way of note to the accounts.

QUESTIONS

1 Identify the three major legal forms of business trading operations.
   What are the main legal and accounting characteristics of each of these forms?

2   Identify any three user-groups.
    Discuss the respective accounting information needs of each of these users.
3   The Statement of Principles notes that financial statements should be relevant
    and reliable.
    What do you understand by these terms?
4   What are the four key accounting concepts?
    Why are they treated with such a high degree of respect?

REFERENCES

Accounting Standards Board, *Statement of Principles Exposure Draft*, London, 1995.
Accounting Standards Committee, *Disclosure of Accounting Policies*, Statement of Stand-
    ard Accounting Practice 2, London, 1971.
Accounting Standards Steering Committee, *The Corporate Report*, London, 1975.

2 | Regulatory Framework of Company Reporting

This chapter examines:

- nature of accounting regulation;
- control and monitoring of company accounting.

All limited companies in the UK operate within an extensive legal and accounting framework. Limited companies are particularly subjected to the accounting requirements of company legislation and the accounting requirements that are established by the ASB. In addition, if a company is listed on a Stock Exchange, there will be other requirements that have to be met.

ACCOUNTING REQUIREMENTS

In addition to legal requirements, there are numerous and significant accounting rules and regulations. These rules have been issued in the form of Statements of Standard Accounting Practice – typically termed Accounting Standards and, more recently these accounting standards are now issued under their revised name – Financial Reporting Standards.

The system of introducing and monitoring accounting standards changed fundamentally in 1991. Prior to this date, accounting standards were designed and issued by the Accounting Standards Committee (ASC). This was a Committee comprising of representatives of the accountancy bodies who could only implement an Accounting Standard if it had unanimous support from all the representative accounting bodies. The organizational and control mechanisms of this Committee were however subject to a number of serious criticisms during the 1980s. In particular, the ASC was regarded as being too slow, too cumbersome and rather unresponsive to pressures to introduce change. In an attempt to issue accounting standards, the ASC was frequently too ready to accept compromise, resulting in some loosely defined and poor quality standards. Subsequent enforcement of these standards was weak and haphazard.

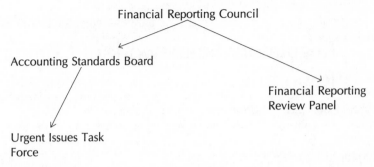

Figure 2.1 Accounting constitution – reporting structure

Political, accounting and auditing pressure led to an impetus for a revision to the standard setting process. In 1987 a working party under the chairmanship of Sir Ron Dearing, and combined with Governmental support, led to the creation of a substantially revised standards setting constitutional process (see fig. 2.1 above).

This Dearing Report led to the formation in 1990, of a completely re-organized framework. The structure was dominated by the creation of two key organizations: the Financial Reporting Council (FRC) and the Accounting Standards Board (ASB). These two bodies were assisted by the creation of two further supplementary authorities: the Financial Reporting Review Panel (FRRP) and the Urgent Issues Task Force (UITF).

FINANCIAL REPORTING COUNCIL

Although the FRC has significant governmental support it is not government controlled. It forms part of the self-regulatory process which is reflected in its constitution, financing and membership. These bodies have a total budget of over £2 million and with a legal contingency budget of a similar amount to enforce legal action against companies not complying with accounting regulations.

The FRC's prime function is to determine policy for the standards setting process. It is comprised of a chairman and three deputy chairman who are appointed jointly by the Secretary of State for Trade and by the Governor of the Bank of England. It is comprised of 30 members who represent the users, preparers and auditors of financial statements. Its members are drawn from senior levels in accountancy, industry, commerce, trade unions, the Law, Universities, the Bank of England and Government.

In particular the FRC was established to implement sound accounting practice, to provide policy guidance and to ensure that the new arrangements were adequately funded.

In particular, the Council has codified its role as being:

1   'to promote good financial reporting . . . and make public reports on reporting standards'. This role will include making 'representations to Government on the current working of legislation and on any desirable development . . .';
2   'to provide guidance to the ASB on work programmes and on broad policy issues';
3   'to verify that the new arrangements are conducted with efficiency and economy, and that they are adequately funded'; (Council Meeting May 1990 (from: State of Financial Reporting FRC Annual Review 1994).)

The FRC's funding arises from three major sources. The funds are raised in approximately equal proportions from the accountancy profession, City financial institutions, and the Government.

ACCOUNTING STANDARDS BOARD

The second organization, the Accounting Standards Board (ASB) which is consti-tutionally a subsidiary of the FRC, is concerned with the responsibility of initiat-ing, designing, revising and withdrawing accounting standards. The ASB has been prescribed as the standard-making body for this purpose and as such its Account-ing Standards are effectively given statutory recognition under sec 256 (1) the Companies Act 1985.

The ASB is a smaller body than its predecessor (the ASC). The ASB is tot-ally independent and does not need approval for its actions from either the FRC or any other source. It will not normally have more than ten members and will have a full time chairman and technical director and be supported in its work by a technical staff of accountants. It can now formally issue accounting standards with a two-thirds majority. Although this organization is under the auspice of the FRC, it nevertheless has independent powers and autonomy to issue pronouncements on the substance of accounting matters.

Since the Companies Act 1985, accounting standards issued by the ASB have been formally recognized by the legislation. Accordingly directors of public companies are now required to disclose in the financial statements if their company has materially departed from the requirements of an accounting stand-ard. The ASB has been subject to criticism. Some argue it has become too prescriptive, its pronouncements are too detailed and it has undermined the professional judgement of many accountants. Critics also argue that greater emphasis should be placed on the importance of user groups and less on the needs of accountants.

URGENT ISSUES TASK FORCE

The ASB has created another committee – the Urgent Issues Task Force (UITF) – whose major purpose is primarily to operate in the form of a rapid response force. Its principal objective is largely to investigate very urgent accounting matters for which no existing accounting standard is applicable or where the interpretation of a standard is in doubt. Urgency of response is a key feature of its activities and, at times, it has issued its pronouncements (or Abstracts) – in a matter of hours rather than weeks. In due course most of the contents of Abstracts may be incorporated into revised and updated Accounting Standards. With a maximum of 15 members on the Committee, an abstract will be issued unless more than two members dissent. The pronouncements of the UITF are regarded as good accounting practice and it is intended that the Abstracts will form part of the body of accounting knowledge that helps form a true and fair view.

FINANCIAL REPORTING REVIEW PANEL (FRRP)

The policing and monitoring of the Accounting Standards is predominantly performed by the FRRP. The Panel is recognised by the Secretary of State for Trade and will concentrate on examining material departures from Accounting Standards that result in a company's financial statements not providing a 'true and fair' view. If necessary, it can seek an order from the High Court which, in turn, may require a company to change its financial statements. In such instances, the cost of any revision of the non-conforming company can be assessed on the directors personally. Although the FRC has no direct or detailed input into the construction of Accounting Standards it nevertheless oversees and supervises the whole standard-setting procedure. The companies which fall within the authority of the Review Panel are: public limited companies; companies within a group headed by a plc; and large private companies (in other words, any company not qualifying as small or medium-sized under sec 247 of 1985 Companies Act). The Panel does not routinely examine all companies' financial statements but concentrates on matters drawn to its attention by users, the press or the accountancy profession. Normally the Panel aims to achieve its objectives by seeking voluntary agreements to any revisions needed to the accounts. Although the Panel has not, as yet, taken a company through all the legal processes, most company directors have regarded an investigation by the Panel as sufficient warning and have revised their financial statements.

LEGAL STATUS

Large limited companies are legally obliged to state in their financial statements whether their accounts have been prepared in accordance with applicable accounting standards. The Companies Act 1989, (modifying schedule 4 of Companies Act 1985) noted:

> It shall be stated whether the accounts have been prepared in accordance with applicable accounting standards and particulars of any material departure from these standards and the reasons for it shall be given.

Although non-compliance with an accounting standard is not directly regarded as a breach of statute as such, it nevertheless has very significant indirect implications. Legal opinion supplied to the ASB has indicated that compliance with accounting standards is necessary to ensure that a company meets its statutory obligations in providing accounting statements that are regarded as being true and fair. The presumption is now that compliance is necessary to show a true and fair view and that departure must be so abnormal that separate explanation will be required. In exceptional circumstances it is justifiable for companies to depart from the provisions of the Companies Act when preparing their accounts. This departure from legislation can only occur when compliance with the legislation would result in a company's accounts being inconsistent with its obligation to ensure its accounts give a true and fair view. This is termed the 'true and fair override principle'. If such a departure does occur, the particulars of any departure, the reasons for it and its effects shall be given in a note to the accounts. Indeed if this override provision is claimed, then UITF Abstract 7 requires additional information to be included in the notes to the financial statements. This will include the need to provide a statement of the treatment required by the Act and a description of, and the reasons for, the treatment being adopted. Additionally an explanation is required as to why the treatment required by the Act would not give a true and fair view. The effect on the financial statements of departure should be quantified.

Under the former ASC, accounting standards were termed Statements of Standard Accounting Practice (SSAPs). When the ASB was formed the existing SSAPs were adopted. Since its formation, when the ASB issues an accounting standard the Accounting Standards are now termed Financial Reporting Standards (FRSs). For the time being the SSAPs will exist side by side with the newly issued FRSs. Over the course of time, the SSAPs should gradually be removed as the ASB withdraws existing SSAPs and replaces them by FRSs.

The ASB also issues Financial Reporting Exposure Drafts (FREDs) which are usually proposed or draft FRSs. Their purpose is to invite comment and provoke discussion on accounting issues that ASB is considering issuing an FRS upon. In addition to FRSs, the ASB issues Statements of Recommended Practices (SORPs). These are Statements that are to provide accounting guidance to specific areas of commerce and industry. Typical areas include the pension industry, charities and oil and gas accounting. These statements are not mandatory but provide good examples of professional practice.

STATEMENTS OF STANDARD ACCOUNTING PRACTICE AND FINANCIAL REPORTING STANDARDS ISSUED OR ADOPTED BY THE ACCOUNTING STANDARDS BOARD

The SSAPs and FRSs issued or adopted by the ASB are as follows:

SSAP 1   Accounting for Associated Companies
SSAP 2   Disclosure of Accounting Policies
SSAP 3   Earnings per Share
SSAP 4   Accounting for Government Grants
SSAP 5   Accounting for Value Added Tax
SSAP 6   Superseded by FRS 3
SSAP 7   Withdrawn
SSAP 8   The Treatment of Taxation under the Imputation System in the Accounts of Companies
SSAP 9   Stocks and Long-term Contracts
SSAP 10   Superseded by FRS 1
SSAP 11   Superseded by SSAP 15
SSAP 12   Accounting for Depreciation
SSAP 13   Accounting for Research and Development
SSAP 14   Superseded by FRS 2
SSAP 15   Accounting for Deferred Tax
SSAP 16   Withdrawn
SSAP 17   Accounting for Post Balance Sheet Events
SSAP 18   Accounting for Contingencies
SSAP 19   Accounting for Investment Properties
SSAP 20   Foreign Currency Translation
SSAP 21   Accounting for Leases and Hire Purchase Contracts
SSAP 22   Accounting for Goodwill
SSAP 23   Withdrawn
SSAP 24   Accounting for Pension Costs
SSAP 25   Segmental Reporting

FRS 1   Cash Flow Statements
FRS 2   Accounting for Subsidiary Undertakings
FRS 3   Reporting Financial Performance
FRS 4   Accounting for Capital Instruments
FRS 5   Reporting for the Substance of Transactions
FRS 6   Acquisitions and Mergers
FRS 7   Fair Values in Acquisition Accounting
FRS 8   Related Party Disclosures

URGENT ISSUES TASK FORCE (UITF)

Abstracts

Abstract 4: presentation of long-term debtors in current assets   Where the figure of debtors due after more than one year is material in the context of the total net current assets then it should be disclosed on the face of the balance sheet rather than just by way of a note (as has been the practice in the past where long-term debtors were included in current assets).

Abstract 5: transfers from current assets to fixed assets   This abstract requires transfers from current assets to fixed assets to be made at the lower of cost and net realizable value. This prevents the practice of transfers being made at a value higher than NRV. This avoids charging the profit and loss account with any diminution in value of what are, in effect, unsold trading assets. Once transferred to fixed assets, the CA 1985 alternative accounting rules could be used to take the debit reflecting the diminution in value to a revaluation reserve.

Abstract 6: accounting for post-retirement benefits other than pensions   Post-retirement benefits other than pensions are liabilities, which, in accordance with the accruals concept of SSAP 2 and CA 1985, should be recognized in financial statements, i.e. similar to SSAP 24.

Abstract 7: true and fair override disclosures   Where the directors depart from provisions of CA 1985 to the extent necessary to give a true and fair view, the Act required that 'particulars of any such departure, the reasons for it and its effect shall be given in a note to the accounts'. Abstract 7 seeks to clarify the meaning of that sentence as follows.

1   Particulars of any such departure.
2   The reasons for it: a statement as to why the treatment prescribed would not give a true and fair view.
3   Its effect: a description of how the position shown in the accounts is different as a result of the departure, with quantification if possible, or an explanation of the circumstances.

The disclosures required should either be included in or cross referenced to the note required about compliance with accounting standards, particulars of any material departure from those standards and the reasons for it (paragraph 36 A Sch 4).

Abstract 8: repurchase of own debt   This abstract addresses the situation where an entity buys its own debt at a price different from the amount of the liability shown in its balance sheet. The abstract requires the difference to be taken into the profit and loss account immediately (rather than carried forward and amortized) except in either of two cases. These are:

1   where the debt has been refinanced with very similar debt, so that in sub-
    stance no real change has taken place; or
2   where the new debt is not at market rates of interest.

Abstract 9: accounting for operations in hyper inflationary economies This
abstract concerns the consolidation of foreign subsidiaries in high inflation countries. The translation of the accounts of such subsidiaries using the closing rate
method is likely to give distorted results, and the abstract broadly says that the
local accounts should either be adjusted for inflation first or be prepared using a
strong currency (rather than the local currency) as the functional currency.

Abstract 10: disclosure of directors' share options If a company grants share
options to directors – their value should be included in the aggregate of directors'
remuneration. However, no agreement exists as to how to place a meaningful
money value on options.
    The UITF has concluded that it is not always practicable for it to specify an
appropriate valuation method for options as a benefit in kind. It recommends that
information concerning the option prices application to individual directors,
together with market price information at the year end (and also at the date of
exercise), should be disclosed in the notes.

Abstract 11: capital instruments: issuer call options The conditions of a capital
instrument may include an issuer call option (i.e. a right of the issuer but not the
investor) to redeem the instrument at an early date, usually on the payment of a
premium. The question arises as to how to account for an instrument that includes
an issuer call option following FRS 4.
    The issuers of capital instruments should *not* have to account for *possible
payments* that they are not obliged to make, and may very well elect not to make.
Payment of a premium on exercise of an issuer call option is a *cost* that stems
directly from the decision to exercise the option and should be reported in the
period in which exercise *occurs.*
    Note that the payment required on exercise of such an option does not form
part of the finance costs which have to be spread over the instrument's term – see
FRS 4.

Abstract 12: lessee accounting for reverse premium and similar incentives This
abstract requires benefits received by a lessee as an incentive to sign a lease to be
spread on a straight-line basis over the term of the lease.

Abstract 13: accounting for ESOP trusts Assets/liabilities of the ESOP (Employees
Share Ownership Plan) trust must normally be brought onto the balance sheet of
the sponsoring company.

Abstract 14: disclosure of changes in accounting policy When there is a change
of accounting policy, in addition to information required by FRS 3, an indication
should be given of the effect of the change on the current year's results. If the
effect is immaterial, then this should be pointed out in a simple statement.

Abstract 15: disclosure of substantial acquisitions This is a technical change which specifies shareholding levels at which additional disclosures may be necessary in the cases of substantial acquisitions.

STOCK EXCHANGE

Companies that are listed (sometimes termed 'quoted') on the London Stock Exchange have to meet additional accounting requirements. The listing authority in the UK, the London Stock Exchange, attempts to ensure that users of financial statements are given additional information and protection by insisting that companies who wish to obtain a listing comply with additional financial requirements. Listed companies will then have a continuing obligation to meet the Stock Exchange's regulation during the period of their membership.

Companies must satisfy the Stock Exchange that they can offer users evidence concerning their financial performance, the quality of management, future prospects and trading potential. These detailed rules are contained in the Stock Exchange (Listing) Regulations and also in the Admission of Securities to Listing (the so-called Yellow book).

Companies that fail to comply with the Stock Exchange requirements once they are listed may find, that in extreme circumstances, their listing can be suspended until compliance with the regulations is achieved.

The Stock Exchange Regulations insist, *inter alia* that:

*   The published financial statements are sent to shareholders within six months of the company's financial year end.
*   More detailed information in the Directors' Report concerning significant departures from accounting standards, explanations of material variations between profit forecasts and actual results, analysis of turnover and profit on a geographical basis, more detailed information on debentures and loans, information regarding directors' shareholdings, members having more than 5 per cent of issued shares, and any remuneration and dividends that are waived by directors.
*   The company must produce interim accounts which are to be sent to all members or alternatively published in two national newspapers.
*   Companies meet stringent regulations over the public release of 'price sensitive' company news.

INTERNATIONAL ACCOUNTING STANDARDS COMMITTEE

Attempts at standardizing accounting standards have come from the international front. In 1973 the International Accounting Standards Committee was formed (IASC). The founder members comprised of Australia, Canada, France, Germany,

Japan, Mexico, the Netherlands, the UK, Republic of Ireland and the USA. Since this date the number of representative countries has grown to reach over 100 in number.

The objective was initially stated to be 'to formulate and publish in the public interest basic standards to be observed in the presentation of audited accounts and financial statements and to promote their world wide acceptance and observance'. However their objectives were widened later to include working 'generally for the improvement and harmonisation of regulations, accounting standards and procedures'.

The IASC has no legal or other powers as such. Its major value lies in acting as a force to implement change in companies. It has produced over 30 International Accounting Standards (IASs) which provide an 'off-the-shelf' package of accounting standards for countries with less formally developed accounting systems (see also chapter 13, International Influences on Company Reporting).

QUESTIONS

1   Explain the constitutional structure of corporate reporting regulation in the UK. Discuss what you consider to be major advantages and fundamental weaknesses of this system.
2   What are Accounting Standards? Discuss what purposes you believe these standards perform.
3   What is the purpose of the Urgent Issues Task Force?
4   Explain to what extent you believe that company accounting is over regulated in the UK.
5   Discuss to what extent you believe that accountants should be regulated. Suggest improvements to the UK accounting regulatory regime.

3 | Format of Financial Statements

This chapter examines:

- the form and content of company accounts;
- reporting financial performance.

The format of a company's financial statements was largely determined by the European Community (EC) Fourth Directive which was adopted by the Council of Ministers in 1978. Referring extensively to existing and highly regulated accounting practice in Germany and France, the Fourth Directive attempted to standardize the format of the profit and loss account and balance sheet throughout all Member States. This standardization policy meant that a profit and loss account and balance sheet would comprise of the same format whether, for example, the accounts were published in France, Germany, Spain or the UK. Within narrowly defined limits, the Fourth Directive allows companies in the Member States to modify their format to a choice of two balance sheet formats and four profit and loss layouts. However, individual countries could allow companies to choose from all formats or restrict the choice. The Companies Acts in the UK have allowed companies the widest choice of formats. This choice has had the resulting effect of still providing some difficulty in comparing the financial statements of companies – albeit on a more restricted scale prior to the issue of the 4th Directive.

In the UK, company financial statements will normally comprise of the following *legal* requirements:

- directors' report;
- profit and loss account;
- balance sheet;
- auditors' report;
- notes to the accounts.

In addition to these statements the financial statements will have to include accounting statements, imposed or recommended by the Accounting Standards Board. In particular these statements will include:

- a cash flow statement;
- a statement of recognized gains and losses;
- a reconciliation statement of shareholders' funds;
- operating and financial review;
- business review.

FORMAT

In 1978, after the EC issued the Fourth Directive, all Member States of the EC were required to adopt its contents into their own legislation.

These European requirements were adopted by the UK in the 1981 Companies Act – later incorporated into 1985 Companies Act. The standardized format of published accounts was a novel innovation for UK companies. Prior to this Directive, the UK legislation merely stipulated the content of accounts. However, most of continental Europe already had a legal requirement specifying detailed attention to the format. The EC adopted this highly prescriptive approach and implemented this as a European-wide requirement.

Although some authorities prefer the adoption of a standardized approach on the grounds of allowing European financial statements to be more easily compared, many opponents of standardization lamented the loss of flexibility and individualism that standardization brought.

FORMAT OF PROFIT AND LOSS AND BALANCE SHEET

The detailed format requirements are specified in section 226 of the 1985 Companies Act and sec 4 of 1989 Companies Act. Although the format is standardized, the Act permits a certain degree of choice.

There are four formats permitted (see appendix 3.1). Two of these formats can be produced in what is known as 'vertical' format, which is the more modern and most commonly used method. The alternative format is termed 'horizontal', which, in the UK, is adopted only very infrequently. In essence the visual effect of the vertical format is to produce the profit and loss account in a single columnar form with both the debit and credit entries in the profit and loss account listed in a single column. In contrast, the horizontal form of the profit and loss account lists the credit entries of the profit and loss account on one side of the page and the debit entries on the other side.

Two of the formats (formats 1 and 3) analyse expenses by function and disclose the company's cost of sales, administrative expenses and distribution costs. The other two layouts (formats 2 and 4) disclose a company's expenses and indicate the cost of raw materials purchased, staff costs and depreciation charges.

There are two permitted formats for the balance sheet. Each format has the same headings but one format is in the commonly used vertical format whereas the alternative is presented on a horizontal basis. The vertical form 'stacks' the assets and liabilities in one column – effectively 'mixing' the debit and credit entries in one statement. The horizontal style lists the asset (debit) entries and liability (credit) entries and also shows the asset totals separately from the liability totals.

All items in the formats are prefixed by an alphabetical letter to indicate the major headings, and a Roman numeral to denote subheadings. Arabic numerals are used to indicate a detailed breakdown of a sub-heading.

The 1985 Companies Act requires that once a standard format has been chosen, it must be consistently adopted in future years – unless the directors consider that there are special reasons for a change. Additionally the items shown in the standard format (and prefixed by either an alphabetical letter or Roman numeral) must be shown in the financial statements in the same order and under the same headings and sub-headings – unless there are no amounts to include under that heading.

It must be stressed that the legal requirements are the minimum information that must be shown. It is legally permitted for companies to add or expand descriptions and additional headings or sub-headings may be incorporated. Any items that are indicated in the format by an Arabic numeral may be combined in the profit and loss account or the balance sheet on the condition that the individual item is shown separately in the notes to the accounts. This provision, which is frequently used by many companies, allows only the important details to be displayed on the face of the profit and loss account and balance sheet.

When presenting the accounts for a specific year, it is a legal requirement that corresponding figures are provided for the previous year. If specific corresponding figures are not comparable with the current year's figures then a full explanation must be provided in the notes.

It is also important that 'netting-off' is not used. Income should not be netted-off against expenditure and assets should not be netted-off against liabilities. For example, unless there is a legal right of set-off, overdraft and loans should not be set-off against cash balances.

MODIFICATION

It is important to realize that provided a company complies with the legal and accounting regulations, a degree of modification and flexibility is permitted. A very large number of companies voluntarily provide more information and add further description to items than is legally required. The Companies Act 1985 provides for any item in the chosen legal format to be expanded and shown in greater detail. Additional headings or sub-headings may be expanded and analysed in greater depth. New headings may be inserted if no adequate description is suitable in the standard format. Immaterial items can be combined under another heading.

The Companies Act attempts to ensure that only the most significant detail is placed on the face of the profit and loss account or balance sheet. The Act provides for items represented by an Arabic number in the standard format to be combined either on the profit and loss account or on the balance sheet – provided the individual items are shown in the notes (but only if such combination aids comprehension of the financial statements). In other words, many companies' final accounts will not necessarily exactly resemble the standard formats. The Act has provided scope for companies to only show key items on the face of the final accounts, provided that the remainder of the information is shown in the notes to the accounts.

All the items are assigned Arabic numerals which implies that the items, if appropriate, may be combined together on the face of the profit and loss account.

In addition to the items specified in the format every profit and loss account must show:

- profit or loss on ordinary activities before taxation;
- amounts transferred to reserves;
- the amount of any net dividends paid or proposed.

FRS 3, REPORTING FINANCIAL PERFORMANCE

The format and content of the financial statements was also changed by FRS 3 which came into effect for accounting periods ending on or after June 1993. FRS 3 applies to all companies whose accounting statements are required to give a true and fair view. (FRS 3 amends SSAP 3 and supersedes SSAP 6.)

The major features and changes implemented by FRS 3 are:

- The provision of multi-column analysis of the profit and loss account.
- A very strict definition of extraordinary items and an amendment of the definition of EPS.
- Redefining the requirements for the calculation and disclosure of exceptional items.
- The introduction of a new primary accounting statement: A Statement of Recognized Gains and Losses (SORG).
- A reconciliation of opening and closing balances of shareholders' funds.
- A note indicating the amount of the profit that would have been calculated if historical cost had been used.
- Prior year adjustments should be accounted for by restating the comparative figures for the preceding year in the primary accounting statements and by adjusting the opening balance of reserves in the current and previous period for the cumulative total effect.

Although the earnings per share (EPS) figure is a significant figure it is not the only information on which to judge the performance of a company. The ASB issued FRS 3 with the intention of trying to persuade users from merely using the conventionally calculated EPS.

The ASB believes that there is an array of other information that should be examined in addition to the EPS. FRS 3 requires companies 'to highlight a range of important components of financial performance to aid users of financial performance in understanding the performance achieved . . . and to assist them in forming a basis for their assessment of future results and cash flows' (FRS 3, para 1).

TIERED OR MULTI-LAYERED PROFIT AND LOSS ACCOUNT

The introduction of multi-column analysis has led to the sales and operating profit of a company being split between *continuing operations* (including separate disclosure of *acquisitions* during the year) and *discontinued operations*. Analysts will particularly find the split between continuing and discontinued items of special value. This split will help to allow the estimation of future earnings potential (from continuing activities) as opposed to those activities which have recently been curtailed (from the discontinued activities). To assist in the determination of discontinued activities FRS 3 identifies a number of conditions that must be satisfied (para 4):

1 The sale or termination of business operations is completed either in the financial period or before the earlier of three months after the commencement of the subsequent period and the date on which the financial statements are approved.
2 If a termination, the former activities have ceased permanently.
3 The sale or termination has a material effect on the nature and focus of the firm's operations and represents a material reduction in its operating facilities.
4 The assets, liabilities, and results of operations are clearly distinguishable, physically and operationally and for financial reporting purposes.

Although these conditions are by no means clear-cut in practice, they do at least attempt to bring a degree of standardization to the interpretation of this information.

EXTRAORDINARY AND EXCEPTIONAL ITEMS

Before the issue of FRS 3, a company's EPS was calculated by using profit *after* deducting exceptional items but *before* taking into account extraordinary items. In practice the definition of exceptional and extraordinary items was rather flexible and subject to considerable interpretative variations. In many instances where an item had a negative impact on reported earnings there was a temptation to classify the item as extraordinary so as to exclude its impact from the EPS. Conversely, where an item had a positive effect on earnings, companies frequently attempted to classify it as exceptional rather than extraordinary. In other words debit items were taken 'below the line' but credit items were taken 'above the line'.

Exceptional items

These are defined as 'material items which derive from events or transactions that fall within the ordinary activities of the reporting entity and which individually or, if a similar type, in aggregate, need to be disclosed by virtue of their size or incidence if the accounts are to give a true and fair view'. Exceptional items do not normally have to be disclosed on the face of the profit and loss account unless they fall within a limited number of categories (para 20). These specific exceptional items are commonly termed 'super-exceptionals'. They consist of:

- profit or loss on sale of or termination of an operation;
- fundamental reorganization or restructuring – which has a material effect on the operation;
- profit or loss on disposal of fixed assets.

Extraordinary items

The ASB believes that extraordinary items will be 'extremely rare in practice' as they 'relate to highly abnormal events or transactions that fall outside the ordinary activities of a reporting entity and which are not expected to recur'.

In practice the ASB does not envisage that companies will normally have any extraordinary items. The ASB has considerably tightened up the definition of an extraordinary item as: 'Material items possessing a high degree of *abnormality* which arise from events or transactions that fall outside the ordinary activities of the reporting entity and which are not expected to recur'. By including abnormal items in the definition, the ASB intends to ensure that only extremely restricted use is made of extraordinary items. In fact, the definition is so restricted, that the ASB fails to provide any examples of extraordinary items in FRS 3.

FRS 3 now requires a company to calculate the EPS *after* the inclusion of exceptionals and also *after* extraordinary items. The classification of an item now as exceptional or extraordinary will be irrelevant in so far as the calculation of the EPS is concerned.

STATEMENT OF RECOGNIZED GAINS AND LOSSES

FRS 3 introduced a new primary accounting statement: The Statement of Recognized Gains and Losses (SORG). This Statement is designed to highlight all gains and losses – both *realized* and *unrealized* that have been recognized by the company (see table 3.1 below). *Realized* gains and losses have been traditionally taken and shown in the profit and loss account whereas *unrealized* gains and losses will have often been taken to the company's reserves. In many cases it was considered that a number of companies were effectively 'hiding' unrealized gains and losses in the reserves. In particular the 'hiding' of unrealized losses in the reserves frequently led to many unsophisticated users of financial statements failing to appreciate their significance. A recognized gain or loss is any item that has been accounted for in the period, irrespective of when the gain or loss has occurred.

For example, the revaluation of a property illustrates the relevance of a SORG. A building, acquired in 1980 for £100,000 may have remained at its original historical figure in the balance sheet until 1994. But in 1995 the property is revalued to £150,000. Although the actual gain may have occurred over the last 15 years, it is accounted for when it is revalued, i.e. in 1995. At this point the gain will be recognized and appear in the company's SORG. If, in due course, the property is sold then the profit will be realized and the profit on disposal of the asset will appear in the 1995 profit and loss account.

FRS 3 regards the SORG as providing information that is useful for combining information about operating performance with other aspects of a company's financial performance and also for assessing the return on investment. It is regarded by the ASB as a primary financial statement – which effectively means that it is given the same degree of respect and credence as the other, more conventional financial accounting statements such as the profit and loss account and the balance sheet. (The Statement is not intended to reflect the realization of gains recognized in previous periods nor does the statement deal with transfer between reserves.)

EXAMPLE TABLE 3.1 STATEMENT OF RECOGNIZED GAINS AND LOSSES

Profit for the financial year	100
Unrealized surplus on revaluation of properties	10
Unrealized (loss)/gain on trade investment	(5)
	105
Currency translation differences on foreign currency net investments	(3)
Total recognized gains and losses relating to the year	102
Prior year adjustment	(8)
Total gain and losses recognized since last annual report	94

NOTE ON HISTORICAL COST PROFIT AND LOSS ACCOUNT

There is a wide variety of practice when companies account for land and buildings in the balance sheet. Some companies adopt a strict historical cost basis for the valuation of buildings but many companies use a form of 'modified historical cost' accounting where only land and buildings are periodically revalued. When a company sells any of its assets, FRS 3 requires the profit (or loss) on disposal to be calculated by comparing the sale proceeds against the 'carrying value' of the asset (the carrying value being the value at which the building is shown in the balance sheet). For example, a firm purchases a building for £10,000 in 1950 and revalues the building in 1990 to £50,000. It subsequently sells the building in 1995 for £75,000. The profit on sale, carried to the profit and loss account will be the difference between the sale proceeds of £75,000 and its carrying value in the balance sheet of £50,000, i.e. a realized profit of £25,000.

To assist in comparing the results of companies who have revalued assets at different times (or perhaps have not revalued at all) FRS 3 requires an additional note on the historical cost profit, i.e. the difference between sale proceeds and the original historical cost. In the above example the historical cost profit will be £65,000 (£75,000 – £10,000). (This £65,000 is shown by way of note and it does not appear in the profit and loss account.) (See table 3.3.)

MEASURING PERFORMANCE

Earnings per share

For many years a company's results were often interpreted by the placing of undue reference on a company's EPS. The ASB has attempted to distract attention away from this sole indicator by minimizing scope for distortion through misinterpretation and misclassification of extraordinary items. But in addition, a number of substantial amendments have also been implemented.

The ASB notes that 'it is not possible to distil the performance of a complex organisation into a single measure' (FRS 3, para 52). The ASB does not want undue significance to be placed on any one such measure which purports to do so. The ASB requires a range of factors to be considered. Towards this end, FRS 3 requires the EPS to be calculated on the basis of profit attributable to equity shareholders. In other words the EPS is calculated after the inclusion of both exceptional and extraordinary items.

In particular, FRS 3 has been criticized for the inclusion of extraordinary items in the EPS. A number of analysts argue that there are many virtues in having the EPS only calculated on the basis of the 'maintainable' (or 'core') earnings of the organization. Any 'one-off' item which would, in all probability, be classified as an exceptional item would distort the core results of the firm. So to obtain a 'typical' or 'representative' figure of the firm's trading activities a number of analysts have tended to recalculate the earnings per share by still excluding what they determine to be extraordinary items.

FRS 3 also requires the profit and loss account to be tiered (or multi-layered).

In effect this tiering means splitting the company's total turnover and profits in the profit and loss account into:

1 *Continuing operations:* The sales and profits of a company that will be continuing in a company must be highlighted. The user can identify those 'core' parts of the business that must remain as a part of the business and are expected to be a part of the business in the coming year.
2 *Acquisitions:* By identifying those parts of the business that have been acquired during the current year, the user can expect these new parts to generate returns in the coming year.
3 *Discontinuing operations:* Items under this heading have been disposed of during the year and will not be generating any returns in the coming financial year.

Total turnover

The total turnover is the total sales from all sources for the current financial year. The profit and loss account must also highlight:

• any profit or losses on the sale or termination of an operation;
• profits or loss on the disposal of a fixed asset;
• the cost of a fundamental reorganization.

RECONCILIATION OF MOVEMENTS IN SHAREHOLDERS' FUNDS

The shareholders' funds of an entity will predominantly consist of share capital and reserves. FRS 3 recognizes that shareholders' funds may change other than for reasons related to its financial performance.

In practice most shareholders' funds will change because the company has issued new share capital and in companies which have written-off goodwill to reserves. FRS 3 requires companies to prepare a statement that reconciles the opening and closing balance of shareholders' funds either in the form of a primary accounting statement or in the form of a note to the accounts. FRS 3 requires that the opening balance of shareholders funds is reconciled with the closing balance (see table 3.2).

As part of the reconciliation, the statement would include such items as:

• the recognized gains and losses for the year;
• goodwill written off immediately to reserves during the year;
• any share capital redeemed or issued.

EXAMPLE TABLE 3.2 RECONCILIATION OF MOVEMENT IN SHAREHOLDERS' FUNDS

Profit for financial year	100
Dividends	(20)
	80
New share capital subscribed	25
Goodwill written-off	(30)
Net addition to shareholders' funds	75
Opening balance of shareholders' funds	300
Closing balance of shareholders' funds	375

EXAMPLE TABLE 3.3 NOTE ON HISTORICAL COST PROFITS AND LOSSES

	£
Reported profit on ordinary activities before taxation	**50**
Realization of property revaluation gains of previous years	10
Differences between a historical cost depreciation charge and the actual depreciation charge of the year calculated on the revalued amount	5
Historical cost profit on ordinary activities before taxation	**65**
Historical cost profit for the year retained after taxation, minority interests, extraordinary items and dividends (say)	42

(Note: In addition to the legally required profit and loss account and balance sheet, the financial accounts must also contain two additional primary statements. These two statements are a Statement of Recognized Gains and Losses (required by FRS 3) and a Cash Flow Statement.)

CLASSIFICATION BY COMPANY SIZE

Small and medium-sized companies

The 1985 Companies Act introduced another classification of limited companies by defining two specific types of limited companies: small and medium sized. (If a company does not fall within the definition of these two categories it is, by default, classified as a large company.) An individual company is defined as small or medium if it meets at least two of the following three conditions in table 3.4.

If a company is classified as small or medium then a number of legal and accounting exemptions and modifications will apply and companies will only have to file 'abridged' or 'abbreviated' accounts. In the case of a 'small' company, the general headings and items identified by a Roman numeral in the balance sheet will remain unchanged. It is possible to combine many of the headings that

TABLE 3.4

	Small company	Medium company
Turnover		
Not exceeding	£2.8 million	£11.2 million
Balance sheet total		
Not exceeding	£1.4 million	£5.6 million
Average number of employees		
Not exceeding	50	250

are preceded by Arabic numerals into new headings. Additionally the extent of the provision in the notes to the accounts can be reduced. In effect, these provisions mean that a small company does *not* have to file: a complete profit and loss account, a directors' report, details concerning directors' emoluments, and in the balance sheet, the small company can omit all items that are not prefixed by a Roman numeral.

The exclusions permitted to a medium company are considerably less than for a small company. A medium-sized company must file a full balance sheet and notes but it is allowed to file a modified profit and loss account – which largely omits showing turnover, cost of sales and other operating income. It must be emphasized that these special requirements only apply for filing purposes (i.e. the sending of financial statements to the Registrar of Companies). Directors are still required to send to each shareholder and debenture holder the full accounts. Additionally small and medium companies are not legally required to take advantage of the exemptions. Companies can, if they so wish, continue to file full accounts. Indeed, because of the cost and time involved in producing modified accounts, many companies still choose to file the same set of accounts that are sent to their shareholders (i.e. the full accounts).

SUMMARY FINANCIAL STATEMENTS

There is yet another category of published financial statements – termed summary financial statements.

These summary statements apply only to listed companies and enable such companies to send a simplified version of their accounts to those shareholders who do not require the full report and accounts. This provision of limited accounting information to shareholders was created by the Companies Act 1985 (sec 251) and Companies Act 1989 (sec 15) in response to the demands of large listed companies who had a very substantial shareholder register. These companies believed that many shareholders were not interested in receiving detailed and complex sets of published accounts. These companies considered that publishing and postage costs could be minimized by not sending out detailed accounts to all shareholders. Only those shareholders who requested full statements would receive a copy. However, it must be stressed that companies taking advantage of this provision must still file a full set of accounts with the Registrar of Companies and send the full published accounts to all shareholders who request a copy.

The summary accounts must:

- state that the information is only a summary, and;
- contain a statement by the company's auditors stating whether in their opinion, the summary statements are consistent with the full annual report and accounts; whether the summary statements comply with the requirements of the relevant section of the Companies Act; and state whether the auditors' report in the annual accounts was qualified.

TRUE AND FAIR

In all company reporting there is an overriding requirement that the accounts must provide a true and fair view (sec 226 (2) 1985 Companies Act).

Directors are required to provide additional information, either in the accounts or in the notes, in circumstances where compliance with the standard prescribed format would not be sufficient to provide a true and fair view. The directors can also depart from the standard format where compliance would be 'inconsistent with the requirement to give a true and fair view' (s226 (5)). In such instances there is an accounting requirement (UITF 7) that the directors give the reasons for the departure.

QUESTIONS

1 State the components of a set of financial statements.
   What function does each of the components serve?
2 The EC Fourth Directive allowed a degree of choice in the presentation of the format of published annual accounts.
   Describe the formats that the UK has adopted for the profit and loss account and balance sheet.
3 Explain the difference between 'abridged' (or 'abbreviated') accounts and summary accounts.
4 What are summary financial statements?
5 What is the earnings per share? Why is it often perceived to be of significance? What changes has FRS 3 made to the definition of the EPS figure?
6 What is the difference between extraordinary and exceptional items?

REFERENCES AND FURTHER READING

Accounting Standards Board, *Reporting Financial Performance 3*, London, 1993.

Appendix 3.1

Balance sheet and profit and loss account formats

The balance sheet and profit and loss account formats are set out in the schedule 4 to the Companies Act 1985. The formats, with certain amendments, apply to group accounts and to the accounts of individual companies. Small companies may modify the profit and loss account and balance sheet formats. These precise modifications are outside the scope of this book.

Balance sheet format 1

A   Called up share capital not paid
B   Fixed assets
    I   Intangible assets
        1   Development costs
        2   Concessions, patents, licences, trade marks and similar rights and assets
        3   Goodwill
        4   Payments on account
    II   Tangible assets
        1   Land and buildings
        2   Plant and machinery
        3   Fixtures, fittings, tools and equipment
        4   Payments on account and assets in course of construction
    III   Investments
        1   Shares in group undertakings
        2   Loans to group undertakings
        3   Participating interests (excluding group undertakings)
        4   Loans to undertakings in which the company has a participating interest
        5   Other investments other than loans
        6   Other loans
        7   Own shares

C Current assets
   I Stocks
      1 Raw materials and consumables
      2 Work in progress
      3 Finished goods and goods for resale
      4 Payments on account
   II Debtors
      1 Trade debtors
      2 Amounts owed by group undertakings
      3 Amounts owed by undertakings in which the company has a partici-
         pating interest
      4 Other debtors
      5 Called-up share capital not paid
      6 Prepayments and accrued income
   III Investments
      1 Shares in group undertakings
      2 Own shares
      3 Other investments
      4 Cash at bank and in hand
D Prepayments and accrued income
E Creditors: amounts falling due within one year
      1 Debenture loans
      2 Bank loans and overdrafts
      3 Payments received on account
      4 Trade creditors
      5 Bills of exchange payable
      6 Amounts owed to group undertakings
      7 Amounts owed to undertakings in which the company has a partici-
         pating interest
      8 Other creditors including taxation and social security
      9 Accruals and deferred income
F Net current assets (liabilities)
G Total assets less current liabilities
H Creditors: amounts falling due after more than one year
      1 Debenture loans
      2 Bank loans and overdrafts
      3 Payments received on account
      4 Trade creditors
      5 Bills of exchange payable
      6 Amounts owed to group undertakings
      7 Amounts owed to undertakings in which the company has a partici-
         pating interest
      8 Other creditors including taxation and social security
      9 Accruals and deferred income
I Provisions for liabilities and charges
      1 Pensions and similar obligations

        2   Taxation, including deferred taxation
        3   Other provisions
J   Accruals and deferred income
    Minority interests
K   Capital and reserves
     I   Called-up share capital
     II   Share premium account
     III   Revaluation reserve
     IV   Other reserves
        1   Capital redemption reserve
        2   Reserve for own shares
        3   Reserves provided for by articles of association
        4   Other reserves
     V   Profit and loss account
    Minority interests

Balance sheet format 2

Assets

A   Called-up share capital not paid
B   Fixed assets
     I   Intangible assets
        1   Development costs
        2   Concessions, patents, licences, trade marks and similar rights and assets
        3   Goodwill
        4   Payments on account
     II   Tangible assets
        1   Land and buildings
        2   Plant and machinery
        3   Fixtures, fittings, tools and equipment
        4   Payments on account and assets in course of construction
     III   Investments
        I   Shares in group undertakings
        2   Loans to group undertakings
        3   Participating interests (excluding group undertakings)
        4   Loans to undertakings in which the company has a participating interest
        5   Other investments other than loans
        6   Other loans
        7   Own shares

C   Current assets
    I   Stocks
      1   Raw materials and consumables
      2   Work in progress
      3   Finished goods and goods for resale
      4   Payments on account
    II   Debtors
      1   Trade debtors
      2   Amounts owed by group undertakings
      3   Amounts owed by undertakings in which the company has a partici-
         pating interest
      4   Other debtors
      5   Called up share capital not paid
      6   Prepayments and accrued income
    III   Investments
      1   Shares in group undertakings
      2   Own shares
      3   Other investments
    IV   Cash at bank and in hand
D   Prepayments and accrued income

Liabilities

A   Capital and reserves
    I   Called-up share capital
    II   Share premium account
    III   Revaluation reserve
    IV   Other reserves
      1   Capital redemption reserve
      2   Reserve for own shares
      3   Reserves provided for by the articles of association
      4   Other reserves
   Minority interests
    V   Profit and loss account
B   Provisions for liabilities and charges
      1   Pensions and similar obligations
      2   Taxation including deferred taxation
      3   Other provisions
C   Creditors
      1   Debenture loans
      2   Bank loans and overdrafts
      3   Payments received on account
      4   Trade creditors
      5   Bills of exchange payable

      6   Amounts owed to group undertakings
      7   Amounts owed to undertakings in which the company has a participating interest
      8   Other creditors including taxation and social security
      9   Accruals and deferred income
D   Accruals and deferred income

Profit and loss account format 1

1   Turnover
2   Cost of sales
3   Gross profit or loss
4   Distribution costs
5   Administration expenses
6   Other operating income
7   Income from shares in group undertakings
8   Income from participating interests (excluding group undertakings)
9   Income from other fixed asset investments
10 Other interest receivable and similar income
11 Amounts written off investments
12 Interest payable and similar charges
13 Tax on profit or loss on ordinary activities
14 Profit or loss on ordinary activities after taxation
     Minority interests
15 Extraordinary income
16 Extraordinary charges
17 Extraordinary profit or loss
18 Tax on extraordinary profit or loss
     Minority interests
19 Other taxes not shown under the above items
20 Profit or loss for the financial year

Profit and loss account format 2

1   Turnover
2   Change in stocks of finished goods and work in progress
3   Own work capitalized
4   Other operating income
5   (a)   Raw materials and consumables
     (b)   Other external charges
6   Staff costs:
     (a)   Wages and salaries
     (b)   Social security costs
     (c)   Other pension costs

7 (a) Depreciation and other amounts written off tangible and intangible fixed assets
   (b) Exceptional amounts written off current assets
8 Other operating charges
9 Income from shares in group undertakings
10 Income from participating interests (excluding group undertakings)
11 Income from other fixed asset investments
12 Other interest receivable and similar income
13 Amounts written off investments
14 Interest payable and similar charges
15 Tax on profit or loss on ordinary activities
16 Profit or loss on ordinary activities after taxation
   Minority interests
17 Extraordinary income
18 Extraordinary charges
19 Extraordinary profit or loss
   Minority interests
20 Tax on extraordinary profit or loss
21 Other taxes not shown under the above items
22 Profit or loss for the financial year

(Note: Format 1 and Format 2 of the profit and loss account can also each be expressed in 'horizontal format'. However, most companies choose not to adopt this horizontal format.)

4 | Verification of Financial Statements

This chapter examines:

* the nature and significance of an auditors' report;
* accountability and corporate governance;
* significance of true and fair.

As discussed in chapter 1, the directors have the effective power of control in most large limited companies but the legal ownership of these companies lies with another party – the shareholders.

The major means of communication by which directors account for the stewardship of the shareholders' assets is through the issuing of the annual report and accounts. So that the shareholders can have a degree of confidence in these accounting statements, independent accountants report to the shareholders. These independent accountants acting in their capacity as auditors are legally required to examine the financial statements of all larger-sized limited companies.

In practice the auditors are appointed by the company's directors but this decision must be ratified by the shareholders. All statutory audit reports are addressed to the company's shareholders.

DEFINITION AND EXTENT OF AN AUDIT

Until 1994 all businesses that were limited companies were legally obliged to have an audit. Throughout the 1980s there was growing pressure to remove the cost and administrative burden of statutory audits for smaller-sized companies.

In effect, for audit purposes limited companies were split into three categories:

1   Companies with annual turnover under £90,000. This category of companies are no longer required to be subject to an annual audit.
2   Companies with annual turnover between £90,000 and £350,000. These companies are not required to be subject to a full audit but need to have a

compilation report. (A compilation report is not a full audit, but a more superficial and briefer examination of the company's accounts.)
3   Companies with an annual turnover over £350,000 are still required to be subject to a full statutory audit.

In May 1993 the Auditing Practices Board (APB) issued Statement of Auditing Standards, *Auditors' Reports on Financial Statements* (SAS 600). This Statement identified the key elements of an auditors' report:

1   a title identifying the person or persons to whom the report is addressed – the shareholders in the case of limited companies;
2   an introductory paragraph, identifying the financial statements that have been audited;
3   separately headed sections, consisting of:
    (a)   respective responsibilities of directors and auditors;
    (b)   the basis of the auditors' opinion;
    (c)   the auditors' opinion;
4   auditors' signature and date.

Here is an example of an auditors' unqualified opinion:

EXAMPLE 4.1   AUDITORS' REPORT TO THE SHAREHOLDERS OF ABC PLC
We have audited the financial statements on pages X to Y which have been prepared under the historical cost convention, as modified by the revaluation of certain fixed assets and the accounting policies set out on pages X to Y.

Respective responsibilities of directors and auditors
As described on page X the company's directors are responsible for the preparation of financial statements. It is our responsibility to form an independent opinion, based on our audit, on those statements and to report our opinion to you.

Basis of opinion
We conducted our audit in accordance with Auditing Standards issued by the Auditing Practices Board. An audit includes examination on a test basis, of evidence relevant to the amounts and disclosures in the financial statements. It also includes an assessment of the significant estimates and judgements made by the directors in the preparation of the financial statements, and of whether the accounting policies are appropriate to their company's circumstances, consistently applied and adequately disclosed.
    We planned and performed our audit so as to obtain all the information and explanations which we considered necessary in order to provide us with sufficient evidence to give reasonable assurance that the financial statements are free from material mis-statement whether caused by fraud or other irregularity or error. In forming our opinion we also evaluated the overall adequacy of the presentation of information in the financial statements.

Opinion
In our opinion, the financial statements give a true and fair view of the state of the company's affairs as at 31 December 1996 and of its profit (or loss) for the year

then ended and have been properly prepared in accordance with the Companies Act 1985.

Signature
Registered auditors

Date

Address

If the auditors cannot issue an unqualified report, the above report must be amended. If the auditors' opinion on financial statements is to be qualified (perhaps because the company has not complied with an accounting standard) the area of difficulty or non-compliance with the accounting standard must be clearly highlighted. In extreme instances the auditors may consider that the financial statements do not give a true and fair view and accordingly, the auditors' report will reflect this opinion.

ACCOUNTABILITY AND CORPORATE GOVERNANCE

Report of the Committee on The Financial Aspects of Corporate Governance (the so-called Cadbury Committee)

The Code of Best Practice   In an attempt to improve accountability and govern-ance the Cadbury Committee was established in 1991 by the Financial Reporting Council, the London Stock Exchange, and the accountancy profession to 'address the financial aspects of corporate governance'.

The Committee's Code applies to all listed companies registered in the UK and the Committee encourages other companies to comply with the Code.

The Committee requires that:

1   all listed companies should make a statement in their report and accounts about their compliance with the Code and identify any areas of non-compliance;
2   companies' statements of compliance should be reviewed by the auditors before publication.

The publication of this statement of compliance is a continuing obligation of listing by the London Stock Exchange.

Board of Directors   The Code requires that the Board of Directors 'meet regu-larly, retain full and effective control over the company and monitor the executive management'.

There should be a clear division of responsibilities at the head of the company which will help ensure 'a balance of power and authority, such that no one individual has unfettered powers of decision'.

The Board should include non-executive directors of 'sufficient calibre and number for their views to carry significant weight in the board's decisions'. Adequate provision should be made for the directors to take independent professional advice if necessary and all directors should have access to the advice and services of the Company Secretary.

Non-executive directors   The Cadbury Report places considerable emphasis on the importance of companies having non-executive directors who can bring an independent judgement to bear on issues of strategy, performance, resources and standards of conduct. The Code requires the majority of non-executives to be independent of the management and free from any business or other relationship which could materially interfere with the exercise of their independent judgement.

Executive directors   The service contracts of executive directors should not normally exceed three years. There should be full and clear disclosure of directors' total emoluments and those of the Chairman and highest paid director, including pension contributions and stock options. The Code requires separate figures be given for salary and performance related elements of the emoluments. The basis on which performance is measured should be explained.

Reporting and controls

It is the Board's duty to present a balanced and understandable assessment of the company's position.

- The Board should ensure that an objective and professional relationship is maintained with auditors.
- The Board should establish an audit committee consisting of at least three non-executive directors.
- The directors should explain their responsibility for preparing the accounts next to a statement by the auditors about their reporting responsibilities.

In particular The Statement of Directors' Responsibilities should cover the following:

- The legal requirement for directors to prepare financial statements for each financial year which give a true and fair view of the state of affairs of the company and of the profit and loss account.
- The responsibility of the directors for maintaining adequate accounting records, for safeguarding the assets of the company and for preventing and detecting fraud and other irregularities.
- Confirmation that suitable accounting policies, consistently applied and supported by reasonable and prudent judgements and estimates have been used in the preparation of the financial statements.
- Confirmation that applicable accounting standards have been followed, subject to any material departures disclosed and explained in the notes to the

accounts. (This statement will normally be placed immediately before the auditors' report.)

- The directors should report upon the effectiveness of the company's system of internal control.
- The directors should also report that the business is a going concern, with supporting assumptions or qualifications as necessary.

EXAMPLE 4.2 EXTRACT FROM BRITISH TELECOMMUNICATIONS

Corporate governance

The directors consider that during the year BT has fully complied with the Code of Best Practice published by the Committee on the Financial Aspects of Corporate Governance (the 'Cadbury Committee') and complies with Section A of the best practice provisions of the Stock Exchange Listing Rules introduced following the publication of Directors' Remuneration – Report of a Study Group chaired by Sir Richard Greenbury (the 'Greenbury Report')

The Board

The Board meets regularly to consider matters specifically reserved for its attention. It sets the strategic direction of the group and monitors overall performance.

The majority of the directors are non-executive and, between them, have a wide range of experience at a senior level in international, legal, marketing, government and diplomatic affairs. Seven of the nine non-executive directors are independent of the management of BT, either being free from any business or other relationships which could materially interfere with the exercise of their judgement or not previously involved in the management of BT.

Non-executive directors have normally been appointed for periods of three years. Towards the end of that period, the Board has considered whether to continue the appointment for a further period. The Board has now agreed that non-executive directors will normally be appointed initially for three years. At the end of that period it will consider whether to continue the appointment, which will then become terminable on twelve months' notice from either BT or the director. Appointments will be reviewed again by the Board at the end of the sixth year. Normally, appointments will be for a maximum of ten years.

The non-executive directors provide a strong independent element on the Board, with Sir Colin Marshall, Deputy Chairman, as senior member. However, the Board operates as a single team.

The executive directors have service agreements which are reviewed by the Board Committee on Executive Remuneration. Information about the periods of these contracts is in the report of the Board Committee on Executive Remuneration.

The Board has agreed and established a procedure for directors, in furtherance of their duties, to take independent professional advice, if necessary, at the company's expense. In addition, all directors have access to the advice and services of the company secretary, the removal of whom would be a matter for the whole Board.

Board committees

Following Sir Peter Bonfield's appointment as Chief Executive, the Board set up an Executive Committee which he chairs. In addition to Sir Peter, the members of the

Committee are the Deputy Chief Executive, the Group Finance Director and other senior executives responsible for BT's operations and central functions. These executives include the heads of BT's three customer divisions and the network and systems division, together with the Secretary and Chief Legal Adviser, the Group Personnel Director and two executives responsible for developing the group's strategy and plans. The Committee develops the group's strategy, for Board approval, and oversees implementation. It also finalizes (before Board approval) annual quality plans and budgets and reviews operational activities.

The Nominating Committee of the Chairman, Deputy Chairman and three other non-executive directors ensures the Board has an appropriate balance of expertise and ability among the non-executive directors. For this purpose it has agreed, and regularly reviews, a profile of the required skills and attributes. This profile is used to assess the suitability as non-executive directors of candidates put forward by the directors and outside consultants. Candidates short-listed for appointment are met by the Committee before it recommends an appointment to the Board.

The Committee also assesses candidates for executive directorships before it recommends an appointment.

The Board Audit Committee, consisting solely of non-executive directors, is chaired by Sir Colin Marshall. Its terms of reference include reviewing BT's internal controls and published financial reports for statutory compliance and against standards of best practice, and recommending appropriate disclosure to the Board. It also reviews annually the services and fees of the company's auditors, to ensure that an objective and professional relationship is maintained.

Internal financial control

The directors are responsible for the group's systems of internal financial control. Such systems can provide only reasonable and not absolute assurance against material financial mis-statement or loss. Key elements are:

- Formal policies and procedures are in place, including the documentation of key systems and rules relating to the delegation of authorities, which allow the monitoring of controls and restrict the unauthorized use of the group's assets.
- Experienced and suitably qualified staff take responsibility for important business functions.
- Annual appraisal procedures have been established to maintain standards of performance.
- Forecasts and budgets are prepared which allow management to monitor the key business and financial activities and risks and the progress towards financial objectives set for the year and the medium term.
- Monthly management accounts are prepared promptly providing relevant, reliable and up to date financial and other information; significant variances from budget are investigated as appropriate.
- All investment projects are subject to formal authorization procedures, with an investment committee, comprising members of the Board, considering major investment projects.
- The Board Audit Committee reviews reports from management, from the internal auditors and from the external auditors, to provide reasonable assurance that control procedures are in place and are being followed.
- Formal procedures have been established for instituting appropriate action to correct weaknesses identified from the above reports.

On behalf of the Board, the Board Audit Committee has reviewed the effectiveness of the systems of internal financial control in existence in the group for the year ended 31 March 1996 and for the period up to the date of approval of the financial statements.

Statement of BT business practice

BT will comply with the laws and regulations of the territories in which it operates. However, we aim to go further and maintain high international standards of business integrity and professional competence in all our activities world-wide, in our drive to become the most successful world-wide telecommunications group.

The Board has adopted a Statement of Business Practice which sets out the principles that the group will observe. BT requires its employees, agents and contractors to apply these.

Pension fund

BT's main pension fund – the BT Pension Scheme – is not controlled by the Board, but by trustees, who are company and union nominees, with an independent chairman. The trustees look after the assets of the pension fund, which are held separately from those of the company. The pension scheme funds can only be used in accordance with its rules and for no other purpose.

Reporting

A statement by the directors of their responsibilities for preparing the financial statements is included on page X.

The auditors, Coopers & Lybrand, have reported to the company that, in their opinion, the directors' comments on internal financial control above and on going concern on page X provide the disclosures required by paragraphs 4.5 and 4.6 of the Code of Best Practice (as supplemented by the related guidance) and are not inconsistent with the information of which they are aware from their audit work on the financial statements, and the statements above appropriately reflect the company's compliance with the other paragraphs of the Code specified by the London Stock Exchange for their review. The auditors were not required to carry out the additional work necessary to, and do not express any opinion on, the effectiveness of either the group's systems of internal financial control or its corporate governance procedures, nor the ability of the group or the company to continue in operational existence.

AUDITORS AND THE CADBURY CODE

Since the implementation of the Stock Exchange's Code of Best Practice for Corporate Governance, auditors are now required to report on whether a listed company has complied with the requirements of this Code.

Most companies either incorporate this requirement in the main auditors' report or else display the information in a separate self-contained report, usually adjacent to the main auditors' report.

EXAMPLE 4.3 REPORT OF AUDITORS TO ABC PLC ON CORPORATE GOVERNANCE MATTERS

In addition to our audit of the financial statements, we have reviewed the directors' statement on page X on the company's compliance with the paragraph of the code of best practice specified for our review by the London Stock Exchange. The objective of our review is to draw attention to non-compliance with those paragraphs of the Code where such non-compliance is not disclosed.

We carried out our review in accordance with Bulletin 1995/1 'Disclosures relating to corporate governance' issued by the Auditing Practices Board. That Bulletin does not require us to perform the additional work necessary to, and we do not, express any opinion on the effectiveness of either the company's corporate governance procedures nor on the ability of the company to continue in operational existence.

Opinion

With respect to the directors' statements on going concern on page X, in our opinion the directors have provided the disclosures required by paragraph 4.6 of the Code (as supplemented by the related guidance for directors) and such statement is not inconsistent with the information of which we are aware from our audit work on the financial statements.

Based on enquiry of certain directors and officers of the company and examination of relevant documents, in our opinion the directors' statements on page Y appropriately reflects the Company's compliance with the other paragraphs of the Code specified for our review.

Signed

Chartered Accountants

Address
Date

Statement of directors' responsibilities in relation to financial statements

The following statement which should be read in conjunction with the auditors' statement of their responsibilities set out on page X, is made with a view to distinguishing for shareholders the respective responsibilities of the directors and of the auditors in relation to the financial statements.

The directors are required by the Companies Act 1985 to prepare financial statements for each financial year which give a true and fair view of the state of affairs of the company and the group as at the end of the financial year and of the profit or loss for the financial year.

The directors consider that in preparing the financial statements on pages X to Y, the group has used appropriate accounting policies, consistently applied and supported by reasonable and prudent judgements and estimates and that all applicable Accounting Standards have been followed. The financial statements have been prepared on a going-concern basis.

The directors have responsibility for ensuring that the group keeps accounting records which disclose with reasonable accuracy the financial position of the group and which enable them to ensure that the financial statements comply with the Companies Act 1985.

The directors have general responsibility for taking such steps as are reasonably open to them to safeguard the assets of the group and to prevent and detect fraud and other irregularities.

The above report of the auditors to ABC plc on corporate governance matters makes reference to the directors' statements on page X. In particular, directors are required to comment on whether the going-concern concept is applicable and also the nature of internal financial controls within the company.

Directors' comments on the company's ability to continue as a going concern and also on the internal controls in place within the company are frequently found in the directors' report.

Examples of these two instances are:

EXAMPLE 4.4(a)   GOING CONCERN

Corporate governance
Throughout the financial year the company fully complied with the Cadbury Code of Best Practice (the 'Code') as in force.

After making enquiries, the directors have a reasonable expectation that the Company has adequate resources to continue operating for the foreseeable future. For this reason, the going concern was adopted in preparing the accounts.

EXAMPLE 4.4(b)   INTERNAL FINANCIAL CONTROLS
The directors have overall financial responsibility for the system of internal financial control throughout the group. In discharging that responsibility, the directors have evolved a system of financial controls which is designed to safeguard the assets of the group and the integrity of its accounting records, though such a system can only provide reasonable, as opposed to absolute assurance against material mis-statement or loss. The directors have reviewed the effectiveness of the system of internal financial control for the financial year and the period to the date of approval of the financial statements and have considered the major business risks and the control environment. The review revealed nothing which in the opinion of the Board indicated that the system was inappropriate or unsatisfactory. These controls include:

- Formal policies and procedures are established, including the documentation of key systems and rules relating to the delegation of authority.
- Forecasts and budgets are prepared which allow the management to monitor key business and financial activity and the progress towards the financial objectives set for the year and the medium term; monthly management accounting are prepared promptly; significant variations from budgets are investigated.
- All investment projects are subject to authorization procedures, with an investment board considering major investment projects.

(Include other controls as appropriate to the company.)

The company's auditors will review the company's statements concerning its compliance with those paragraphs of the Code currently in effect and specified for their review. The auditors will then report on whether the directors' statements appropriately reflect the company's compliance with the Code of Best Practice.

What is true and fair?

A vital term found in the auditors' report is that of 'true and fair'. Unfortunately from the auditors' standpoint, this term has not been comprehensively and legally defined. The Companies Acts place an overriding obligation for financial statements to provide a 'true and fair view' (1985 Companies Act, sec 226 (2) and 1989 sec 4).

In particular the 1985 and 1989 Companies Acts require the directors of companies to:

1   provide additional information where compliance with the standard formats and disclosure provisions would not be sufficient to provide a true and fair view, and;
2   depart from the format and disclosure rules in those circumstances where compliance would be inconsistent with the requirement to give a true and fair view.

Until the Companies Act 1989 (sec 36A, Sch 4), there was no specific legal obligation to comply with any accounting standard – it was only a professional requirement. The Companies Act 1989 required companies to state 'whether the accounts have been prepared in accordance with applicable accounting standards and particulars of any material departure from those standards and the reasons for it shall be given.' Since the legislation defining truth and fairness has been so lacking, accountants have sought to obtain further legal opinion.

Legal opinion, supported by Leonard Hoffmann QC and Mary Arden QC (in 1983/4) believed that Accounting Standards represented sound professional practice and because accountants were professionally compelled to comply with these accounting standards, then it would be expected by the users of the accounts that the financial statements would comply with them. In other words, their legal opinion was that the courts would regard compliance with accounting standards as prima facie evidence that the financial statements showed a true and fair view. And conversely if the financial statements were regarded as being true and fair – then the financial statements will have been compiled under the requirements of the Accounting Standards.

Shortly after the 1989 Companies Act came into effect, a new opinion was sought by the ASB from Mary Arden in 1993. Arden reinforced and extended her earlier opinion by giving stronger support to the importance of SSAPs and FRSs and some degree of support to the UITF Abstracts. Stronger legal support was given to accounting standards because:

• It was considered that accounts must be prepared in accordance with applicable accounting standards – and these standards would be issued by an authority recognized by legislation – i.e. the ASB.
• There is a presumption that compliance with accounting standards is necessary to give a true and fair view – because any departures from applicable accounting standards should be disclosed and recognized.

- The 1989 Companies Act has given the Review Panel power to apply to Courts in the case of plcs and 'public interest companies' to determine whether the accounts are true and fair.
- The ASB has adopted a policy of widespread discussion and consultation before a standard is adopted. This procedure of consultation will add authority to their pronouncements.

Additionally the 1993 opinion notes that the courts are likely to treat 'UITF Abstracts as of considerable standing even though they are not envisaged by the Companies Acts'.

Departure from true and fair

Arden believes that departure from accounting standards can only be justified if departure has been 'appropriate in the particular case' in order to give a true and fair view. The Companies Acts allow companies to depart from the legislation, when preparing their accounts, if to comply with the legal provisions would be incompatible with the requirement for the accounting statements to be true and fair. This provision is termed the 'true and fair override'. In the instance of companies citing truth and fairness as a reason for not complying with aspects of the Companies Acts, the UITF has issued Abstract 7. This Abstract insists that companies provide additional information over and above what is required under legislation.

In essence UITF 7 requires companies to:

1 Provide details of the departure and a statement of the accounting treatment that the Companies Acts require.
2 Reasons for the departure and why compliance with the legal treatment will not give a true and fair view.
3 An explanation of how the position in the accounts is different as a result of the departure – normally with quantification. If the effect cannot be quantified, the directors should explain the circumstances.

QUESTIONS

1 What do you understand by the term 'true and fair'?
2 Explain the circumstances in which a company can depart from the normal requirement to give a true and fair view.
3 What do you understand by the term 'corporate governance'?
  Explain the major intentions of the Cadbury Committee.
4 Discuss the reasons why the financial statements need to be audited.
5 What do you consider to be the more significant features of an auditors' report?

REFERENCES AND FURTHER READING

Report of the Committee on the financial aspects of corporate governance: compliance with the code of best practice ('Cadbury Report'), by Adrian Cadbury, HMSO, 1995.

5 | Profit and Loss Account

This chapter examines:

- the nature, format and content of the profit and loss account;
- disclosure provisions.

The profit and loss account provides a historical record of a company's financial performance during the course of its last financial year. In essence, the profit and loss account records and compares a firm's revenue and expenses to determine whether a profit (i.e. revenue exceeding expenses) or loss (i.e. expenses exceeding revenue) has occurred.

For their own internal accounting purposes, a company's management will provide a comprehensive profit and loss account which itemizes and provides a detailed breakdown of all the income received and all the forms of expenses which the company needs to pay. This detailed information is produced largely to assist management to record, operate and control the company's business affairs. Much of this detailed information is for the benefit of the firm's own managers and is produced to an in-depth degree. If the information was published in this complex form it would provide a vastly (often over) complex profit and loss account. This high level of detail would also provide competitors with a substantial amount of valuable information. Therefore limited companies only produce, for shareholder and public availability, a less complex (or published) profit and loss account.

After the European Commission issued the Fourth Directive in 1978, all Member States were required to adopt the contents of this Directive into their own legislation. This Directive required all Member States to implement legislation that required limited liability companies to publish financial statements in a *standardized format* which contained specified information. (Most of continental Europe already had a legal requirement specifying detailed attention to the format. The European Union (EU) adopted this highly prescriptive approach and implemented this requirement on a European-wide basis.)

These European requirements were adopted by the UK in the 1981 Companies Act – later incorporated in 1985 Companies Act (with some amendments by the 1989 Companies Act). The standardized format of published accounts was a novel innovation for UK companies. Prior to the Fourth Directive and the 1981 Companies Act, UK legislation merely stipulated the content of accounts and not a detailed format.

Although some authorities prefer the adoption of a standardized approach on the grounds of allowing European financial statements to be more easily compared, many of the opponents of European standardization lamented the loss of flexibility and individualism that this standardization has brought.

The detailed format requirements are specified in Schedule 4 of the 1985 Companies Act. Although the format is standardized, a certain degree of choice is permitted.

There are four different formats of profit and loss account permitted. There are two permitted versions of the balance sheets; one option is in vertical (or columnar) format and the other is the (less commonly used) horizontal format.

In addition to the items required by these formats, the Companies Act 1985, (sec 4) requires every profit and loss account to show three additional features:

1   profit or loss on ordinary activities;
2   any amount that is (or proposed to be) transferred to or from reserves;
3   the total amount of net dividends paid or proposed.

Of all the items in a profit and loss account the depreciation expense causes the most difficult conceptual problem.

DEPRECIATION

The fixed assets of a firm will usually be purchased in one accounting period but will normally last for many future years. These fixed assets, largely comprising of buildings, plant and machinery and fixtures and fittings, will be used in the business to generate future earnings for many years – and in the case of buildings, perhaps for many decades.

Legally and also in accordance with accounting standards, the cost of an asset must be allocated over the period of time expected to benefit from its use.

Depreciation is defined as:

> a measure of the wearing out, consumption or other loss of value of a fixed asset whether arising from use, effluxion of time or obsolescence through technology and market changes. (SSAP 12.)

Depreciation should be allocated to accounting periods so as to charge a fair proportion to each accounting period during the expected useful life of the asset. In the assessment and allocation of depreciation to accounting periods, there are three factors that need to be considered:

1   Cost (or valuation – if the asset has been revalued).
2   Nature of the asset and the length of its expected useful life to the business having due regard to the incidence of obsolescence.
3   Estimated residual (or scrap) value.

SSAP 12 notes that 'the allocation of depreciation to accounting periods involves the exercise of judgement by management in the light of technical, commercial and accounting considerations and accordingly require annual review'.

In a conceptual sense, depreciation is an intrinsic requirement to assist in ensuring that a company does not deplete its capital base.

If a company does not provide for depreciation of its fixed assets in its profit and loss account then the company's earnings will, in relative terms, be overstated. If the earnings are overstated, excessively high levels of dividends could be distributed by the company (i.e. in real terms, it is possible that dividends will be distributed from non-trading profits). Accordingly, if dividends are distributed from non-trading profits the accounting danger is that the dividends are being distributed from the company's capital base (i.e. from its shareholders' funds); which in turn signifies that the company is, in effect, depleting its capital – the heart or substance of its very existence. Ultimately, if this depletion continues, the original shareholders' funds will be returned to shareholders in the form of dividends.

To assist in maintaining the capital base of shareholders' funds, companies are required to make provision for the deterioration, ageing and erosion etc. of their fixed assets that were originally acquired. The accounting process of making this provision is by including a depreciation charge in the company's profit and loss account – which will reduce the amount of earnings potentially available for distribution. This 'artificial' restriction of earnings is necessary to maintain the capital base of the company (i.e. depreciation is part of the process of capital maintenance).

(Note: It is important to realize that the depreciation concept is not designed to provide a means or method to replace ageing assets. Depreciation is not intended to be a 'savings-scheme' by which the company can fund purchases of new assets. Its purpose is to maintain the original capital base of the company by restricting the amount of profits available for distribution.)

Two of the most common methods of depreciation are:

1   Straight line method.
2   Reducing balance method.

STRAIGHT LINE METHOD

Under this commonly used method of depreciation, an equal charge for depreciation is entered into the profit and loss account each year.

This method can be illustrated by the following formulae:

Annual depreciation charge (to profit and loss account)

$$= \frac{\text{Original cost (or value) of fixed asset} - \text{estimated residual (scrap) value}}{\text{Estimated useful economic life (years)}}$$

In the company's balance sheet, the fixed asset will be shown at its net amount (i.e. less depreciation).

For example, company A purchased a machine for £1,000 in 1995. It decides that the machine has a useful life of ten years, with nil scrap value.

In its profit and loss account, the depreciation charge every year between 1995 and 2004 will be £100:

i.e.
$$\frac{£1000 - nil}{10 \text{ years}}$$

In the balance sheet, the machine would be recorded:

As at 1995	Cost (£)	*Depreciation (£)	Net (£)
Machine	1,000	100	900
1996			
Machine	1,000	200	800
1997			
Machine	1,000	300	700

(*Note: This depreciation figure is the aggregate depreciation balance and not merely the depreciation of a given year.)

REDUCING BALANCE METHOD (SOMETIMES TERMED THE DIMINISHING BALANCE METHOD)

Under this less commonly selected method, a fixed percentage rate of depreciation charge is applied to the fixed assets. Although the actual percentage charge can be mathematically calculated, most companies choose to use a reasonably practical percentage figure to use for calculation.

Each year's depreciation charge in the profit and loss account will vary in size and become progressively less as the years pass.

For example, Company B purchases a machine in 1995 for £1,000. It has decided to use the reducing balance method with an annual charge of 20 per cent.

In the profit and loss account, the entries would be:

1995 ... £200 (20% of £1,000)
1996 ... £160 (20% of £800)
1997 ... £128 (20% of £640)
etc.

In the balance sheet:

As at 1995	Cost (£)	Depreciation (£)	Net (£)
Machine	1,000	200	800
1996			
Machine	1,000	360	640
1997			
Machine	1,000	488	512
etc.			

Legislation requires companies to state any charges for depreciation in the notes – if the amount for depreciation has not already been shown in the relevant profit and loss account.

It is important, when analysing financial statements, to have regard for the company's depreciation policy. The amount of depreciation charged in the profit and loss account and information from the supporting 'notes to the accounts' concerning depreciation methods and policies should be carefully examined. Particularly in the case of land and buildings, the user should note whether the depreciation is being charged on the original cost of the asset or (in the instance of companies revaluing their fixed assets) on the new revalued figure. (In some circumstances, there have been examples in the past of a small number of UK companies attempting not to depreciate their buildings on the grounds that these assets have been considered appreciating assets. This practice has been largely abandoned.)

SEGMENTATION

The 1985 Companies Act and SSAP 25, *Segmental Reporting*, require that companies provide segmented information to support the figures given in the profit and loss account. (The provision of segmental information may entail, for example, the 'splitting-up' of sales, earnings and assets into such categories as business activities and geographical location.)

For each class of business which the directors deem to be 'substantially different' from other businesses the company must disclose:

1   the turnover of that class of business;
2   the profit or loss (before taxation) attributable to that class.

Additionally for each substantially different geographical market, the company must identify the turnover that is attributable to that market.

In addition, SSAP 25 requires companies to segment:

1 turnover, distinguishing between
   (a) turnover derived from external customers, and;
   (b) turnover derived from other segments;
2 the company's profits before taxation, minority interests and extraordinary items;
3 net assets.

Segmental information need not be provided if, in the opinion of the directors, disclosure would be seriously prejudicial to the interests of the company. The Stock Exchange requires more detailed segmented information for listed companies. A geographical analysis of net turnover and profit that is derived from operations outside the UK should be provided, namely an analysis of turnover by continent and if any continent accounts for more than 50 per cent of turnover derived from overseas operations then a more detailed breakdown is required, normally on a country by country basis.

SSAP 13 *ACCOUNTING FOR RESEARCH AND DEVELOPMENT*

The accounting treatment of research and development has been standardized by SSAP 13, *Accounting for Research and Development.* Under the heading Research and Development, the following would normally be included:

- experimental, theoretical or other work aimed at the discovery of new knowledge or the advancement of existing knowledge;
- searching for application of knowledge;
- formulation and design of possible applications for such work;
- testing in search for, or evaluation of, product, service or process alternatives;
- design, construction and testing of preproduction prototypes and models;
- design of products, processes or systems involving new technology or substantially improving existing facilities.

SSAP 13 classifies all research and development into three categories:

1 *Pure or basic research:* Pure or basic research is experimental or theoretical work undertaken primarily to acquire new scientific or technical knowledge for its own sake.
2 *Applied research:* Applied research is defined as original or critical investigation undertaken in order to gain new scientific or technical knowledge and directed towards a specific or practical aim or objective.
3 *Development research:* Development research is the use of scientific or technical knowledge in order to produce new or substantially improved materials, devices, products or services prior to the commencement of commercial production or commercial applications or to improving substantially those already introduced or installed.

The accounting difficulty for companies is whether research expenditure should be written-off to the profit and loss account when incurred or whether the research is to be capitalized in the balance sheet as an asset. Many companies engage in research in the expectation that ultimately the research will lead to future enhanced earnings. Some companies believe that because the research may lead to additional profits it should accordingly be treated as an asset. Against this view there is the danger that the capitalized research expenditure does not yield the expected benefits or earnings, in which case the concept of conservatism will be breached.

To protect the concept of conservatism, SSAP 13 requires both pure research and applied research to be written-off as an expense directly to the profit and loss account when incurred.

SSAP 13 notes that development expenditure should be written-off in the year of expenditure *except* in the following circumstances, when it may be deferred to future periods:

1   there is a clearly defined project, and;
2   the related expenditure is separately identifiable, and;
3   the outcome of such a project has been assessed with reasonable certainty as to;
    (a)   its technical feasibility, and;
    (b)   its ultimate commercial viability, considered in the light of such factors as likely market conditions, public opinion and legislation, and;
4   the total of all development costs, (including any further development costs) is expected to be exceeded by related future sales or other revenues, and;
5   adequate resources exist, or are reasonably expected to be available, to enable the project to be completed and to provide for any future increases in working capital.

If these explicit conditions apply, then the research and development expenditure can be deferred and capitalized in the balance sheet as an asset.

SSAP 13 requires companies to disclose:

• their accounting policy on research and development;
• the total amount of research and development charged in the profit and loss account – which is analysed between current year's expenditure and amounts amortized from deferred expenditure;
• movements on deferred expenditure and the amount carried forward at the beginning and end of the period.

Deferred development expenditure should be disclosed under intangible fixed assets in the balance sheet.

PENSION COSTS

Since the introduction of SSAP 24, *Accounting for Pension Costs*, the subject of accounting for the pension contributions for employees (paid by the company) has become an increasingly complex subject for many companies.

SSAP 24 *Accounting for Pension Costs*

This Standard applies where the employer has a legal or contractual commitment under a pension scheme, to provide or contribute to pensions for his employees. It also addresses discretionary and *ex gratia* increases in pensions and *ex gratia* pensions. The same principles apply irrespective of whether the scheme is funded or unfunded. A funded scheme is typically where the pension contributions are held in a clearly identifiable fund of investments. An unfunded scheme is typified by the contributions of employees and employers not being specifically identifiable or 'ear-marked' – as is the case with some public sector employees.

This standard applies to the two major types of pension schemes: *defined contribution schemes* and *defined benefit schemes*. Although SSAP 24 primarily addresses pensions, its principles may be equally applicable to the cost of providing other post-retirement benefits (e.g. post-retirement medical expenses.) This Standard does not apply to either state social security contributions or redundancy payments.

Pension cost: General Principle.

The accounting objective is that: the employer should recognise the expected cost of providing pensions on a systematic and rational basis over the period during which he derives benefit from the employees' services. (SSAP 24, para 77.)

1 *Defined contribution schemes:* In some company pension schemes the pension payable to an employee on retirement is not related to years of service or final salary. Where an employee is a member of a defined contribution scheme the pension will be dependent on the value of the employee's total accumulated pension fund. The company may or may not contribute to the employee's fund – but, if the fund is at an inadequate level at retirement – the company incurs no further legal liability. There are few major accounting difficulties with this type of scheme.

For defined contribution schemes the charge against profits should be the amount of contributions payable to the pension scheme in respect of the accounting period.

2 *Defined benefit schemes:* In a defined benefit scheme, the employee's pension is determined by the amount of the final salary on retirement and the number of years of service provided by the employee. Irrespective of the value of the pension on retirement, the company pension scheme must legally pay a pension based on the employee's salary and years of service. If there is a shortfall in the pension fund the company (not the employee) must make good the deficit. Accordingly there is a potential liability that needs to be accounted for. (Note: there could also be an asset – if the pension scheme is in surplus.)

For defined benefit schemes the pension cost should be calculated using actuarial valuation methods which are consistent with the requirements of this Standard. The actuarial assumptions and method, taken as a whole, should be compatible and should lead to the actuary's best estimate of the cost of providing the pension benefits promised. The method of providing for expected pension costs over the service lives of employees in the scheme should be such that the regular pension cost is a substantially level percentage of the current and expected future pensionable payroll in the light of the current actuarial assumptions.

Subject to the provisions of the following paragraphs, variations from the regular cost should be allocated over the expected remaining service lives of current employees in the scheme. A period representing the average remaining service lives may be used if desired.

The provisions of the above paragraph should not be applied where, and to the extent that, a significant change in the normal level of contributions occurs because contributions are adjusted to eliminate a surplus or deficiency resulting from a significant reduction in the number of employees covered by the enterprise's pension arrangements. Amounts receivable may not be anticipated; for example, the full effect of a contribution holiday should not be recognized at the outset of the holiday, but rather spread over duration.

Balance sheet If the cumulative pension cost recognized in the profit and loss account has not been completely discharged by payment of contributions or directly paid pensions, the excess should be shown as a net pension provision. Similarly, any excess of contributions paid over the cumulative pension cost should be shown as a prepayment.

Disclosures The following disclosures should be made in respect of a *defined contribution scheme*:

1   the nature of the scheme (i.e. defined contribution);
2   the accounting policy;
3   the pension cost charge for the period;
4   any outstanding or prepaid contributions at the balance sheet date.

In addition to the above, in the case of a *defined benefit scheme*, the following must be stated:

1   whether the pension costs and provisions (or asset) are assessed in accordance with the advice of a professionally qualified actuary and, if so, the date of the most recent formal actuarial valuation or later formal review used for this purpose;
2   the pension cost charge for the period together with explanations of significant changes in the charge compared to that in the previous accounting period;
3   any provisions or prepayments in the balance sheet resulting from a difference between the amounts recognized as a cost and the amounts funded or paid directly;
4   the amount of any deficiency on a current funding level basis, indicating the action, if any, being taken to deal with it in the current and future accounting periods;
5   an outline of the results of the most recent formal actuarial valuation or later formal review of the scheme on an on-going basis.

Also further disclosures should include: the actuarial method used; a brief description of the main actuarial assumptions; market value of scheme assets and the level of funding expressed in percentage terms.

EMPLOYEES

In many ways the extent and quality of information disclosed about employees is very restricted. The average number of staff employed during the year must be disclosed in the notes.

Additionally the average number of employees within each classification or category of business must be recorded. Although these categories are not made explicit, these categories could be:

- geographical analysis;
- functional or sectional analysis;
- analysis by product category.

Total staff costs must disclose:

- wages and salaries paid or payable during the year;
- social security costs incurred by the company on their behalf;
- other pension costs.

DIVIDENDS

The Companies Act 1985 requires the aggregate amount of any dividends to be disclosed on the face of the profit and loss account.

These dividends will include both paid and proposed. Any dividends that have been proposed by the Board but not yet actually paid will be shown as a current liability in the balance sheet.

It must be borne in mind that to declare a dividend a company:

- must have legal capacity, and
- be physically able to pay.

In the instance of legal capacity there are many complex legal requirements as to the level of dividends that a company can distribute to its shareholders. Company legislation is concerned with ensuring that a company does not distribute its capital back to its shareholders. It is essential that the firm's capital is not depleted by dividend distributions. To ensure that this depletion does not occur, the legislation requires that a company must conform to strict legal rules.

The general requirement for all limited companies is that:

a company's profits available for distribution are its accumulated, realised profits . . . less its accumulated realised losses. ((CA Act 1985), sec 263/4.)

However, in the case of a public limited company there are additional legal restrictions on dividend distribution, namely:

A public limited company cannot pay a dividend which would reduce the amount of its net assets below the aggregate of its called-up share capital plus its undistributable reserves. (sec 264 (1).)

The Companies Act defines undistributable reserves as:

1 Share premium.
2 Capital redemption reserve.
3 Excess of accumulated unrealized profits over accumulated unrealized losses.
4 Any other reserves which the company may not distribute (such as a reserve specifically prohibited in its articles).

In the case of public companies, the dividend must not exceed accumulated realized profits less accumulated realized losses and less accumulated net unrealized losses. Secondly, in a practical sense, a company may have legal capability to pay a dividend but it may not actually have sufficient liquidity with which to pay the dividend. In other words, there is insufficient cash resources from which to issue the dividend payment warrants.

(For layout of published profit and loss accounts see chapter 3 Format of Financial Statements.)

QUESTIONS

1 Explain the purpose of a profit and loss account.
2 Discuss the formats of a profit and loss account that are permitted by the legislation.
3 What is the purpose of depreciation?
4 Why is the treatment of pension costs so significant for most companies?
5 Discuss how SSAP 13 requires research and development to be treated in company accounts.
6 What are distributable profits?

6 | Balance Sheet

This chapter examines:

- the nature and significance of the balance sheet;
- the nature of assets and liabilities;
- the valuation of assets.

WHAT IS A BALANCE SHEET?

A balance sheet provides a list of a company's assets and liabilities. The balance sheet will identify in monetary terms, what a company *owns* (its assets) and what it *owes* (its liabilities) at *a given point in time*.

The Companies Act 1985 allows companies to choose between *two* formats of the balance sheet in the published format. Although the format of each option contains a number of differences, the content is identical. The most common form of balance sheet that is adopted by UK companies is the 'vertical' format – legally termed format 1. (Alternatively a very small minority of companies choose the horizontal format – termed format 2, see chapter 3 Format of Financial Statements.)

VALUATION OF ASSETS

Interpretation and analysis of the balance sheet can be extremely misleading if the user does not appreciate the basis on which a company's assets are stated. In the UK, companies have a choice as to whether they wish to periodically revalue their fixed assets. The Companies Act 1985 allows companies to either show assets at their original cost (termed historical cost accounting) or alternatively assets can be disclosed at their current value (called replacement cost). Some companies use a mixture of historical cost and replacement cost valuation methods, the combination of which is termed *modified historical cost accounting*. Under this modified method the majority of a company's non-fixed assets will be shown at their original or historical cost, whilst their fixed assets may be periodically revalued to their current replacement cost.

Under UK current legislation and accounting requirements there is no specific obligation for companies to revalue upwards any of their assets. For example, two companies may each have purchased a freehold office building in 1980 for £1 million. If a similar building were to be purchased today, a property surveyor might suggest that the current value is £3 million. One company may have decided to periodically revalue its building to reflect the increasing value. So, consequently the building in its balance sheet is now at £3 million, whereas the other company may decide to keep its building at the original cost (i.e. £1 million). Unless the reader of the financial statements is aware of these differences in valuation policy, it can be extremely difficult to compare and analyse a company's balance sheet.

To a certain extent, the user is not totally left unaware of these valuation problems. There can be indications in a company's balance sheet that it has revalued some or all of its assets at some point in time. The user can sometimes identify entries in the balance sheet when an asset has been revalued by the creation of a revaluation reserve.

For example:

EXAMPLE 6.1

Company A purchased a building for £100,000 in 1986. In 1994 a surveyor estimates that the building is worth £150,000.

The accounting entries would be: the company increases the value of the building by £50,000 and subsequently shows the asset in its 1994 balance sheet at £150,000. The corresponding entry on the liability side of the balance sheet would be the creation of a revaluation reserve of £50,000. It is important to stress that because this revaluation gain is *unrealized* (i.e. the building has not actually been physically sold) the gain of £50,000 cannot legally be taken to the profit and loss account.

Additionally in accordance with FRS 3, the gain of £50,000 would be shown as a recognized gain in the Statement of Recognized Gains and Losses. When and if the building is actually sold, the amount arising from profit on sale would be transferred from the revaluation reserve and subsequently taken to the profit and loss account.

The amount of profit that could be shown on disposal of the asset in the profit and loss account is also explained in FRS 3, *Reporting Financial Performance*. In the above example, if the company sells the building in 1996 for £175,000, the profit on disposal would be calculated by comparing the sale proceeds with the *carrying value* of the asset. (The carrying value is the amount at which the asset is shown in the balance sheet, which, in this example, is £150,000.) Therefore the profit on sale would be £25,000 (£175,000 − £150,000). In accordance with FRS 3, the historical cost profit, of £75,000 (£175,000 − £100,000) would need to be disclosed in the notes to the financial statements.

Likewise if an asset has fallen in value, companies will need to provide for this reduction where the diminution is expected to be permanent. The user can also obtain further evidence that the fixed assets are not stated at their current values in the balance sheet by examining the notes. The 1985 Companies Act (sec 7) requires the directors to disclose any substantial differences between the market values and book values in land and buildings. This disclosure is necessary, if in the directors' opinion the difference between the book and market value is of such significance that it should be brought to the attention of shareholders and debenture holders.

FIXED ASSETS

The 1985 Companies Act (sch 4) requires companies to disclose fixed assets under three headings:

1 intangible assets;
2 tangible assets;
3 investments.

   In respect of each of these items, companies are required to:

- state the amount of the item at cost or where the alternative accounting rules (using current values) are used, at revaluation or current cost at the beginning and end of the financial year, and;
- state the effect on that item of any acquisitions or disposals during the year.

   In addition companies must also disclose:

- for each item, the accumulated depreciation or diminution in value made in the financial year;
- any provisions for depreciation made in the financial year, and;
- any adjustments that need to be made to such provisions that result from the disposal of any asset during the financial year.

   SSAP 12, *Accounting for Depreciation* requires that all fixed assets that are subject to depreciation should disclose:

1 the depreciation method used, and;
2 the useful economic lives used in the depreciation rates, and;
3 total depreciation charged for the financial period, and;
4 the gross amount of depreciable assets and the related accumulated depreciation (para 25).

Additionally the effect, if material, of any change in the depreciation method and changes in depreciation caused by any revaluation of assets must be disclosed (paras 26–7). (See chapter 5 Profit and Loss Account.)

   If any capital has been borrowed to finance the building of an asset, and the interest on these borrowed funds has been capitalized this fact must be disclosed. (Capitalization of interest can occur where, for example a company borrows funds to finance the construction of the building. Whilst the building is under construction it is permitted to add the interest that has accrued on the borrowed funds to the cost of the building – instead of showing the interest payable in the profit and loss account.) There promises to be substantial changes in the ASB practice in regard to the valuation of fixed assets. Building upon ED 51, *Accounting for Fixed Assets and Revaluations*, it seems that the ASB will, in the interests of comparability eventually make it necessary for companies to periodically and compulsorily revalue some types of their fixed assets.

INTANGIBLE FIXED ASSETS

The Companies Act 1985 identifies three main categories of intangible assets:

1 Development costs.
2 Concessions, patents, licences, trademarks, and similar rights.
3 Goodwill.

Most companies write-off research and development costs to their profit and loss account in the financial year in which it is incurred. The legislation allows development costs to be capitalized in the balance sheet in 'special circumstances' provided full reasons are given for doing so. Some companies invest extremely heavily in research and developmental expenditure which is expected to be of economic benefit to the company in subsequent years. Some companies object to writing-off all the research and development expenditure in the actual financial year in which it is incurred. Such companies see their research and development expenditure as being effectively an investment in an asset that will provide a source of revenue in future years. Accordingly, these companies may wish to treat research and development costs as an asset that is to be gradually written-off in the future. The potential accounting and business danger for companies that capitalize research and development is that this process shows an asset that may not necessarily lead to a future earning stream (i.e. the research and development fails to provide any benefits and it turns out not to be an asset at all). To minimize this risk the conditions whereby research and development can be capitalized are contained in SSAP 13, *Accounting for Research and Development*. SSAP 13 defines precisely and extensively the conditions when companies are permitted to capitalize research and development costs.

In the interests of prudence, SSAP 13 normally requires research and development to be written-off to the profit and loss account when incurred. If the research and development is classified as 'developmental research' it is possible to capitalize research and development provided that:

1 there is a clearly defined project, and;
2 the related research expenditure is separately identifiable, and;
3 the outcome of the project has been assessed with reasonable certainty as to its
   (a) technical feasibility, and;

(b)   ultimate commercial viability considered in the light of factors such as market conditions, public opinion and consumer and environmental legislation;
4   total developmental costs are expected to be exceeded by future sales, and;
5   adequate resources exist or will exist to complete the project and to provide for any consequential increases in working capital.

Developmental research is the use of scientific or technical knowledge in order to produce new or substantially improved materials, devices, products or services prior to the commencement of commercial production or commercial applications or to improve substantially those already produced or installed (SSAP 13).

CONCESSIONS, PATENTS, LICENCES, TRADE MARKS AND SIMILAR ASSETS

These items can only be shown in the balance sheet if they were acquired for valuable consideration and are not to be shown as goodwill.

GOODWILL

Goodwill is defined in SSAP 22, *Accounting for Goodwill* as:

the difference between the value of the business as a whole and the fair value of its separable net assets. (SSAP 22, para 26.)

SSAP 22 and Companies Act 1985 prohibit companies from leaving goodwill as a permanent feature in the balance sheet.
SSAP 22 requires companies to:

1   Write-off goodwill to reserves immediately on acquisition – the so-called 'immediate write-off method', or;
2   Write-off (amortize) the goodwill to the company's profit and loss account over its useful economic life.

For example, if company A acquires company B for £100 in total, and the total net fair value of the individual assets of B was £80, the difference of £20 would be defined as goodwill. (The use of the term fair value in this definition means that the assets of B must be based on their current value and not their historical cost.)
Goodwill can only be shown in the balance sheet if it has been *acquired* for valuable consideration – normally for cash or by issuing additional shares or some combination of these two means (i.e. the goodwill must be purchased). Although *self-generated* goodwill may frequently exist in many businesses, (perhaps arising

from the reputation, skills, location etc. of a company), it is ignored in accounting. It is not possible for the company's directors to consider that there exists a certain amount of self-generated or inherent goodwill within the business and place this figure in the balance sheet. The showing of self-generated goodwill is considered to be neither objective, nor accurate, nor verifiable and so consequently this process is forbidden. Most companies adopt the immediate write-off method in treating goodwill because it has no impact on earnings.

However, the ASB has proposed that this option is abolished. ED 47, *Accounting for Goodwill* (to be superseded by FRED 12) proposed that companies should be compelled to choose the amortization method. The use of this method would standardize the treatment and allow better comparison – especially with companies in other countries that do not allow immediate write-off (see appendix 6.1).

Until the ASB issued UITF Abstract 3, *Treatment of Goodwill on Disposal of a Business* the treatment of goodwill on the disposal of a company was extremely vague. For example, company A acquired company B for £100. At the date of acquisition the net tangible assets of B were £70 implying that the goodwill was £30 (£100 – 70). In 1996 company B was sold for £120.

If company A wrote-off the goodwill of £30 to reserves then the profit on disposal would be £50 (£120 – £70). Abstract 3 now requires that the £30 goodwill previously written-off be reinstated and written-off against the profit on disposal, giving a profit now of £20 (£120 – (£70 + £30)).

BRAND NAMES

One particular asset that is not referred to in the Companies Acts is that of brand names. The topic of brand names came to the forefront of accounting debate in the late 1980s. Although the Companies Act requires trade marks to be shown in the balance sheet, it does not make specific reference to brand names. Brand names are not just trade marks. The concept of a brand is far more extensive and comprehensive than a trade mark. A brand will encompass a number of complex and interwoven factors, including such features as a recognized name, a product or range of products, an established market position, specialist know-how, marketing techniques, and product image. These characteristics are expected to generate increased earnings for companies. Critics of brand accounting argue that brand names are an integral part or subset of goodwill. Brands should not be allocated their own identity as an asset but should be accounted for in the same manner as goodwill.

The supporters of brand capitalization believe that brands do have their own specific identity which is separate from that of goodwill. Many companies pay considerable sums in purchasing companies that contain significant brands and argue for the right to state brands separately in the balance sheet as an independent asset.

In addition to purchasing brands, a company may also create its own brands. In the late 1980s a number of companies were strengthening their corporate asset base by putting a value on their self-developed or home-grown brands. One of the first companies to do so was the food manufacturer, Rank, Hovis McDougall. Just as a surveyor would value a company's property portfolio, so specialist brand valuation experts would provide an estimate of a company's own brand names. In the case of RHM a brand valuation of £678m was determined by reference to two factors:

1 *Brand profitability:* This involves the examination of individual brand profitability and smoothing out annual earnings' fluctuations by using a weighted average post tax profit figure based upon the last three years.
2 *Brand strength:* which considers a number of factors:
   (a) market leadership;
   (b) stability of brand;
   (c) market and nature of products;
   (d) internationality of products;
   (e) trend of growth;
   (f) support for products;
   (g) protection.

A product that is a market leader in its field will be accorded a greater weighting than a brand that has only limited recognition. Likewise, a brand for which demand remains stable or growing over the years is more valuable than a brand for which demand is variable or falling. The markets in which a brand competes and the actual nature of the brand is significant. A brand that only has limited competition or is a staple and sought-after commodity, such as food lines, will attract a higher branding value. A brand that is recognized in world markets is potentially more valuable than brands merely competing in national or localized positions. A brand that has a year-on-year trend pattern of growth, especially if this growth is supported by legal protection, by heavy advertising and by intense marketing, will assist in enhancing the brand's value.

The next stage is for the company to calculate a 'brand strength score' by allocating arithmetical and confidential weightings to each of the above factors. Once a small number of companies commenced capitalizing their own home grown brands (and seemingly, with the approval of their auditors) the accounting fashion rapidly spread to many other sectors of industry. The next accounting difficulty was deciding whether their values should be amortized. In an attempt to resolve the dilemma relating to the amortization of goodwill and intangible assets the ASB expects that its Discussion Draft will stimulate public debate and hopes some generally acceptable solutions will emerge.

The ASB in ED 52, *Accounting for Intangible Assets* (to be superseded by FRED 12), has laid down a number of conditions before brands could be granted separate recognition in the balance sheet, namely:

1 the historical cost incurred in creating the brand is known or it can demonstrated that it is readily ascertainable and;
2 its characteristics can be clearly distinguishable from those of goodwill and other assets and;

3 its costs are capable of being measured independently of goodwill. There will normally have 'to be an active market in intangible assets of the same kind that is undertaken independently of the purchase and sale of businesses or business segments'.

It is this final point that is most contentious – for if ED 52 is ultimately accepted then most companies would be effectively banned from capitalizing brands – largely because brands are not routinely bought and sold.

TANGIBLE ASSETS

Under the historical cost accounting rules the amount to be included in the balance sheet will be its purchase price or production cost. The purchase price must include the incidental costs of acquisition, such as legal costs. Production costs shall include the purchase price of raw materials and consumables used, together with other costs incurred which are directly attributable to the production of the asset. The production cost can also include interest on borrowed capital that is used to finance the production of the asset, provided the interest element is disclosed in the notes.

The 1985 Companies Act (sec 4, sch 18) and SSAP 12 require all fixed assets having a limited economic life to be depreciated on a systematic basis over their useful economic life.

SSAP 12 requires the depreciation charge in the profit and loss account to be based on the carrying amount of the asset in the balance sheet. The whole of the depreciation charge must be charged to the profit and loss account and must not be offset against reserves in the balance sheet. Any fixed assets whose value is considered to have permanently diminished must write the value of the asset down to its estimated recoverable value, which should then, if appropriate, be depreciated over its remaining useful life.

INVESTMENT PROPERTIES

Special accounting provisions apply in the case where companies have properties that are held for their investment potential.

An investment property is defined in SSAP 19, *Accounting for Investment Properties* as an interest in land and/or buildings:

a) in respect of which construction and development has been completed and;
b) which is held for its investment potential with any rental income being negotiated on an arm's length basis. (Para 8.)

Investment properties must be carried in the balance sheet at an open market value – and the carrying value must be prominently displayed. Investment properties do not need to be subject to a periodic depreciation charge. Any changes in the values of investment during the course of the financial year should be recognized in the Statement of Recognized Gains and Losses.

Assets appearing in the balance sheet may, at least in part, be financed by a variety of government grants for the purposes of encouraging investments in various assets and locations. The accounting requirements of government grants are defined in SSAP 4, *Accounting for Government Grants*. Where a government grant is provided to assist a company to purchase a capital asset, SSAP 4 allows two accounting treatments.

These are:

1   to treat the amount of the grant as deferred income which is credited to the profit and loss account by instalments over the expected useful economic life of the asset, or;
2   to deduct the amount of the grant from the purchase price or production cost of the asset – with a consequential reduction in depreciation.

Although both options are acceptable to SSAP 4, there are potential legal difficulties for limited companies using option 2. Legal advice is that it may be illegal to deduct the amount of the grant from the cost of the asset because the resulting net figure does not indicate the actual purchase price or production cost. Accordingly, the accounting practice is for companies to adopt option 1.

LEASED ASSETS

Finance and operating leases

If a company has assets acquired under the terms of a lease, then the company must comply with the requirements of SSAP 21, *Accounting for Leases and Hire Purchase Transactions*.

SSAP 21 defines two types of leases: finance (or capital) leases and operating leases. The accounting treatments and balance sheet entries differ in each case. A finance lease is defined as 'a lease that transfers substantially all the risks and rewards of ownership of an asset to the lessee'.

It should be presumed that this transfer of risks occurs, if at the inception of the lease, the present value of the minimum lease payments, including any initial payment, amounts to substantially all (normally 90 per cent or more) of the fair value of the asset.

An operating lease is a lease that is not a finance lease.

A finance lease should be recorded in the balance sheet of a lessee as a tangible fixed asset and also as an obligation to pay future rentals. In addition, further information must be disclosed either on the balance sheet or more commonly in the notes concerning:

- gross amount of leased assets;
- accumulated depreciation;
- depreciation allocated for the financial year.

A finance lease should be depreciated on the shorter of the term of the lease and the leased asset's useful life. An operating lease will not be capitalized in the lessee's balance sheet and only the lease rental payments will be entered in the profit and loss account (SSAP 21, para 15).

INVESTMENTS

Investments may be included in the balance sheet as either a fixed or current asset. Investments held on a long-term basis should normally be classified as a fixed asset and investments of a relatively temporary nature should be accounted for as a current asset. The aggregate value of investments listed on a recognized stock exchange must be stated. Any difference between the market value and the value stated in the balance sheet must be disclosed.

CURRENT ASSETS

Current assets which predominantly includes stocks, work-in-progress, trade debtors, cash and bank balances must normally be shown in the balance sheet at their purchase price or production cost. The 1985 Companies Act, (sch 23) requires that if the net realizable value of an asset is lower than the purchase price or production cost then it must be shown at net realizable value. The Companies Act requires the use of FIFO, LIFO or Weighted Average cost – although SSAP 9 does not normally permit the use of LIFO (because of its rather 'illogical' nature and it is frequently at variance with the provision of a fair approximation of cost).

Stocks should be sub-divided into:

- raw materials and consumables;
- work-in-progress;
- finished goods;
- payments on account.

SSAP 9, *Stocks and Long-term Contracts*, requires that a statement shall be provided that describes the amount at which stocks are stated in the financial statements. (A typical statement would be that 'stocks are shown at the lower of cost and net realisable value.') If there is a material difference between the value of stocks as stated in the balance sheet and the value of stocks at replacement cost then the amount of the difference should be stated in the notes.

LONG-TERM CONTRACTS

A long-term contract is where the company is involved in contract work that is extended over more than one accounting period. The most common examples are buildings or road construction.

Long-term contracts must be accounted for on an individual basis. As the contract progresses, the work (turnover and costs) of the contract should be proportionately reflected in the profit and loss account. In the balance sheet the amount by which turnover is in excess of payments on account should be included in the headings: 'amounts recoverable on contracts' and then disclosed within the company's debtors figure.

Additionally the cost of long-term contracts, (net of the amounts transferred to the cost of sales and) after deducting any foreseeable losses should be shown as a 'long-term contract' under the general heading of 'stocks'.

(Long-term contracts is a specialized area of accounting. For further information, readers are advised to consult *Advanced Financial Accounting* by Lewis and Pendril, see the Further Reading section at the end of this chapter.)

UITF 5 requires that if a current asset is transferred from being a current asset to a fixed asset classification then the transfer must occur at the lower of cost or net realizable value. If the transfer occurs at a net realizable value (which is lower than its previous carrying value) then the diminution should be charged to the profit and loss account. This requirement was introduced to prohibit companies (such as construction companies) having potential development land banks that were stated as stock within current assets – where the value of the land had fallen since purchase. To avoid writing the land bank down to its net realizable value (resulting in a loss being charged to the profit and loss account) a number of firms 'reclassified' the asset as fixed by transferring it to land and buildings in the fixed asset section of the balance sheet. Once the potential building land is classified as a fixed asset the more flexible and less stringent rules for writing down a fixed asset apply.

In general terms, it is crucial that the stock valuations are calculated as accurately and as objectively as possible. Whilst the end-user of financial statements has little choice (from the available information provided in published format) but to accept the stock valuation figures, it is important to appreciate the impact on profits that stock discrepancies and valuation differences can cause. (Stock valuation procedures and controls will form a significant role in the internal accounting controls of a company's financial systems.)

For every £1 that stocks are undervalued, the profits will be £1 understated (and vice versa). This direct relationship arises because the lower the closing stock valuation – the higher will be the cost of sales. Accordingly, the higher the cost of sales figure – the lower will be profits.

EXAMPLE TABLE 6.2
Company A has sales of £100; opening stock of £20, and purchases of £60.

1 Assuming closing stocks are valued at £25 the earnings will be:

Trading accounts for period ending 19xx

Sales		£100
Opening stock	20	
Add		
Purchases	60	
	80	
Less		
Closing stock	**(25)**	
Cost of sales		(55)
Gross profit		**45**

---

2   If closing stocks are calculated to be £15, then in the above example, the cost of sales will be £65 and the gross profit will be £35 (£100 − £65).

The user of financial statements should also be aware that the choice of a stock valuation may critically affect the company's profit. Although the calculation of stock valuations is outside the scope of this book; readers who are interested in this area are suggested to refer to a management accounting text. A recommended text is *Management and Cost Accounting* by Drury: see Further Reading section at the end of this chapter.

DEBTORS

Debtors (also known as 'receivables') state the amounts that are owed to the company and should be shown under the headings (1985 Companies Act, Schedule 4):

1 Trade debtors – these debtors arise from the credit sale of goods to customers and are frequently the largest item contained within the general heading of debtors.
2 Amounts owed by group undertakings.
3 Amounts owed by undertakings in which the company has a participating interest.
4 Other debtors – these are trade debts, such as a debt arising from the sale of a fixed asset. Under this heading any loans to directors and company officers must be included.
5 Prepayments and accrued income (for example, this would include any expenses such as the rent or insurance that has been paid in advance).

The amounts falling due after more than one year should be shown separately under each of the above headings.

From a company's liquidity position, it is extremely important that the debtors' balances are kept under close review. The greater the debtor balances and the longer these debts remain unpaid then the longer a company will carry not only the risk of default, but also the cost of carrying the debtors. In other words, the longer that debtor balances are left outstanding – then the longer the company has to await for the cash inflows. As a result the company may have to turn elsewhere for funding such as expensive overdraft finance. Accordingly, companies should have general policies of sound credit control. In practice, a sound credit control management will include such actions as: investigating the creditworthiness of a company before agreeing to undertake business on credit terms; having and enforcing strict payment terms and conditions for debtors; and periodically examining ageing debtor balances – with appropriate follow-up action.

FRS 4, *ACCOUNTING FOR CAPITAL INSTRUMENTS*

FRS 4 came into effect for companies whose accounting year ends after June 1994. This rather complex standard examines the methods by which companies are financed and explains how financial and capital instruments should be accounted for and shown in company accounts.

In essence, it defines capital instruments, in rather wide terms, as methods that a business uses in order to obtain finance.

Before FRS 4 was issued there was a great variety of methods by which companies accounted for rather complex financial instruments and also considerable variety in the extent and quality of information provided in the financial statements.

Objective

The objective of FRS 4 is to ensure that the financial statements provide 'a clear, coherent and consistent treatment of capital instruments' (FRS 4, para 1). FRS 4 defines capital instruments as 'all instruments that are issued . . . as a means of raising finance, including shares, debentures, loans and debt instruments, options and warrants that give the holder the right to subscribe for or obtain capital instruments' (para 2).

FRS 4 splits capital instruments into two major categories:

1 debt;
2 shareholders' funds.

As regards debt, FRS 4 requires that any capital instrument that creates a liability should be regarded as debt. Even if the liability depends on a future event – such as a contingent liability – the capital instrument is still debt (rather than part of shareholders' funds). So if a capital instrument gives the bearer the right to receive cash or shares at a future time the instrument should be treated as debt – and shown accordingly on the balance sheet. Shareholders' funds are effectively defined by default. Any capital instruments that do not fall within the definition of debt are considered to be part of shareholders' funds. FRS 4 requires these shareholders' funds to be split between:

- non-equity interests;
- equity interests.

Non-equity interests include:

- any rights of the shares to receive payments for a limited amount that is not calculated by reference to the company's assets or profits or the dividends on any class of equity share;
- any rights to participate in a surplus in a winding-up that are limited to a specific amount that is not calculated by reference to the company's assets or profits;
- shares that are redeemable either because they were issued as redeemable shares or because the issue may require their redemption.

Equity shares are defined as any shares other than non-equity shares.

In the financial statements FRS 4 requires companies to analyse shareholders' funds between equity interests and non-equity interests.

For example:

EXAMPLE TABLE 6.3

Item	Analysed between	
Shareholders' funds	Equity interests	Non-equity interests
Minority interests	Equity interests in subsidiaries	Non-equity interests in subsidiaries
Liabilities	Convertible liabilities	Non-convertible liabilities

Any dividends should be divided between dividends payable on equity shares and dividends payable on non-equity shares. The company needs to provide a brief summary of the rights of each class of shares. This summary should include the rights to dividends, the dates on which shares are redeemable, amounts payable on redemption, and voting rights.

The company should also disclose the total amount of dividends for each type of shares and any other appropriation of profits in respect of non-equity shares. Any warrants that a company has issued should be shown separately in the balance sheet. FRS 4 explains the treatment of scrip dividends. (Some companies issue additional shares to shareholders – termed scrip dividends, instead of distributing dividends.) Companies that issue scrip dividends should treat the cash foregone as the net proceeds.

ACCOUNTING TREATMENT OF DEBT

If a company issues debt the resulting liability should be shown in the balance sheet at the net amount that has been received after all issue costs have been deducted (i.e. the liability should be stated at the net proceeds). The finance cost of the debt should be allocated to periods over the term of the debt at a constant rate on the net carrying amount. All finance costs should be charged to the profit and loss account. The carrying amount of the debt should be increased by the finance cost in respect of the financial year and reduced by payments made in respect of the debt in that period.

For example:

EXAMPLE TABLE 6.4

Company A issues £10 million of 5% loan stock that will be repayable in 3 years at a premium of 4%. Company A's merchant bank charges issue costs of £100,000.

The finance costs are comprised of:

	£
Interest for 3 years (3 years × £500,000)	1,500,000
Premium (4% × £10 million)	400,000
Issue costs	100,000
Total	2,000,000

Company A receives (net): £9,900,000 (£10 million less issue costs of £100,000). The difference between the financing cost and the amount paid should be added to the liability. At the end of 3 years the liability will have increased to £10,400,000 (i.e. the original debt of £10 million plus the premium on redemption).

Any gain or loss the company makes arising from the repurchase of the debt should be recognized in the profit and loss account.

A company is also required to disclose an analysis of the maturity of debt by showing the amounts falling due:

1 in one year or less or on demand;
2 between one and two years;
3 between two and five years;
4 five years or more.

The maturity of the debt should refer to the earliest date on which the lender can require repayment.

Convertible debt

Convertible loan stock is debt that, at the lender's option can be converted to equity at a predetermined date and rate. Prior to FRS 4, some companies antici-pated that the lender would convert their debt into equity and accordingly classified convertible debt as part of shareholders' funds. FRS 4 has now prohib-ited this anticipatory course of accounting treatment. Conversion of debt should not be taken for granted and should be reported within the liabilities of the company. The finance cost should be calculated on the basis that the debt will not be converted into shares but will be redeemed for cash. No gain or loss should be recognized on conversion.

FRS 5, *REPORTING THE SUBSTANCE OF TRANSACTIONS*

During the 1980s an increasing number of companies attempted to utilize a number of accounting techniques and practices to minimize or completely eliminate the amount of information that was shown in the financial statements. In particular, some companies attempted to comply with the strict and literal interpretation of various provisions of the Companies Acts and the content of accounting standards. In essence, companies were disguising certain transactions and removing a number of transactions which should have resulted in liabilities appearing in the balance sheet. These transactions gave rise to terminology that came to be called *'off balance sheet finance'*.

In an attempt to counter this growing use of 'off balance sheet finance' the accounting profession has increasingly adopted an accounting remedy termed *'substance over form'*.

In essence, this term implies that the practical substance of a transaction should be accounted for rather than its legal formalities. In other words, the practicalities of a transaction should take priority over the strict legal position. The application of substance over form has been criticized by lawyers for allowing accountants to promote their interpretation of transactions above the position of the law. Nevertheless, the application of substance over form is seen by accountants as essential in their attempts to ensure the financial statements report all transactions. To further the development of this term, the Accounting Standards Board issued FRS 5, *Reporting the Substance of Transactions* in 1994.

FRS 5 requires companies 'to report the substance of the transactions into which it has entered . . . (and to) . . . determine the substance of a transaction, whether any resulting assets and liabilities should be included in the balance sheet, and what disclosures are appropriate' (FRS 5, p. 4).

The FRS will not change the vast majority of transactions but will affect the more complex transactions whose substance may not be readily apparent. FRS 5 identifies transactions that may require particularly careful analysis which will often possess the following features:

1 the party that gains the principal benefit generated by an item is not the legal owner of the item;
2 a transaction that is linked with others in such a way that the commercial effect can be understood only by considering the series of transactions as a whole, or;
3 an option is included on terms that make its exercise highly likely.

FRS 5 establishes general principles that apply to all transactions and, in addition it identifies five specific Application Notes. In these Application Notes, five transactions, commonly used by companies, and are selected for detailed analysis. They consist of:

1 consignment stock;
2 sale and repurchase agreements;
3 factoring;
4 securitized assets;
5 loan transfers (see FRS 5 for further information).

The general principle involved in determining the substance of any transaction is to identify whether a transaction has given rise to new assets or liabilities for the company and whether it has increased or decreased the company's assets or liabilities. (Assets are broadly defined as rights or other access to future economic benefits controlled by the company; whereas liabilities are a company's obligations to transfer economic benefits as a result of past transactions or events.)

Once an asset or liability has been identified it should be recognized in the balance sheet – provided that there is sufficient evidence that an asset or liability exists and the asset or liability can be measured at a monetary amount with sufficient reliability.

In particular FRS 5 requires the use of a special form of presentation, termed a 'linked presentation' for certain non-recourse finance arrangements. On the face of the balance sheet, the finance should be deducted from the gross amount of the asset that it finances. The conditions for its use require, *inter alia*, that the finance will be repaid from the proceeds generated by the specific item it finances and there is no possibility of a claim on the company being established other than against funds generated by the asset. Additionally there must be no provision whereby the company may keep the item on repayment of the finance.

FRS 5 also makes reference to 'quasi-subsidiaries'. Prior to the Companies Act 1989 and FRS 5, a number of companies created what became known as quasi-subsidiaries. These were companies that were not subsidiaries in the legal definition but were in a practical sense.

By distorting and carefully circumventing the legal definition of a subsidiary, companies could implement the use of off-balance finance. Since these companies were not legally classified as a subsidiary the holding company did not have to prepare consolidated accounts. In effect this lack of a consolidation requirement allowed companies to channel debt and obtain finance through what was effectively a subsidiary which did not require to be consolidated. Although the 1989 Companies Act substantially tightened the definition of a subsidiary, FRS 5 provided a 'fail-safe' definition in the event that the 1989 Companies Act definition of subsidiary was circumvented.

FRS 5 defines a quasi-subsidiary as 'any company, trust, partnership or other vehicle that, though not fulfilling the definition of a subsidiary is directly or indirectly controlled by the reporting entity and gives rise to benefits for the entity that are in substance no different from those that would arise were the vehicle a subsidiary' (FRS 5, para 7).

FRS 5 requires that all 'assets, liabilities, profits, losses and cash flows of any quasi-subsidiaries should be included in the consolidated financial statements of the group that controls it as if they were those of a subsidiary'.

FRS 8 *RELATED PARTY DISCLOSURES*

Objective

The objective of this FRS is to ensure that financial statements contain the disclosures necessary to draw attention to the possibility that the reported financial position and results may have been affected by the existence of related parties and by material transactions with them.

Summary

1   Financial Reporting Standard 8 'Related Party Disclosures' requires the disclosure of:
    (a)   information on related party transactions and;
    (b)   the name of the party controlling the reporting entity and, if different, that of the ultimate controlling party whether or not any transactions between the reporting entity and those parties have taken place.
    Aggregated disclosures are allowed subject to certain restrictions.
2   Two or more parties are related parties when at any time during the financial period:
    (a)   one party has direct or indirect control of the other party, or;
    (b)   the parties are subject to common control from the same source, or;
    (c)   one party has influence over the financial and operating policies of the other party to an extent that other parties might be inhibited from pursuing at all times its own separate interests, or;
    (d)   the parties, in entering a transaction, are subject to influence from the same source to such an extent that one of the parties to the transaction has subordinated its own separate interests.
3   No disclosure is required in consolidated financial statements of intragroup transactions and balances eliminated on consolidation. A parent undertaking is not required to provide related party disclosures in its own financial statements when those statements are presented with consolidated financial statements of its group.
4   Disclosure is not required in the financial statements of subsidiary undertakings, 90 per cent or more of whose voting rights are controlled within the group, of transactions with entities that are part of the group or investees of the group qualifying as related parties provided that the consolidated financial statements in which that subsidiary is included are publicly available.

Definition of related party

The following definitions shall apply in this FRS and in particular in the Statement of Standard Accounting Practice set out in paragraphs 3–7.

* Close family: Close members of the family of an individual are those family members, or members of the same household, who may be expected to influence, or be influenced by, that person in their dealings with the reporting entity.
* Control: The ability to direct the financial and operating policies of an entity with a view to gaining economic benefits from its activities.
* Key management: Those persons in senior positions having authority or responsibility for directing or controlling the major activities and resources of the reporting entity.

Persons acting in concert   Persons who, pursuant to an agreement or understanding (whether formal or informal), actively co-operate, whether by the ownership by any of them of shares in an undertaking or otherwise, to exercise control or influence over that undertaking.

Related parties   These are:

1   Two or more parties are related parties when at any time during the financial period:
    (a)   one party has direct or indirect control of the other party, or;
    (b)   the parties are subject to common control from the same source, or;
    (c)   one party has influence over the financial and operating policies of the other party to an extent that the other party might be inhibited from pursuing at all times its own separate interests, or;
    (d)   the parties, in entering a transaction, are subject to influence from the same source to such an extent that one of the parties to the transaction has subordinated its own separate interests.

2   For *the avoidance of doubt*, the following are *related parties* of the reporting entity:
    (a)   its ultimate and intermediate parent undertakings, subsidiary undertakings, and fellow subsidiary undertakings;
    (b)   its associates and joint ventures;
    (c)   the investor or venturer in respect of which the reporting entity is an associate or a joint venture;
    (d)   directors of the reporting entity and the directors of its ultimate and intermediate parent undertakings, and;
    (e)   pension funds for the benefit of employees of the reporting entity or of any entity that is a related party of the reporting entity.

3   The following are presumed to be related parties of the reporting entity unless it can be demonstrated that neither party has influenced the financial and operating policies of the other in such a way as to inhibit the pursuit of separate interests:

(a) the *key management* of the reporting entity and the key management of its parent undertaking or undertakings;

(b) a person owning or able to exercise control over 20 per cent or more of the voting rights of the reporting entity, whether directly or through nominees;

(c) each person acting in concert in such a way as to be able to exercise control or influence over the reporting entity under a management contract.

Disclosure of transactions and balances Financial statements should disclose material transactions undertaken by the reporting entity with a related party. Disclosure should be made irrespective of whether a price is charged. The disclosure should include:

1 the names of the transacting related parties;
2 a description of the relationship between the parties;
3 a description of the transactions;
4 the amounts involved;
5 any other elements of the transactions necessary for an understanding of the financial statements;
6 the amounts due to or from related parties at the balance sheet date and provisions for doubtful debts due from such parties at that date, and;
7 amounts written off in the period in respect of debts due to or from related parties.

Transactions with related parties may be disclosed on an aggregated basis (aggregation of similar transactions by type of related party) unless disclosure of an individual transaction, or connected transactions, is necessary for an understanding of the impact of the transactions on the financial statements of the reporting entity or is required by law.

The accounting practices set out in the FRS should be regarded as standard in respect of financial statements relating to accounting periods commencing on or after 23 December 1995.

CALLED UP SHARE CAPITAL

When a company is initially formed, its authorized and issued share capital must be stated. The authorized share capital is the maximum amount of share capital that the company can theoretically issue to its shareholders. It must be stated at the time that the company is formed in the company's Memorandum of Association. It is possible to increase the authorized amount of share capital subject to the procedures stated in the company's Articles of Association and ratification by existing shareholders. The issued share capital is the amount of shares that have actually been taken up by shareholders.

A company's ordinary share capital is frequently termed the equity, (or risk or venture capital) of the company. The shareholders have to carry the risk of the business activities. If the company succeeds the shareholders will gain – whereas company failure will mean the shareholders stand potentially to lose all their share capital. Subject to legal and other constraints in the company's Articles, a company's directors can decide on the level of dividend that is payable to shareholders – whereas if the company is wound-up, the ordinary shareholders will receive their share capital back (if any) only after all other debts and forms of capital have been repaid. In effect the ordinary shareholders stand potentially to gain the most in times of prosperity and stand to lose the most if the company fails.

Preference shares

The preference share capital usually has an attached fixed dividend rate. For example, a company might have 9 per cent preference share capital. This dividend is fixed and does not normally vary with the profitability of the company. The directors usually have the option of not paying the 9 per cent dividend – but if non-payment occurs the company cannot pay a dividend on any other type of shares. Normally preference shareholders do not have a vote at shareholders' meetings – but if their dividend is unpaid then the shareholders are usually entitled to vote during the duration of the non-payment.

Cumulative or non-cumulative shares

In the case of cumulative preference shares, if the directors do not pay a dividend then the dividends that should have been paid are 'rolled-up'. When the dividends are eventually paid again these arrears must be paid before any other class of dividend. In the case of non-cumulative shares, the non-payment of dividends in a particular year will mean that the dividend to shareholders is lost. Arrears will never be distributed.

Redeemable shares

Redeemable shares are repaid to shareholders at the date stated in their description. For example: 1999, 9 per cent preference shares will be repaid to the shareholders in 1999. Sometimes redemption is between a range of dates: e.g. 2005–2010, 9 per cent preference shares will be repaid at the company's option any time between the years 2005 and 2010. Convertible preference shares are convertible by their holders, normally at their option, to ordinary share capital at a predetermined date.

Bonus issue

A bonus (sometimes termed a scrip or capitalization) issue of shares is the granting of 'free' shares to existing shareholders. The existing shareholders do not have to pay for these shares. A bonus issue is often expressed in the form of a ratio – such as a 1 for 5 bonus issue. Shareholders will be given one 'free' share for every five shares that they currently possess.

In effect, a bonus issue is a way of formally allocating the company's reserves to shareholders in the form of share capital. (Note: it is legally permissible to use a share premium account to issue bonus shares.)

The accounting entries to record a bonus issue are to debit reserves and to credit share capital (i.e. no cash transactions are involved). A company may issue bonus shares for a number of reasons but it must be remembered that a bonus issue of shares will normally reduce the market value of existing shares. (The mere fact of a company issuing additional shares from its reserves does not by itself increase the value of the company.)

For example, a company has a 1 for 1 bonus issue. Before the bonus issue the shares have a market value of £2 each. By announcing a 1 for 1 bonus issue, the company has converted reserves into equity and doubled the number of shares held by shareholders. The effect is that shareholders now hold twice the number of shares but at half the value (i.e. now £1 and not £2). Although the accounting or economic benefits of issuing bonus issues of shares are often difficult to recognize, many companies believe 'physiological' benefits of seemingly awarding a 'gift' of shares combined with the effect of reducing the market price of some shares may often tend to make the shares more 'marketable'.

A bonus or scrip issue of shares should not be confused with a scrip dividend. Some companies now choose to issue shareholders with additional shares (instead of paying dividends) termed scrip dividends.

Rights issue

A rights issue of shares is where a company invites existing shareholders to subscribe to additional shares in their company. Unlike bonus shares, a rights issue of shares is not 'free' – shareholders must pay to take-up the rights issue. Rights issues are expressed as a ratio such as (say) 2 for 5. For every 5 shares currently owned, the shareholder will have the right to *purchase* an additional two shares. The ratio can be set at whatever level the company considers necessary. The more shares that a company wishes to issue will affect the price at which they can be issued. An issue of 4 for 5 will normally require greater incentives to shareholders to take-up the shares than would a issue of 1 for 10. The incentives to buy normally take the form of discounts on the price of the shares. A company will frequently have a rights issue when it wishes to raise additional funds for expansion or perhaps to redeem some of its debt.

RESERVES

In general terms, reserves can be defined as the net assets of a company that are not represented by share capital.

Reserves can arise from three main sources:

1 by retaining profits in the business;
2 issuing of shares at a premium (share premium account);
3 revaluation of assets.

Any movements to and from reserves of whatever category must be disclosed in the notes (1985 Companies Act, sch 4, para 46).

Retained profits

Retained profits will arise when only some of a company's earnings are distributed as a dividend. The remainder will be ploughed back into the company's reserves and frequently shown under the heading of a 'profit and loss account balance' or as 'retained earnings' (or even as 'unappropriated profit') in the company's balance sheet.

Share premium

A company is legally obliged (Companies Act 1985, sec 130 (1)) to have a share premium account if it issues shares at a value that is greater than their nominal value. The difference between the issue price and the nominal value is taken to a share premium account.

A share premium can only be used for the following major purposes:

• to issue fully paid bonus (scrip issue) shares;
• writing-off preliminary expenses (such as legal and stockbroking costs);
• writing-off any expenses on issuing shares or debentures.

Unlike some countries, all shares of UK companies must legally have a 'par' or 'nominal' value (occasionally termed 'face' value) on being initially issued. The par or nominal values have little significance in themselves; their significance only arises in the need to create a special legal reserve – the share premium account. For example, company A's shares have a par value of £1. If company A issues additional shares for £3 each, the £2 premium (issue price minus par value) must be credited to a share premium reserve. It must not be distributed as a dividend but only used for the purposes specified above.

Revaluation reserve

A revaluation reserve will arise when an asset is revalued. For example, a building is purchased in 1990 and is shown in a company's balance sheet at a net value of £100,000. A surveyor's opinion regards the building's current market value as £150,000. The accounting entries in the company's balance sheet will be to increase the value of the buildings to £150,000 and to credit an amount of £50,000 to a revaluation reserve, i.e. debit buildings with an additional amount of £50,000 and credit the revaluation reserve with £50,000.

If a company has a revaluation deficit it should be charged to the profit and loss account to the extent that it exceeds any previously created revaluation reserve of the same assets. A revaluation reserve can be reduced if any amounts that are transferred to it are no longer required. It is not permitted to write-off goodwill against a revaluation reserve. (Although prior to the 1989 Companies Act a number of companies used their revaluation account for goodwill write-off, but the 1989 Act forbids this procedure.)

Capital redemption reserve

A company is only able to redeem or purchase its own shares from its distributable reserves or from the new issue of share capital.

If the shares are redeemed or purchased, other than by a new issue of shares, a company must transfer an equivalent amount from distributable reserves to a 'frozen' non-distributable reserve – termed a capital redemption reserve. The purpose of this transfer is to offer a degree of protection to other shareholders and creditors. This procedure creates a 'buffer' or safety zone whereby other shareholders and creditors can be assured that the company's capital cannot be totally redeemed (i.e. it offers a degree of protection for other shareholders and creditors by preserving the share capital and undistributable reserves).

Classification of reserves

Reserves can be classified as distributable and non-distributable. Generally, the only major reserves that will be distributable are the profit and loss account balance (retained profits). The remainder of reserves, including the share premium and revaluation reserve are non-distributable.

Reserves can also be classified as either capital or revenue. Although capital reserves are not distributable, revenue reserves can be so used.

The undistributable reserves of a company are:

1 share premium account;
2 revaluation reserves and other unrealized profits;
3 capital redemption reserve;
4 any other reserve that the company's Articles of Association prohibit a company from distributing.

Until recently, the classification of some forms of finance, notably convertible loan and debenture stock frequently caused difficulties in classification. Some companies classified convertible debt as part of shareholders' funds on the basis that many such debenture holders will, in the normal course of business, exchange their 'convertibles' into equity. FRS 4, *Accounting for Capital Instruments* has now standardized the procedure. All convertible debt must be accounted for and disclosed as a liability on the face of the company's balance sheet and supported by further information concerning redemption dates and details of conversion into equity.

FRS 4 also extends the legal disclosure provision of all types of debt by requiring companies to provide analysis of debt maturity in categories of:

- immediate repayment and in one year's time or less;
- between one and two years;
- between two and five years;
- five years or more.

See FRS 4 for disclosure requirements.

Creditors

A company that has adopted format 2 for its published accounts must split and disclose its creditors between the amount of liabilities payable within one year and after one year in the notes. Those companies choosing format 1 must place this split on the face of the balance sheet. In addition, for both formats, the aggregate amount of debts that are payable (other than by instalments) and falling due for payment in more than five years' time; and also any amount that is payable by instalments after the end of this five year period must be disclosed.

Provision for liabilities and charges

The Companies Act 1985 regards a provision as an amount retained as being reasonably necessary for the purpose of providing for any liability or loss which is either likely to be incurred, or certain to be incurred, but there exists a degree of uncertainty as to the amount or the date when it will actually arise. An example of an item found within this category might be a provision for an environmental liability. A company might have caused, or perhaps inherited environmentally contaminated land which has to be rectified and compensation paid at an amount and date yet to be fully determined.

The Companies Act 1985 specifically requires provisions to be identified under the following headings:

- pensions and similar obligations;
- taxation including deferred taxation;
- other provisions.

The Companies Act requires that companies specifically disclose contingencies relating to:

- arrears of cumulative dividends;
- charges on companies' assets and;
- state the nature of any contingency not provided for in the accounts.

SSAP 17, *ACCOUNTING FOR POST BALANCE SHEET EVENTS*

Although companies need to prepare a balance sheet at a given date, it is also important to consider post-balance sheet events. SSAP 17 defines 'post balance sheet events' as:

> those events, both favourable and unfavourable, which occur between the balance sheet date and the date on which the financial statements are approved by the Board of Directors. (Para 18, SSAP 17.)

Post-balance sheet events are split into two categories: adjusting and non-adjusting events.

An adjusting event provides additional evidence of conditions *existing* at the balance sheet date; whereas a non-adjusting event concerns conditions which did *not* exist at the balance sheet date. Examples of adjusting events are the subsequent determination of the purchase price or the proceeds of a sale of assets purchased or sold before the year end; or the valuation of property which provides evidence of a permanent diminution in value.

A non-adjusting event could be the announcement of a merger or acquisition after the balance sheet date; issue of shares and debentures and strikes or labour disputes. A material post-balance sheet event will require *changes* to be included in the financial statements of the company – if it is an adjusting event or if the event indicates the going-concern concept is inapplicable.

A material post-balance sheet event only needs to be disclosed in the financial statements if it is a non-adjusting event or if the transaction is primarily concerned with 'window dressing' (i.e. where the transaction is designed to reverse shortly after the year end – with the purpose of artificially enhancing the company's accounting position).

For every post-balance sheet event it is important that the following are disclosed in the financial statements:

- the nature of the event, and;
- an estimate (before taxation) of its financial effects, and;
- the taxation implications.

SSAP 18, *ACCOUNTING FOR CONTINGENCIES*

In the preparation of the financial statements consideration must be given to the possible existence of contingencies.

SSAP 18 defines a contingency as:

a condition which exists at the balance sheet date, where the outcome will be confirmed only on the occurrence or non-occurrence of one or more future uncertain events. (Para 14.)

A contingent loss should be accrued in the financial statements if it is *probable* that a future event will confirm a loss which can be estimated with reasonable accuracy at the date on which the financial statements are signed by the directors. A contingent loss that is not accrued should be disclosed, unless the possibility of loss is *remote*. Contingent gains should *never* be accrued but they may be disclosed in the notes, if it is probable that the gain will be realized.

In respect of each contingency, the following information should be supplied:

1 the nature of the contingency;
2 the uncertainties which are expected to affect the ultimate outcome, and;
3 a prudent estimate of the financial effect, or a statement that it is not practicable to make such a estimate.

Possible contingencies include a company guaranteeing an overdraft or a loan; the existence of performance bonds (perhaps where a parent company guarantees to complete a contract); or a product guarantee or warranty.

EXAMPLE TABLE 6.5   EXTRACT FROM BOC GROUP PLC: CONTINGENT LIABILITIES AND BANK GUARANTEES

	Group 1995 (£ million)	Parent 1994 (£ million)
Guarantees of related undertakings' borrowings	8.4	2.7
Guarantees of wholly-owned subsidiaries' borrowings	–	725.8
Other guarantees and contingent liabilities	18.5	–

Various Group undertakings are parties to legal actions and claims which arise in the ordinary course of business, some of which are for substantial amounts. While the outcome of some of these matters cannot readily be foreseen, the directors believe that they will be disposed of without material effect on the net asset position.

QUESTIONS

1 Explain what you understand by modified historical cost accounting?
   When examining a balance sheet, what implications does the use of historical cost accounting have for user-groups.
2 What do you understand by a brand name?
   Discuss to what extent you consider that brand names are a integral part of goodwill or do they have a separate identity?

3 Explain what you understand by the term reserves in a company's balance sheet.
4 The accounting treatment for goodwill has always caused conceptual and accounting problems for accountants.
   In the context of SSAP 22 discuss the nature of these problems. Explain your preferred treatment.
5 Discuss the reasons why it is so important for most companies to carefully monitor and control their stock and debtor balances.
6 Explain the difference between a bonus or scrip issue of shares and a rights issue. Discuss the circumstances when each method would be appropriate.
7 Some companies show buildings in their balance sheet on a historical cost basis, whereas other companies periodically revalue their assets to current values. Consequently it is impossible to analyse company financial statements in any meaningful way. Do you agree?

Appendix 6.1

Goodwill and intangible assets

The Accounting Standards Board (ASB) has recently attempted to stimulate debate by publishing a Discussion Draft on these issues. Although the ASB does not produce definitive solutions, it discusses the inherent conceptual difficulties and practical implications of accounting for goodwill and identifies a number of possible solutions. The extent to which these accounting remedies will find popular acceptance in the company board room is open to significant doubt.

To the non-accountant, goodwill is often perceived as one of great mysteries of the accounting universe. As if by a wave of a magician's wand, goodwill can vanish just as rapidly as it was created. The problem centres upon the very nature and substance of goodwill. It is an intangible asset, intrinsic and inherent to the business and incapable of separate realization from the business itself. Even though the non-accountant may be mystified, the position is not much better for the specialist. Many accountants are equally perplexed and divided as to the appropriate accounting treatment for goodwill.

Traditionally, goodwill has been split into two major categories: purchased and non-purchased (or sometimes termed internally-generated) goodwill. To the accountant, purchased goodwill is defined 'as the difference between the fair value of consideration for an acquisition less the net sum of fair values of recognised assets and liabilities acquired'. Quite simply, if company A acquires company B for £100 and company B's net assets are £70, then the difference, (i.e. £30) is termed purchased goodwill.

The current accounting treatment of purchased goodwill (that is also consistent with the provisions of the Companies Act 1985) is expounded in SSAP 22. It permits two different treatments for goodwill:

1   immediate elimination of goodwill against reserves or;
2   the capitalization of goodwill as an asset that is subsequently amortized over its useful economic life.

The overwhelming majority of companies write-off goodwill to reserves immediately on acquisition. (One recent survey reported that the proportion was over 96 per cent.) The major reason for using the immediate write-off to reserves method is that it avoids having to implement the alternative amortization method – which would have a negative impact on reported corporate earnings. But even this immediate write-off method to reserves is causing many companies serious problems. Companies that follow an aggressive acquisition policy are particularly having difficulties. As the amounts paid for purchased goodwill have increased dramatically in recent years, so the immediate 'write-off' method has led to a significant erosion of companies' reserves.

However, there is now one small consolation. The choice of accounting method is not as fundamental in the case of disposal of a company as it was previously. Presently, the ASB requires the related goodwill on disposal of a company to be written-off to the profit and loss account – even if the purchased goodwill was originally written-off to reserves.

In an attempt to bypass the need to write-off goodwill to either reserves or to earnings, many companies have been extracting intangible assets from goodwill itself. The intangibles can include patents, licences, trade marks, concessions and brand names. These intangible assets are then shown separately in the balance sheet. Since the present SSAP 22 is interpreted as applying only to goodwill – the remaining intangible assets can be left, virtually untouched in the balance sheet. But there is no consensus of opinion concerning the accounting treatment. What some companies term brand names other companies term goodwill.

The ASB admits that 'purchased goodwill is an accounting anomaly. Every method of accounting for it results in inconsistencies with other aspects of financial reporting.' Over recent years the amounts paid for goodwill have substantially increased. A survey in 1990 by the Institute of Chartered Accountants in England and Wales reported that the amount paid for purchased goodwill reached 44 per cent as a percentage of the acquirer's net worth.

The ASB does not wish to allow intangible assets that are acquired during the purchase of another company to be identified and individually capitalized. It is thought that it is not realistically possible to separate them without disposing of the underlying business. Additionally, the ASB considers that the methodology for the valuation of the intangible assets can be of questionable accuracy. Supporters of capitalization vigorously dismiss such criticisms. They regard patents, licences and trademarks as possessing a separate and clearly ascertained identity that can be readily attributed with a market value.

Nevertheless the ASB is definite and rather blunt. Intangible assets should be treated just like goodwill. They should be 'subsumed within purchased goodwill and accounted for accordingly'.

In the case of non-purchased goodwill, any costs of developing the goodwill are to be written-off to the profit and loss. Neither the costs of development nor the value to the business of this goodwill are to be recognized as an asset in the balance sheet.

The Discussion Draft also proposes to treat internally-generated intangible assets in the same manner as internally-generated goodwill. For the most part they are to be ignored. The ASB had already proposed to tighten up the requirements for capitalizing internally-generated intangible assets in the form of an earlier exposure draft. ED 52 allowed capitalization only if the cost of creating the intangibles could be clearly identified and measured separately from that of goodwill. However, ferocious opposition from critics has led the ASB to leave ED 52 in abeyance. (FRED 12 is likely to change some of ED 52's requirements.)

The 1985 Companies Act allows companies to show patents, licences and trademarks in the balance sheet. Such assets may be shown under this heading if the assets were acquired for valuable consideration or if the assets were created by the company itself. They are not required to be incorporated under the goodwill heading. The new Discussion Draft provides evidence of a substantial shift of opinion. The ASB is attempting to restrict the extent of these legal boundaries. It is proposed that internally generated intangible assets are to be treated in the same manner as internally generated goodwill and not capitalized.

Options

The ASB initially proposed a number of possible options in the recognition and treatment of goodwill. The methods that are discussed can be divided into two major groups:

1   asset-based methods;
2   elimination methods.

Asset-based methods

1   *Capitalization and predetermined life amortization:* In this method the purchased goodwill is capitalized and then amortized over a predetermined finite life. A maximum life of 20 years is suggested.

2   *Capitalization and annual review:* Purchased goodwill is capitalized and then subject to an annual review. Only if the value of goodwill is deemed to have fallen will the carrying amount of goodwill be reduced. Consequently, in each year there might or there might not be a goodwill charge to the profit and loss account.

The Discussion Draft proposes to introduce rather complex annual review procedures in determining the extent, if any, of the amortization charge. It terms these review procedures as 'ceiling tests' that are designed to ensure that any capitalized goodwill is not carried in the balance sheet at an amount in excess of its value. In its simplest terms, one of these 'ceiling tests' is based on an annual discounted cash flow procedure which compares the estimated discounted future cash flows of the acquired investment with its underlying 'net fair value'. (The net fair value is defined as the fair value of assets, liabilities and goodwill.) The second goodwill ceiling test is 'a comparative test' that compares future cash flow forecasts with past actual results. This latter test is designed to ensure that management is not over optimistic about the future – compared with the actual results achieved in the past.

3   *Combination of methods 1 and 2:* Method 1 would be the method to use for the majority of acquisitions – but method 2 would be used where goodwill has a life expected to be in excess of 20 years.

Elimination methods

4   *Immediate write-off method:* Purchased goodwill would be eliminated against reserves immediately on acquisition. This is a continuation of the practice that is permitted under SSAP 22.

5   *Separate write-off reserve:* The purchased goodwill is transferred to a separate 'goodwill write-off reserve' immediately on acquisition. The shareholders' funds are shown both *before* and *after* the goodwill write-off.

Creation of separate write-off reserve: balance sheet extract

Called up share capital	1,000
Share premium account	350
Revaluation reserve	250
Profit and loss account balance	200
Shareholders' funds before goodwill write-off	1,800
Cumulative goodwill write-off reserve	(100)
Shareholders' funds after goodwill write-off	1,700

The ASB argues that this method will prominently highlight the amount of goodwill for the benefit of users. Its supporters believe that it allows users to see clearly the 'net worth' of the business and allows the company's management to explain that the separate write-off reserve is an accounting adjustment and not related to a physical loss in value.

Critics of this method dislike the concept of displaying a negative reserve and believe that it is almost a self-contradictory methodology. The Discussion Draft retorts by arguing that if such a view prevails then a note could be added explaining that the good-will write-off reserve should be regarded as part of the annual profit and loss account balance.

6 *Variant of method 5 – a separate write-off reserve with recoverability assessment:* Purchased goodwill is transferred to a separate goodwill write-off reserve immediately on acquisition. The balance in this reserve is assessed for recoverability at the end of each year. Any losses that reduce goodwill below the balance in the write-off reserve are charged to the profit and loss account.

Accountants have never really found a widely acceptable accounting treatment for goodwill. Perhaps there is no solution that will ever meet the demand of all companies. When the situation is compounded by the introduction of intangible assets there is an exponential growth in the difficulties. Perhaps part of the answer lies in making the non-specialist more aware of the very abstract nature of goodwill and in the inherent limitations of all the possible accounting treatments. For many years accounting for goodwill has been too erratic and uncertain. The latest Discussion Paper at least provides a forum for the issues to be comprehensively aired and perhaps eventually, firmly resolved.

In July 1996 as a result of discussions of the above proposals the ASB issued FRED 12, *Goodwill and Intangible Assets.* The draft's proposals include the following:

- Purchased goodwill and purchased intangible assets should be capitalized.
- An internally developed intangible asset may be recognized only if it has a readily ascertainable market value.
- There is a rebuttable presumption that the useful economic lives of purchased goodwill and purchased intangible assets are limited and do not exceed 20 years from the date of acquisition.
- Where goodwill or an intangible asset is believed to have a useful economic life of more than 20 years, or less, it should be amortized over the estimated useful economic life.
- Where goodwill or an intangible asset is believed to have a useful economic life of more than 20 years, and its value is not significant or is not expected to be capable of continued measurement in future, it should be amortized over 20 years.
- Where goodwill or an intangible asset is believed to have a useful economic life of more than 20 years, and its value is significant and expected to be capable of continued measurement in future, it should be amortized over the estimated useful economic life or, if this is infinite, not amortized at all, and annual impairment reviews should be performed.
- Where goodwill or an intangible asset is amortized over a period that does not exceed 20 years, impairment reviews need to be performed only at the end of the first full financial year following its initial recognition and, thereafter, if subsequent events or changes in circumstances indicate that its carrying value might not be recoverable in full.
- Where a company's accounts include goodwill that is not amortized, they

should explain that the departure from the statutory requirement to amortize it is necessary for the overriding purpose of providing a true and fair view. The reasons for the departure and its effect should be disclosed.

FURTHER READING

Advanced Financial Accounting, Lewis, R. and Pendrill, D. (Pitman) 1996.
Financial Reporting Exposure Draft 12, ASB, 1996, London.
Management and Cost Accounting, Drury, C., Chapman & Hall, 1992.

7 | Directors' Report and Operating and Financial Review

This chapter examines:

* purpose and contents of directors' report;
* nature and content of an Operating and Financial Review (OFR);
* value of these reports to users.

The directors' report contains a mixture of statutory produced information, details required by the Stock Exchange, and any information that the directors wish to voluntarily comment upon. The directors' report is designed to complement the financial statements and provide a commentary on the financial information and also on the company's general affairs.

The Companies Act 1985 specifies the majority of the required content of a directors' report. Additional disclosure provisions have been called for by the Report on the Financial Aspects of Corporate Governance, the so-called Cadbury Report.

CONTENTS

Principal activities and review

The director's report must contain details of the principal activities of the business during the course of the year and of its position at the year end.

The company must provide a fair review of the development of the business during the year. The Companies Act does not provide any guidance on the form that this review should take and does not specify the degree of detail.

Some companies do not always necessarily put all the required information in the directors' report. It is permissible to place the information elsewhere in the annual report such as in the chairman's statement – provided that the directors' report refers to the location of the information.

Future developments

Directors are also legally required to provide an indication of future developments of the business. This section should include any significant changes in the business's activities that the directors are considering implementing.

Directors should make reference to the following points:

- Dividends:
  - the level of dividends recommended by the directors and any amounts proposed to be carried forward to reserves.
- Significant changes in fixed assets.
- Substantial differences between the book value and market values of fixed assets.
- Post-balance sheet events – these are any significant events which have occurred between the financial year end and the date on which the financial statements are approved by the directors.
- Research and development activities.
- Information on employees:
  - if the company employs more than 250 employees, the directors must state their policy as regards:
    - the regular provision of information to employees;
    - consultation procedures before making decisions that may affect their interests;
    - ensuring employees are aware of factors that may affect the performance of the company;
    - the employment of disabled employees;
    - the continued employment of employees who become disabled whilst employed by the company;
    - training and career development of disabled people.
- Donations of a political or charitable nature made by the company, if together, the total sum exceeds £200. (Donations made outside of the UK need not be disclosed.)

Directors

As regards directors themselves, the directors' report must note:

- The names of any persons who were directors during the year.
- Directors' interests in any of the company's shares or debentures and in any share or debenture options.
- Any insurance (e.g. for negligence) that the company has effected on behalf on the directors.
- The appointment of the company's auditors.

Additionally, the directors must report on any persons having a substantial share holding in the company (currently 'substantial' is defined as 3 per cent or more of any class of voting shares). Listed companies must disclose whether they are a close company for taxation purposes.

The Companies Act does not explicitly require companies to have the directors' report audited. However, auditors must highlight any aspects of a directors' report that are 'inconsistent' with the remainder of the financial statements.

Chairman's statement

Although a chairman's statement is not a legal requirement, virtually all companies will produce this statement usually found at the beginning of a set of financial statements.

In practice, the chairman's statement is frequently issued as a marketing and public relations exercise. The statement often produces an overoptimistic presentation of the company's fortunes by highlighting those areas that present the company in the best possible image.

There is no legal or accounting requirement to produce a chairman's statement, although most companies take the opportunity to include a report by the Chairman. Because there are no requirements as to the format or content of this statement there is a variety of practice.

Generally, companies tend to produce a statement that includes at least reference to the following:

- commentary on the year's financial and operating results;
- features or events that had major trading implications;
- major developments and initiatives that have happened during the year;
- new or different strategies being adopted;
- reference to new or retiring directors, and comments on employee performance;
- prospects for the coming year.

OPERATING AND FINANCIAL REVIEW

In 1993 the Accounting Standards Board (ASB) recommended that all listed companies include an Operating and Financial Review (OFR) as an integral part of their annual report. The objective of the ASB was to introduce more accountability and understanding into the complex world of financial statements.

The annual reports of companies have traditionally been centred upon the provision of a vast array of financial information, largely in numerical form. Over recent years, there has been a continual trend for many companies to publish, as part of their annual report, a considerable amount of non-numerical information in a more expansive and descriptive format.

In the past, these summaries have been produced on an *ad hoc* and voluntary basis with their contents varying in clarity and precision. In an attempt to standardize the structure and content of this information, the ASB has issued advice on the publication of a new narrative statement termed: an Operating and Financial Review. An OFR is defined as:

> a framework for the directors to discuss and analyse the business's performance and the factors underlying its results and financial position, in order to assist users to assess for themselves the future potential of the business. (*Operating and Financial Review: A Statement*, Accounting Standards Board 1993.)

Although the publication of an OFR is neither a mandatory requirement nor an accounting standard, the ASB hopes that the production of an OFR will come to be regarded as an example of 'best practice' for leading companies.

For many of the less sophisticated financial readers, the narrative part is often regarded as one of the more readily understood sections of the annual report. Even in the case of complex businesses, the financial statements alone are frequently inadequate to meet the needs of the most avid and financially informed user. The recent Cadbury Report on Corporate Governance has recommended that all listed companies should produce a 'balanced and understandable assessment' of their position. The ASB has adopted this recommendation and advises companies to produce such a statement in a formalized and structured format – the so-called OFR. Many influential bodies, including the Financial Reporting Council and the Stock Exchange have provided enthusiastic support for its introduction.

The fundamental aim of an OFR is to allow directors to interpret and comment upon the financial statements and not merely provide numerical analysis. Particular emphasis is placed on discussing the trading and financial changes that the business is currently experiencing and any forecast developments to which the business may be exposed. The OFR has been initially drafted with listed companies in mind, but it can be applied to other organizations in which the public has a valid interest. The FRC considers that 'with the increasing complexity of many businesses, there is a growing need for annual reports to include an objective discussion that analyses and explains the main features underlying the results and financial position'.

Essential features

An OFR should be written in a clear and concise style and be readily understandable by the general reader of financial statements. It should only include matters that are likely to be of significant interest to investors.

The OFR should:

- concentrate on providing an analytical rather than numerical discussion;
- explain the reason for, and the effect of any changes in accounting policies on the financial results of the company;
- provide an explanation on how any financial ratios or other numerical information relate to the financial statements;

- provide a discussion of any events, trends and uncertainties that have affected the company's results either during the present year or are expected to do so in the future.

Since 1980 companies in the USA have been required by the Securities and Exchange Commission to publish a Management Discussion and Analysis – the USA equivalent of an OFR. However, its fortune has met with only limited success. Emerging evidence has tended to indicate that these statements are overoptimistic in outlook, and minimize or even ignore news that might have a negative impact on the firm.

In the UK, provision is made for directors not to provide information on the grounds of confidential or commercially sensitive information. If they take advantage of this exemption then they should take particular care that the remaining contents of the statement do not mislead the reader by providing an incomplete and unbalanced version. The ASB effectively splits the contents of the OFR into two major sections; the operating review and the financial review.

Operating review

The purpose of the operating review is to enable the user 'to understand the dynamics of the various lines of business undertaken'. In other words, the OFR highlights and explains the predominant factors that influence and determine the organization's business activities. Significant features that affect trading performance, both internal and external to the firm, should be discussed.

The ASB envisages that the typical areas to be covered would include:

1 *Operating results for the period:* The OFR should discuss the significant features of operating performance for the period covered by the financial statements. In particular the OFR should cover changes in the industry or the environment in which the business operates, developments within the business, and their effect on the earnings results.

In essence the OFR should contain:

- changes in market conditions;
- new products or new services introduced;
- changes in market share, turnover and exchange rates;
- new and discontinued activities.

2 *Dynamics of the business:* The OFR should also discuss the main factors and influences that may have a major effect on future results. This would include identifying the principal risks and uncertainties in the main line of business and a commentary on the approach to managing these risks and in, qualitative terms, the nature of the potential impact on results. Examples will include:

- scarcity of raw materials;
- skill shortages and expertise;
- patents, licences or franchises;

- dependence on major suppliers or customers;
- product liability;
- health and safety;
- environmental protection costs and potential environmental liabilities;
- self-insurance;
- exchange rate fluctuations;
- rates of inflation differing between costs and revenues or between different markets.

3 *Investment for the future:* The OFR should also discuss the extent to which directors have sought to maintain and enhance future income or profits.

This area may encompass a discussion of activities and expenditure that are expected to increase future product and corporate profitability. Detailed analysis is required on capital expenditure plans for both the current financial period and also for planned future expenditure. The definition of capital expenditure is taken in its widest context and includes expenditure on training programmes; marketing and advertising campaigns; and also pure and applied research.

As regards the financial statements, the OFR requires a discussion on the overall returns to shareholders in terms of both dividends and earnings, highlighting performance of individual segments, and any gains or losses taken to the Statement of Recognized Gains and Losses. Reference should be made to dividend policy and to any aspect of accounting policy that is particularly sensitive to subjective financial judgements.

Financial review

The second section is mainly designed to explain:

- the firm's capital structure;
- its treasury policy, and;
- the liquidity position.

This section will require comment on the firm's capital structure, its nature, maturity dates of debt, extent to which borrowings are at fixed interest rates, and its currency and interest rate management strategy. In particular the firm will be expected to reveal the manner in which its treasury activities are controlled, details of borrowings including any foreign currency implications and hedging instruments.

Finally, other information should be provided which concerns any resources of the business that are not explicitly stated in the balance sheet. Included in this section would be a discussion on intangible assets including reference to any existing brand names.

Over recent months a number of companies have already included an OFR as a part of their financial statements. They are a welcome development in attempting to enhance the accountability of directors and in providing greater understanding to the users of financial statements. As in the case of financial statements, the reader should also diligently study the contents of an OFR with an inquiring and critical frame of mind. As evidenced by the American experience, there will always be the temptation that firms will emphasize positive and favourable aspects and quietly understate, disguise or even ignore the adverse news and trends. Nevertheless, the OFR promises to be another step in the long journey to greater accountability and understanding.

QUESTIONS

1 What are the purposes of directors' reports?
   What are the salient features of a directors' report?
2 Do you believe that a chairman's statement has any use?
3 Discuss the advantages or benefits that you believe a user of financial statements can obtain from examining an Operating and Financial Review.
4 State the key features that you consider might be contained within an Operating and Financial Review.
5 'The major difficulty with a company's Operating and Financial Review is that it provides a temptation for the management to present an unduly optimistic view of the company.'
   Explain to what extent you agree with the above quotation.

For an example of an extract from an Operating and Financial Review see chapter 9, part 2.

8 | Cash Flow

This chapter examines the:

- importance of cash;
- nature and significance of cash flow;
- analysis of cash flow statements.

The importance of cash to any business cannot be overemphasized. Cash is the 'life-blood' of all business activity. There are numerous examples of businesses that have failed because of their neglect in recognizing the overriding importance of having sufficient cash balances. Many companies fail not because they are intrinsically unprofitable but because the basic principle of ensuring that cash receipts exceed cash payments is ignored. The importance of cash is expressed in the age-old accounting adage that 'cash is king' – a principle that should underpin most trading activity.

Traditional accounting that is centred on accruals-based principles implies that all revenue and expenses are recorded when they are *earned* or *incurred* (and *not* when they are physically paid or received). This approach contrasts with cash flow accounting where transactions *are* recorded as and when they are *actually* paid or received in cash.

Many businesses trade predominantly on the basis of credit. Sales and purchases may be legally incurred today but it quite feasible that the actual physical cash receipts and payments relating to the transaction will not take place until, perhaps, many months later. A sale of £100 worth of goods on credit that takes place on 1 January will be recorded in the profit and loss account at this date – but it will have no effect on the company's cash balances until the debtor physically pays the company £100 for the goods. In this situation, a profit is being accrued immediately but the firm has to wait to receive the cash. The major differences between cash transactions and accruals-based entries need to be faced when analysing company financial statements.

A company's profit and loss account and balance sheet only record its financial performance and financial position. These statements do not provide answers to a number of vital issues such as:

- the source and destination of a company's cash flows;
- the sources and uses of these cash flows;

- the amount of cash utilized during the year;
- the cash balance at the year end.

There have been numerous instances where companies, that have been showing a profit, have shortly afterwards collapsed. Their demise has frequently come about for the crucial and fundamental reason that they have simply depleted their cash reserves to unsustainable levels. It is vital to remember that although it is possible that profit may equate to cash – it is not necessarily the case. Many of the critics of more traditional accruals-based accounting argue that a form of cash accounting provides greater benefits to the users of financial statements. The major advantage in using cash is that it is clear-cut and a more objective form of measurement. It is not dependent on arbitrary allocations of expenses over time. The firm either possesses cash or it does not – there are few 'grey' areas causing dispute or problems of interpretation. There is considerably less scope for creative accounting or manipulation of cash entries. Cash movements are more easily verifiable than in accruals-based accounting.

Some analysts believe that, since cash flow is a relatively objective figure, it is useful to calculate the *net cash flow per share* from operating activities.

The immense significance of analysing cash flows should never be understated. It is vital to carefully monitor the cash flow position, not only from the internal perspective of the company's management but also from the needs of external users.

Until 1991, the predecessor to the ASB, the Accounting Standards Committee required companies to produce a working capital-based funds flow statement in the now revoked SSAP 10. The content of this funds flow statement, (formally entitled a Statement of Source and Application of Funds) was essentially a re-arrangement of the information given in the profit and loss account and in the balance sheet. It did not define funds in detail and did not lay down a precise and clear definition of funds flow. FRS 1 criticizes a funds flow statement based upon movements in working capital because it can obscure changes relevant to the liquidity and viability of an entity. For example, in a funds flow statement, a significant decrease in cash available may be masked by an increase in stock or debtors. The end result being that companies may run out of cash whilst reporting increases in working capital.

FRS 1, *CASH FLOW STATEMENTS*

The importance for all users to carefully examine a company's cash flow position was recognized by the ASB, with the issue in 1991 of FRS 1[1]. This initial standard was amended and updated by FRS 1 (Revised 1996), *Cash Flow Statements* (CFS).

A number of major advantages can be attributed to the CFS:

- It emphasizes the importance of a company to be profitable and also to generate net positive cash flows.
- It can highlight dependency on external funding and the actual payments needed to service such sources of finance.

- It can stress to investors the inherent risk that the firm is undertaking.
- It provides additional evidence on a company's ability to meet its obligations when they become due for payment.
- It helps to explain a firm's capacity to command resources and to adapt its existing operations in response to business changes or developing opportunities.
- It assists and informs users in analysing a company's dividend record and also identifies cash generated and expended.
- It assists users to make and monitor their decisions.
- It can assist in enhancing the stewardship function of management by making the company's management accountable for the enterprise's solvency and liquidity.
- Although the information contained in a CFS is historical in nature (and so is not totally indicative of future cash flows), it nevertheless can provide a basis for formulating an assessment about future cash flows.

In essence, a CFS records cash in and cash out. Although the information in a cash flow statement is also historical in nature, it can nevertheless assist users of financial statements in making judgements on the amount and degree of relative certainty of future cash flows. Historical information can also be of use in checking the accuracy of past cash flow assessments. A statement can also provide an indication of the relationship between profitability and the cash generating ability of the company – and thus of the 'quality' of its earnings.

FRS 1 (Revised) believes that historical cash flow information is 'a useful addition to the balance sheet and profit and loss account in their portrayal of financial position, performance and financial adaptability. Historical cash flow information gives an indication of the relationship between profitability and cash generating ability and thus of the quality of the profit earned' (FRS 1, p. 55).

In particular, FRS 1 believes that a CFS will assist users to develop models to assess and compare the present value of the future cash flows of organizations. Additionally historical cash flow information could be useful to check the accuracy of past assessments and to highlight the relationship between the entity's activities and its receipts and payments.

Maximum value can be ascertained from a CFS when it is analysed in conjunction with the profit and loss account and balance sheet. By specifying the format of a cash flow statement, FRS 1 (Revised) attempts to report a company's 'cash generation and cash absorption for a period by highlighting the significant components of a cash flow in a way that facilitates comparison of the cash flow performance of different businesses'. A CFS will also 'provide information that assists in the assessment of (a company's) liquidity, solvency and financial adaptability' (para 1(a), (b)).

FRS 1 applies to all companies whose financial statements are intended to provide a true and fair view of their financial position and profit or loss. However, it does not apply to:

1 small limited companies;
2 other entities which would have been classified as a small limited company had they incorporated;

3 wholly owned subsidiary undertakings of a parent company that is established in a European Union member state;
4 other minor categories.

The major objective of FRS 1 is to require companies to report their 'cash generation and cash absorption for a period'. To achieve this aim, FRS 1 requires a CFS to be categorized into eight major sections:

1 operating activities;
2 returns on investment and servicing of finance;
3 taxation;
4 capital expenditure and financial investment;
5 acquisitions and disposals;
6 equity dividends paid;
7 management of liquid resources;
8 financing.

Operating activities

Cash flows from operating activities will include the cash effects of transactions and other events relating to the operating or trading activities of the company.

This section discloses some of the most significant information to be found in a CFS and it is essential for users to analyse this section extremely carefully. Since this part of the CFS highlights movements in cash from the 'core' activities of the business (i.e. the very heart of its operations), it is vital that the reported net cash flows from operating activities are carefully studied. If the net cash flows from operating activities are low (or even negative) the user should be extremely cautious. If the business cannot generate positive and preferably substantial net cash flows (increasing year on year) from its core activities the user needs to analyse the underlying reasons. Additionally a reconciliation between the operating profit (as reported in the profit and loss account) and the net cash flow from operating activities should be given either adjoining the cash flow statement itself or alternatively, as a note. This reconciliation does not, as such form a part of the CFS. The reconciliation should show any movements in stocks, debtors and creditors that relate to operating activities and also include any other differences between cash flow and profits.

Returns on investments and servicing of finance

Returns on investments and servicing of finance are cash receipts resulting from the ownership of an investment and cash payments to providers of finance. In effect, this section will incorporate cash flows arising from a company's own investments. It may perhaps comprise of dividends received from shareholdings in other companies and also from cash flows that arise from servicing its own finance (such as the paying of loan interest to lending institutions and for dividends on non-equity shares).

(Note: under FRS 1 (Revised) equity dividends paid by a company are shown under their own separate heading.)

Taxation

The cash flows to be recorded in this section are cash payments to taxation authorities and any cash receipts in the form of tax refunds. Cash flows in respect of other taxes such as sales taxes are not normally shown in this section but are incorporated under operating activities. Occasionally there may be tax cash inflows arising from tax rebates or returns of tax overpayments.

Capital expenditure and financial investment

Cash flows from investing activities relate to the acquisition or disposal of any fixed asset other than those required to be classified under 'acquisitions and disposals'.
Cash inflows would include:

- cash receipts from sales of property, plant or equipment;
- receipts from the repayment of loans issued by the company.

Cash outflows would include:

- payments to acquire property, plant or equipment;
- loans made by the company and payments to acquire debt of other organizations.

Acquisitions and disposals

Cash flows under this section are related to the acquisition or disposal of any trade or business or investments in another company.
Cash inflows would include:

- cash receipts from sales of investments in subsidiaries (showing separately any balances of cash or overdrafts that have been transferred as part of the sale);
- cash receipts from sales of a trade or business.

Cash outflows include:

- payments to acquire investments in subsidiaries;
- payments to acquire other trades or businesses.

Equity dividends paid

The cash outflows include the equity dividends that are *actually* paid to shareholders.

Management of liquid resources

Liquid resources are defined as current asset investments 'held as a readily disposable store of value' (FRS 1, p. 9). A readily disposable investment can be disposed of by a company without curtailing or disrupting its business and can be readily converted into cash (or traded in an active market).

Every company should explain what it includes as liquid resources and any changes in its policy.

Under this section cash inflows include:

- cash withdrawals from short term deposits (not qualifying as cash);
- cash inflows from the disposals or redemption of any other investments held as liquid resources.

Cash outflows include:

- cash payments into short-term deposits (not qualifying as cash);
- cash outflows to acquire any other investments held as liquid resources.

Financing

Financing includes the cash receipts and cash repayments to external providers of finance. For example, cash receipts would include:

- cash receipts from issuing shares and from issuing debentures and loans.

Cash outflows include:

- repayments of amounts borrowed;
- the acquisition or redemption of the company's shares;
- payments of expenses or commission on the issue of shares, debentures and loans.

Nature of cash

The cash flow statement should include all of a company's inflows and outflows of cash. Cash is defined as cash in hand and deposits repayable on demand. Deposits are deemed repayable on demand if they can be withdrawn at any time without notice and without penalty. (However, if a period of notice is required – it must not exceed 24 hours.) Transactions which do not result in actual cash flows should *not* be included in a cash flow statement.

These standardized categories are to ensure that cash flows are reported in a form that highlights the significant components of cash flow and facilitates comparison of the cash performance between different businesses. A company's cash inflows and cash outflows should normally be included under each of the above individual headings. However, in the case of operating activities it is not necessary to show cash inflows and outflows separately.

The last two headings can be shown as a single section provided a sub-total is provided for each heading. The revised FRS 1 requires a cash flow statement to be prepared on a strict cash flow basis (i.e. by excluding any 'cash equivalents').

Other information to be provided

Reconciliation of operating profit to net cash inflows from operating activities This reconciliation will explain why the operating profit does not agree with cash inflows. For example, some of the differences will be accounted for by a company's depreciation charges.

When an asset is initially purchased there will be cash outflows as far as the cash entries are concerned. But the cost of this asset will be gradually apportioned to the profit and loss account in the form of depreciation – perhaps over many years. Depreciation is usually an annual book-keeping charge against profits in the profit and loss account but no cash exits from the business. For example, in 1996 a firm purchases a machine for £1,000 cash, it will be depreciated over ten years on a constant (straight-line) basis.

In the 1996 CFS there will be an outflow of cash of £1,000 (to purchase the machine) and no entry in later years. But in the profit and loss account there will be a £100 pa depreciation charge (i.e. the £1,000 is spread evenly or accrued over the ten years). In the calculation to obtain the cash flow, the reconciliation statement will show the annual depreciation charge added back to operating profit. In addition, the reconciliation statement will also take account of changes in the levels of stocks, debtors and creditors.

Reconciliation of net cash flow to net debt A CFS should also be accompanied by a note that reconciles the movement in cash in the period with the movement in net debt. This information can be given either adjoining the CFS or in a supporting note. (This reconciliation note does not form part of a CFS as such, rather it is supplementary information.)

The changes in the net debt should be analysed from the opening and closing balances showing separately, any changes resulting from:

* the company's cash flows;
* acquisition or disposal of subsidiaries;
* other non-cash changes;
* recognition of changes in market value and exchange rate movements.

Methods of constructing a cash flow statement

FRS 1 allows the CFS to be prepared under two methods – the direct and indirect method. Although FRS 1 favours the use of the direct method, it also permits the alternative indirect method. The methods only differ in the manner that cash flows from operating activities are identified.

The direct method highlights the actual cash receipts and payments in and out of the company. The indirect method reconciles operating profit to operating cash flows. In both instances the notes must contain a reconciliation statement of cash to operating profit.

Direct method

Specifically, this method returns to first principles of recording cash inflows and cash outflows. It requires the disclosure of cash receipts and payments. For example, it will record cash received from customers and payments made to suppliers, employees and for expenses.

Direct method: calculation of cash flow for operating activities

Cash flow from operating activities	(£m)
Cash received from customers	800
Cash paid to suppliers	(400)
Cash paid to employees	(150)
Cash paid for expenses etc.	(50)
Net cash inflow from operating activities	200

Indirect method

The indirect method is the most commonly adopted method format. It commences with operating profit which is then reconciled to net cash inflows by adjustments for changes in stocks, debtors and creditors (which are shown in the notes).

Indirect method: reconciliation of operating profit to cash flow

Cash flow from operating activities	(£m)
Operating profit	110
Add:	
Depreciation	25
Less:	
Increase in debtors	(40)
Add:	
Increase in creditors	60
Decrease in stocks	45
Net cash inflow from operating activities	200

In the above example, the company generated operating profits of £110m from trading or operating activities but has obtained £200m total net cash flows. Since depreciation is not a cash flow, £25m is added back to operating profit (because it has been retained in the business). The company is taking longer to pay its creditors – which means it has increased cash balances (£60m); it has reduced its stocks thereby releasing £45m in cash; but also it has increased its debtors (i.e. perhaps debtors have been given longer to pay or the company has sold extra production) and thereby reduced its cash flow by £40m. The net result is that, overall net cash inflow is £200m.

Comparison of methods

The direct method explains the actual sources and application of cash flows. It also clearly distinguishes profit from cash. It can provide a basis for estimating future cash flows – especially concerning customers and suppliers that are not obvious from using the indirect method. The direct method presents information in a relatively easy manner to understand and verify.

The indirect method is useful in providing clearer working capital information and for identifying changes in working capital – which are shown explicitly on the face of the CFS.

Model layouts

The ASB in FRS 1 (Revised) has produced model layouts for a single company and for a group of companies. See examples 8.1 and 8.2 below.

LIMITATIONS

Although the CFS is an improvement on the former funds flow statement it is still subject to a number of limitations. The major difficulty is that a conventional CFS is, by its very nature, a backward-looking statement. It is a historical summary recording cash in and out during the last financial year. It would be far more beneficial for most user groups to have access to future projected cash flows. Budgeted cash flow statements are produced by most organizations for internal management use but their content is not normally published. There are problems with accuracy, commercial secrecy and an unwillingness for directors to be subject to criticism – if the actual cash flows differ from projections. Accordingly, future cash estimates have remained solely within the province of the company's internal management.

A CFS will also record cash outflows on expenditure such as plant and machinery – but it will not explain whether the expenditure on a particular piece

EXAMPLE TABLE 8.1

EXAMPLE 1 XYZ LIMITED
CASH FLOW STATEMENT FOR THE YEAR
ENDED 31 DECEMBER 1996

Reconciliation of operating profit to net cash inflow from operating activities

	£000	£000
Operating profit		6,022
Depreciation charges		899
Increase in stocks		(194)
Increase in debtors		(72)
Increase in creditors		234
Net cash inflow from operating activities		6,889

CASH FLOW STATEMENT

Net cash inflow from operating activities	6,889
Returns on investments and servicing of finance (note 1)	2,999
Taxation	(2,922)
Capital expenditure	(1,525)
	5,441
Equity dividends paid	(2,417)
	3,024
Management of liquid resources (note 1)	(450)
Financing (note 1)	57
Increase in cash	**2,631**

Reconciliation of net cash flow to movement in net debt (note 2)

Increase in cash in the period	**2,631**	
Cash to repurchase debenture	149	
Cash used to increase liquid resources	450	
Change in net debt*		**3,230**
Net debt at 1.1.96		**(2,903)**
Net funds at 31.12.96		**327**

---

* *In this example all changes in net debt are cash flows.*

Reproduced with kind permission of Accounting Standards Board.

NOTES TO THE CASH FLOW STATEMENT

Note 1 - GROSS CASH FLOWS

	£000	£000
Returns on investments and servicing of finance		
Interest received	3,011	
Interest paid	(12)	
		2,999
Capital expenditure		
Payments to acquire intangible fixed assets	(71)	
Payments to acquire tangible fixed assets	(1,496)	
Receipts from sales of tangible fixed assets	42	
		(1,525)
Management of liquid resources		
Purchase of treasury bills	(650)	
Sale of treasury bills	200	
		(450)
Financing		
Issue of ordinary share capital	211	
Repurchase of debenture loan	(149)	
Expenses paid in connection with share issues	(5)	
		57

Note 2 - ANALYSIS OF CHANGES IN NET DEBT

	At 1 Jan 1996 £000	Cash flows £000	Other changes £000	At 31 Dec 1996 £000
Cash in hand, at bank	42	847		889
Overdrafts	(1,784)	1,784		
		2,631		
Debt due within 1 year	(149)	149	(230)	(230)
Debt due after 1 year	(1,262)		230	(1,032)
Current asset investments	250	450		700
TOTAL	(2,903)	3,230	–	327

EXAMPLE TABLE 8.2

EXAMPLE 2 XYZ GROUP PLC
CASH FLOW STATEMENT FOR THE YEAR
ENDED 31 DECEMBER 1996

	£000	£000
Cash flow from operating activities (note 1)		16,022
Returns on investments and servicing of finance[*] (note 2)		(2,239)
Taxation		(2,887)
Capital expenditure and financial investment (note 2)		(865)
Acquisitions and disposals (note 2)		(17,824)
Equity dividends paid		(2,606)
Cash outflow before use of liquid resources and financing		**(10,399)**
Management of liquid resources (note 2)		700
Financing (note 2) – Issue of shares	600	
Increase in debt	2,347	
		2,947
Decrease in cash in the period		**(6,752)**

Reconciliation of net cash flow to movement in net debt (note 3)

Decrease in cash in the period	**(6,752)**	
Cash inflow from increase in debt and lease financing	(2,347)	
Cash inflow from decrease in liquid resources	(700)	
Change in net debt resulting from cash flows		(9,799)
Loans and finance leases acquired with subsidiary		(3,817)
New finance leases		(2,845)
Translation difference		643
Movement in net debt in the period		**(15,818)**
Net debt at 1.1.96		**(15,215)**
Net debt at 31.12.96		**(31,033)**

---

[*] *This heading would include any dividends received other than those from equity accounted entities included in operating activities.*

Reproduced with kind permission of Accounting Standards Board.

	£000	£000
Capital expenditure and financial investment		
Purchase of tangible fixed assets	(3,512)	
Sale of trade investment	1,595	
Sale of plant and machinery	1,052	
Net cash outflow for capital expenditure and financial investment		(865)
Acquisitions and disposals		
Purchase of subsidiary undertaking	(12,705)	
Net overdrafts acquired with subsidiary	(5,516)	
Sale of business	4,208	
Purchase of interest in a joint venture	(3,811)	
Net cash outflow for acquisitions and disposals		(17,824)
Management of liquid resources*		
Cash withdrawn from 7 day deposit	200	
Purchase of government securities	(5,000)	
Sale of government securities	4,300	
Sale of corporate bonds	1,200	
Net cash inflow from management of liquid resources		700
Financing		
Issue of ordinary share capital		600
Debt due within a year:		
increase in short-term borrowings	2,006	
repayment of secured loan	(850)	
Debt due beyond a year:		
new secured loan repayable in 2000	1,091	
new unsecured loan repayable in 1998	1,442	
Capital element of finance lease rental payments	(1,342)	
		2,347
Net cash inflow from financing		2,947

* XYZ Group PLC includes as liquid resources term deposits of less than a year, government securities and AA rated corporate bonds.

NOTES TO THE CASH FLOW STATEMENT

Note 1 - RECONCILIATION OF OPERATING PROFIT TO OPERATING CASH FLOWS

	£000	Con-tinuing £000	Dis-continued £000	Total £000
Operating profit		20,249	(1,616)	18,633
Depreciation charges		3,108	380	3,488
Share of profit of associate	(1,420)			
Dividend from associate	350			
Profit of associate less dividends received		(1,070)		(1,070)
Cash flow relating to previous year restructuring provision (note 4)			(560)	(560)
Increase in stocks		(11,193)	(87)	(11,280)
Increase in debtors		(3,754)	(20)	(3,774)
Increase in creditors		9,672	913	10,585
Net cash inflow from continuing operating activities		17,012		
Net cash outflow in respect of discontinued activities			(990)	
Net cash inflow from operating activities				16,022

Note 2 - ANALYSIS OF CASH FLOWS FOR HEADINGS NETTED IN THE CASH FLOW STATEMENT

	£000	£000
Returns on investments and servicing of finance		
Interest received	508	
Interest paid	(1,939)	
Preference dividend paid	(450)	
Interest element of finance lease rental payments	(358)	
Net cash outflow for returns on investments and servicing of finance		(2,239)

Note 3 - ANALYSIS OF NET DEBT

	At 1 Jan 1996	Cash Flow	Acquisition* (excl. cash and overdrafts)	Other non-cash changes	Exchange movement	At 31 Dec 1996
	£000	£000	£000	£000	£000	£000
Cash in hand, at bank	235	(1,250)			1,392	377
Overdrafts	(2,528)	(5,502)			(1,422)	(9,452)
		(6,752)				
Debt due after 1 yr	(9,640)	(2,533)	(1,749)	2,560	(792)	(12,154)
Debt due within 1 yr	(352)	(1,156)	(837)	(2,560)	1,465	(3,440)
Finance leases	(4,170)	1,342	(1,231)	(2,845)		(6,904)
		(2,347)				
Current asset investments	1,240	(700)				540
TOTAL	(15,215)	(9,799)	(3,817)	(2,845)	643	(31,033)

Note 4 - CASH FLOW RELATING TO EXCEPTIONAL ITEMS

The operating cash outflows include under discontinued activities an outflow of £560,000, which relates to the £1,600,000 exceptional provision for a fundamental restructuring made in the 1995 accounts.

---

* This column would include any net debt (excluding cash and overdrafts) disposed of with a subsidiary undertaking.

Note 5 - MAJOR NON-CASH TRANSACTIONS

a. During the year the group entered into finance lease arrangements in respect of assets with a total capital value at the inception of the leases of £2,845,000.

b. Part of the consideration for the purchases of subsidiary undertakings and the sale of a business that occurred during the year comprised shares and loan notes respectively. Further details of the acquisitions and the disposal are set out below.

Note 6 - PURCHASE OF SUBSIDIARY UNDERTAKINGS

	£000
Net assets acquired	
Tangible fixed assets	12,194
Investments	1
Stocks	9,384
Debtors	13,856
Taxation recoverable	1,309
Cash at bank and in hand	1,439
Creditors	(21,715)
Bank overdrafts	(6,955)
Loans and finance leases	(3,817)
Deferred taxation	(165)
Minority shareholders' interests	(9)
	5,522
Goodwill	16,702
	22,224
Satisfied by	
Shares allotted	9,519
Cash	12,705
	22,224

The subsidiary undertakings acquired during the year contributed £1,502,000 to the group's net operating cash flows, paid £1,308,000 in respect of net returns on investments and servicing of finance, paid £522,000 in respect of taxation and utilised £2,208,000 for capital expenditure.

Note 7 – SALE OF BUSINESS

	£000
Net assets disposed of	
Fixed assets	775
Stocks	5,386
Debtors	474
	6,635
Loss on disposal	(1,227)
	5,408
Satisfied by	
Loan notes	1,200
Cash	4,208
	5,408

The business sold during the year contributed £200,000 to the group's net operating cash flows, paid £252,000 in respect of net returns on investments and servicing of finance, paid £145,000 in respect of taxation and utilised £209,000 for capital expenditure.

of machinery was justified in terms of either profitability or necessity. Moreover it may also indicate a large cash outflow on stocks. The CFS will not explain whether this outflow was because of a wasteful or excessive purchasing policy or because the organization was building up its stocks in anticipation of increased production or impending stock price increases. Some critics of the CFS would prefer to be able to identify the nature of the cash and cash equivalent balances and where they are physically located. A CFS will not provide all the answers. It is still necessary for the users to examine the CFS from a critical perspective and with an open and questioning mind.

FREE CASH FLOW

In recent years a number of companies have started to calculate and disclose what is known as a company's *free cash flow*.

The free cash flow of a company is defined as the net cash inflow from operating activities and dividends received from associated undertakings less *net* interest payments, dividends paid to minority shareholders in subsidiary undertakings, net tax payments and net purchases of tangible fixed assets.

In essence, the free cash flow represents the net cash generated during the year which is available for payment of dividends to shareholders, for investment in new businesses or for repayment of borrowings.

QUESTIONS

1   Carefully explain what you understand by a cash flow statement?
    Why is a company's cash flow frequently regarded as being so significant?
2   Explain to what extent you believe that a cash flow statement is of general
    value to user groups.
    With specific reference to any *three* user groups, discuss the benefits that a
    cash flow statement could provide to each of your chosen groups.
3   'In most companies, cash is king'.
    Do you agree?
4   Carefully discuss, with examples, the difference between cash and profit.
5   Carefully examine the cash flow statement of Burton Group plc (below).
    Draft a short report that highlights and discusses the salient features of this
    cash flow statement.
    Clearly state any inferences and conclusions that you can draw. (State clearly
    any assumptions that you make.)

NOTES

1   FRS 1 was revised to take account of public criticism. A number of companies did not
    favour the former definition of cash equivalents – which included only short-term
    highly liquid investments with an original maturity of three months or less. Other
    criticisms included a dislike of the former FRS 1 cash flow format because of the
    inclusion of cash flows relating to purchases or sales of short-term investments under
    the heading of investing activities – together with cash flows arising from the purchase
    or sale of long-term or fixed asset investments. Others considered that the former
    layout of cash flow statements did not always reflect more relevant aspects of cash
    flows of a business.

EXAMPLE TABLE 8.3 BURTON GROUP PLC EXTRACT OF CASH FLOW STATEMENT

Cash flow statement

FOR THE FINANCIAL YEAR ENDED 31ST AUGUST 1996	NOTE	1996 £m	1996 £m	1995 £m	1995 £m
Cash flows from operating activities	25				
Inflow from ongoing activities		**263.8**		212.8	
(Outflow)/inflow from property development and exceptional items		**(6.1)**		10.2	
			257.7		223.0
Returns on investments and servicing of finance					
Interest received		**17.8**		12.7	
Interest paid		**(12.9)**		(6.9)	
Rentals paid under property lease obligations		**(4.1)**		(3.9)	
			0.8		1.9
Taxation paid			**(21.9)**		(8.9)
Capital expenditure and financial investment					
Purchase of tangible fixed assets		**(282.1)**		(118.3)	
Sale of tangible fixed assets		**5.3**		–	
Options exercised over ESOP shares		**1.5**		0.9	
Purchase of shares by ESOP		**(17.6)**		–	
			(292.9)		(117.4)
Acquisition					
Cash balance acquired with Innovations Group	26		**6.7**		–
Dividends paid			**(33.5)**		(28.3)
Cash (outflow)/inflow before use of liquid resources and financing			**(83.1)**		70.3
Management of liquid resources					
Movement in short term deposits with banks			**85.1**		(58.8)
Financing					
Issue of ordinary shares		**5.3**		4.7	
Redemption of loan stocks		**(2.6)**		(1.1)	
Repayment of bank and term loans		**(121.0)**		(61.5)	
New bank and term loans		**121.4**		31.4	
Capital element of finance lease rental payments		**(0.4)**		(0.5)	
			2.7		(27.0)
Increase/(decrease) in cash			**4.7**		(15.5)
Reconciliation of net debt:					
At 3rd September 1995			**(17.1)**		(81.6)
Increase/(decrease) in cash			**4.7**		(15.5)
Decrease in debt			**2.6**		31.7
Movement in short term deposits with banks			**(85.1)**		58.8
Finance leases of Innovations Group			**(0.7)**		–
Non-cash movements in net debt:					
Provision for interest on Zero Coupon Secured Bonds			**(8.7)**		(7.9)
Provision for additional funding costs on property lease obligations			**(2.4)**		(2.6)
At 31st August 1996	25		**(106.7)**		(17.1)

1995 comparatives have been restated to reflect the requirements of FRS1 (revised).

25 Cash flow

	1996 £m	1995 £m

**a Reconciliation of operating profit to
net cash flow from operating activities:**

	1996 £m	1995 £m
Trading profit before exceptional items	161.6	102.1
Depreciation charges	82.8	81.7
Amortisation of own shares	5.3	0.8
Decrease in stocks	0.7	24.3
Decrease in debtors	3.0	6.8
Increase/(decrease) in creditors	10.4	(2.9)
Net cash inflow from ongoing activities	263.8	212.8
Net cash (outflow)/inflow from property development and exceptional items	(6.1)	10.2
Net cash inflow from operating activities	257.7	223.0

	Cash at bank and in hand £m	Funding debt due within one year £m	Funding debt due after one year £m	Net debt £m
b Analysis of net debt				
At 3rd September 1995	249.1	(21.1)	(245.1)	(17.1)
Increase/(decrease) in cash	35.7	(31.0)	–	4.7
Decrease/(increase) in debt	–	12.5	(9.9)	2.6
Movement in short term cash deposits with banks	(85.1)	–	–	(85.1)
Finance leases of Innovations Group	–	(0.1)	(0.6)	(0.7)
Non cash movements in net debt	–	–	(11.1)	(11.1)
Change in maturity of prior year debt	–	(102.2)	102.2	–
At 31st August 1996	**199.7**	**(141.9)**	**(164.5)**	**(106.7)**

26 Acquisition of Innovations Group plc

On 19th August 1996 the Company acquired Innovations Group plc for a total cost of £46.9 million.

	Net book values £m	Fair value adjustments £m	Fair value to the Group £m
Tangible fixed assets	6.5	(2.0)	4.5
Current assets:			
Stock	3.5	(1.4)	2.1
Debtors	7.0	–	7.0
Cash at bank and in hand acquired	6.7	–	6.7
Liabilities:			
Creditors (including finance leases of £0.7 million)	(15.7)	(0.5)	(16.2)
Net assets acquired	8.0	(3.9)	4.1
Goodwill			42.8
Total cost			46.9
Satisfied by:			
Shares to be allotted		23.8	
Cash including acquisition expenses		23.1	
			46.9

Fair value adjustments reflect changes to the open market values of properties and the alignment of stock provisioning policies with the Group. The impact of the acquisition on the results and cashflow for the year was insignificant.
All share allotments and cash payments were made after the year end.

9 | Analysis of Financial Statements

PART 1

This part examines the:

- nature and importance of financial analysis;
- major categories and application of financial ratios;
- interpretation of financial statements.

Apart from meeting legal obligations there are few intrinsic benefits in simply preparing a set of financial statements. The value of financial statements arises from analysing and interpreting the underlying figures and accompanying notes and drawing relevant inferences and conclusions. In many instances a complete understanding of the financial statements is not always possible. The financial statements are prepared on the basis of a large number of assumptions, incorporate a variety of estimates and adopt a range of various accounting policies. On their own, many figures extracted from the financial statements have rather limited value and application. These figures need to be placed in a comparative and meaningful context – which is frequently performed by the application of ratio analysis.

Ratio analysis

An important technique in analysing the figures taken from company financial statements is the use of ratio analysis. Ratios are concerned with the relationships between figures in the financial statements. By using the technique of ratio analysis, data from the accounting statements can be examined and used both internally and externally to the organization. Ratios can not only be calculated within the same company for a specific financial year but they can also be used to establish *a trend* of ratios over the years and also *to compare* figures between different companies. Using comparative ratios will highlight major changes in ratios over the years and assist in identifying possible causes and reasons for these differences.

   It must be stressed that ratio analysis is an extremely crude and approximate technique. The use of ratio analysis without exercising great caution will produce sweeping and often inaccurate conclusions. Ratios are merely approximate indicators; ratios guide, direct and suggest – but they certainly do not provide definitive answers or conclusive statements. The major value of ratios lies in their ability to highlight difficulties, signpost financially deteriorating data, and to assist in waving financial danger-flags to the users. Ratios can also be used in a more positive sense. If ratios are used in a discriminate sense they can assist, for example, in identifying companies that exhibit growth potential in sales and earnings and have effectively utilized their assets. Ratios can also highlight companies with particularly sound (or weak) liquidity and strong (or weak) financial/ investment performance. In short, ratios do not provide definitive conclusions – they merely help to identify topics of concern or interest. They identify areas that should be examined in more depth and suggest areas for more detailed questioning and perhaps further analysis.

The major purposes of ratios can be summarized as:

1 ascertaining the performance of the company;
2 determining the financial strength of the company;
3 using for comparative purposes.

In assessing performance it must be remembered that the figures are, because of the nature of the accounting statements, historical in nature. Ratios can reflect on the financial performance of what *has happened* (i.e. by using historical records) and *not what will happen* in the future. However, performance indicators can be important to the extent that historical performance can provide some prediction of the future. Since the only available ratio data are historically-based then, although the information has severe limitations, it is better than having no information at all.

The financial strength of the business is particularly useful in assessing the degree of security inherent in the business. It is of particular use to external parties such as banks and other lending institutions who can attempt to assess the degree of stability and asset security for lending purposes. Other user groups such as creditors and suppliers are also interested in financial strength as an indicator of credit worthiness and to assist in the assessment of being able to meet their payment demands. Other groups such as shareholders and employees will place importance on the degree of financial strength in the business as an indicator of investment potential and for continuity of trading.

Finally, for comparative purposes, ratios can be of assistance in company interpretation. It is possible to use ratios to compare successive years of data. Within the same company it is possible to establish a trend pattern over the years. It also is possible to determine variations from the norm or highlight particularly favourable or adverse ratios in a time series. If five similar sized businesses in the same line of business have similar ratios (but the sixth company is significantly different) then the analyst should be concerned. Although there may be a genuine business reason for the discrepancy, the analyst should certainly further explore the reasons for the difference. As well as comparing ratios in the same firm over successive years, it is also desirable to compare ratios against similar businesses in the same business area to help analyse the respective and relative performance of each firm. Although it must be stressed that ratios should only be compared against companies of a similar size in a similar line of business. It is meaningless to compare a multi-national corporation with a small regional manufacturing company especially when their business strategies and interests are completely different.

The value from using ratio analysis comes from knowing which ratios to select and being able to interpret them. But whichever ratios are selected, they should be treated with a degree of caution and apprehension. Ratios highlight areas of concern or interest – but the user should only regard them as 'indicators' or 'pointers'. The ratios can identify specific areas of concern or interest – but the user should always attempt to subsequently locate other evidence to substantiate the initial findings or suspicions; a ratio by itself has very little value.

Ratios can be calculated from any figures that are obtained, not only from within a set of accounts, but also from other external sources, including trade and other statistical sources. The ratios must be selected with great care. There is no standard answer – there is no 'right' or 'wrong' solution. Ratios can differ substantially between the size of company, type of business, markets in which the firm operates, and the time of year when the ratios are calculated.

Ratios are particularly useful when a pattern or trend can be established over the years. By identifying and monitoring changes in a ratio over a period, of say five or ten years, any discrepancies or variations from the five or ten year trendline can be easily highlighted. When selecting ratios there should be some connection or relational link between the figures. For example, it would be technically possible to compare profits to annual rainfall, but in the vast majority of businesses (except perhaps umbrella manufacturers) the resulting ratio would be meaningless!

Although there are no definitive classifications of ratios it is often convenient to group ratios into four major categories, namely:

1   profitability;
2   liquidity;
3   efficiency;
4   financial (investment).

The interrelationship of ratios can be expressed in the diagram below:

Structure of ratios

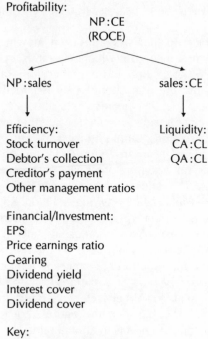

Profitability:

NP:CE
(ROCE)

NP:sales   sales:CE

Efficiency: Liquidity:
Stock turnover   CA:CL
Debtor's collection   QA:CL
Creditor's payment
Other management ratios

Financial/Investment:
EPS
Price earnings ratio
Gearing
Dividend yield
Interest cover
Dividend cover

Key:
NP   = net profit
CE   = capital employed
ROCE = return on capital employed
CA   = current assets
CL   = current liabilities
QA   = quick assets
EPS   = earnings per share

Category 1: profitability ratios

Profitability can be defined as the ability of a company to generate profits. This category of ratios examines the performance of a business in relationship to the amount of assets at a company's disposal. A figure taken from a firm's profit and loss account that reports a business as making a profit of £10,000 has very limited virtue by itself. The size of such a profit may be very reasonable for a small and newly established business but it may be truly disastrous for a multi-national corporation. To be of any significance the profit will need to be related to the size of the business. A common indicator of size can be the assets of the firm that are used in generating these profits. In other words the net profit is compared with the assets, (or sometimes called the capital employed), in the firm. The resulting figure is commonly termed the return on capital employed (ROCE). Because this ratio is often regarded as being so significant it is also often termed the primary ratio:

It can be defined as:

$$\frac{\text{Profit}}{\text{Net assets (or capital employed)}} \times 100\% = x\ \%$$

(Conventionally, this ratio is expressed in the form of a percentage.)

There is often considerable debate as to the definition of the asset base or capital employed figure. Some analysts commonly treat net assets as net capital employed, which can be defined as fixed assets plus current assets minus current liabilities, whilst others use gross capital employed which is defined only as fixed assets plus current assets. Because the net total assets can vary on a month by month basis it is common practice to calculate a simple average figure (i.e. (the opening of net total assets at the beginning of the year *plus* the closing balance of net total assets)/2).

If the resulting return (x% in the above formulae) is (say) 10 per cent then it means that for every £1 invested in the business, the company is generating 10p return. There is no 'right' or 'wrong' figure. The investor must decide whether the 10 per cent return is adequate bearing in the mind the investor's perception of risk inherent in the business. The potential investor will also need to decide on possible alternatives for investing their funds. For example, there might be another business that obtains a 15 per cent return with a higher risk or the investor might consider investing in a (virtually) risk free bank account but which provides only a return of 6 per cent. Ultimately the decision must lie with the investor depending upon the level of risk that is personally acceptable.

The above ratio is rather simplistic and can be modified by using more detailed and specific figures. Although it is often difficult to obtain agreement to standardize the definition it is important to stress that whatever definition is chosen, it must be consistently applied.

The ratio can be modified to calculate the return on capital employed (ROCE). This ratio is frequently regarded as a fundamental indicator of the profitability levels in a company.

It can be defined as:

$$\frac{\text{Operating profit (before tax, interest and exceptional items)}}{\text{Average net total assets}} \times 100\% = x\ \%$$

Sometimes the profit numerator figure selected in the above formulae is defined as profit before interest and tax (termed PBIT) and can be found in the company's profit and loss account under the heading: 'profit on ordinary activities before tax'. The interest payable on the company's long term loans (and sometimes together with exceptional items) is then added back to this 'profit on ordinary activities before tax' figure to determine the PBIT.

(Note: it is common practice to standardize the profit by taking the operating profit before the inclusion of tax, interest or exceptional items. These adjustments will minimize variations and concentrate on highlighting the core or fundamental profits of the firm. This adjustment will facilitate more useful comparisons between companies.)

The ROCE is important because it compares the net profit against the total net assets invested in the business. In other words, the ratio attempts to measure how successfully the firm's management has utilized the assets under its control to generate earnings for the company.

However, caution must be used when interpreting the ROCE. If the ROCE on a business activity is 10 per cent and the firm is largely financed by borrowed funds and the borrowing costs are significantly higher at (say 20 per cent) the user must be placed on alert.

The profitability of a company can not only be examined in the context of its assets but also in relation to its turnover. Firstly, the return on sales can be calculated by comparing profit to sales – to find either gross or net profit margins. That is:

$$\frac{\text{Net profit}}{\text{Sales}} \times 100\% = x \ \% \ \left(\text{net profit margin on sales}\right)$$

It is also possible to recalculate this ratio to find gross profit margin on sales.

$$\text{i.e.} \ \frac{\text{Gross profit}}{\text{Sales}} \times 100\% = x \ \% \ \left(\text{gross profit margin on sales}\right)$$

These ratios will indicate it is receiving x% return on profit. For example, if a company is obtaining a 5% net return then another way of expressing this ratio is to state that for every £1 of sales, the company generates 5p in net profit. The ratio is of special use when comparing profitability on sales in the same company – either establishing a trend or comparing profitability margins in different business segments. It is extremely important to bear in mind that this ratio can vary greatly – depending on the type of business. Some types of business have a relatively low return but the return is compensated by high turnover – whereas other businesses have high profit/sales margins but experience a low turnover. A typical example of the former being a food supermarket – whereas the latter could refer to a jewellery retailer.

This ratio can be easily distorted by the amount of capital employed by each business. Some businesses may obtain a high return on sales – but only at the expense of having enormous amounts of capital employed. To assist in overcoming this problem the asset turnover (or asset utilization) ratio can be calculated:

$$\frac{\text{Sales}}{\text{Assets}} = x \ \text{times}$$

If the sales are £1,000 and the net assets are £250 the resulting figure of 4 (times) would indicate that the assets have been 'turned-over' 4 times during the year. Another way of expressing this ratio would be that for every £1 invested in assets in the last year, £4 worth of sales was achieved. The higher the resulting figure then the more intensively the business is utilizing its assets.

Category 2: liquidity

Although a company must be profitable in the longer term, in the short term at least, it must have sufficient funds to meet day-to-day expenses and commitments. From a company's perspective, liquidity can be viewed as having the cash funds to meet its debts and commitments as and when they become due for payment. In practice a liquid company should have sufficient cash funds to pay its suppliers, pay employees their remuneration and meet its debenture and loan interest payments.

Liquidity can be defined as the ability of a company to meet its debts and obligations as and when they become due for payment.

The importance of liquidity is evidenced from a company's cash cycle. A company will receive cash predominantly from debtors and cash sales. At the same time the cash is being recycled by being paid out to creditors, suppliers, salaries and wages and expenses. The company must aim to keep the cash inflow and the cash outflow under a close degree of control. If the cycle becomes unbalanced or distorted the cash inflow can frequently be insufficient to meet cash outflows. The result can cause liquidity difficulties for the company.

Many businesses find maintaining a liquid position difficult. Many debtors do not pay their debts on time – whilst creditors frequently press the company for urgent payment. In other words, the timing of cash flows is vital for virtually all businesses.

For everyday operations it is imperative that companies maintain a sufficient degree of liquidity. Establishing a sufficient level of liquidity will mean that most companies will need to monitor and control such areas as:

- Debtors: factors to take into account include level and nature of debtors, creditworthiness of debtors, level of bad debts, terms and conditions of credit, credit control policies and practices of the company.
- Stock: levels of stock, monitoring and control of stocks and work-in-progress, obsolete stock and stock write-offs.
- Creditors: monitoring levels and dates of payment, comparing time taken to pay creditors compared with time taken by debtors etc.

In many organizations there can be a clash between a company's profitability and its liquidity. In practice companies arrange a trade-off between these two concepts. To be as profitable as possible a company must invest all its available resources, including most liquid resources into its productive assets (i.e. factories, machinery etc.). If the company overinvests in the productive capacity the company can rapidly reduce its liquid (working capital) funds and become illiquid. On the other hand, if a company has excessively high levels of cash and other liquid resources (i.e. it is too liquid) then the company is underutilizing its resources. In such circumstances the company will easily be able to meet its commitments to creditors and employees but its overall profitability will be reduced because it has failed to invest sufficiently in its productive capacity (i.e. its asset base) – which generates the company's profits.

On the other hand, an excessively high ratio of say 3:1 can equally lead to cause for concern. Such a level of ratio would indicate that the company has 'idle' funds that are not being put to optimal effect. A high ratio might imply that there are excessive levels of stocks, debtors or bank balances in comparison with current liabilities. These excess working capital funds should not be lying idle as part of working capital but rather invested in the productive capacity of the firm, such as in plant and machinery.

In an attempt to determine an appropriate level of liquidity it is possible to calculate two particularly relevant ratios.

Current ratio   One of the most significant indicators of liquidity is the current or working capital ratio.

The ratio is defined as:

current assets : current liabilities
CA : CL

If current assets are £1,000 and current liabilities are £600 then the resulting ratio of 1.67:1 indicates that for every £1 of liabilities there is £1.67 of current assets with which to meet these commitments. Traditional opinion has always regarded a ratio of 2:1 as being a so-called ideal situation since the business can meet its current liabilities twice over. More recent opinion is inclined to regard this figure as being excessively high and nowadays it is common to find a ratio even below 1.5:1 as being acceptable.

The major difficulty is that there is no standard right or wrong answer. The ratio can vary dramatically from business to business. For example, companies whose sales are predominantly on a cash basis, such as high street retailers, can afford to allow this ratio to slip below 1:1.

For example, some large cash based retailers may allow this ratio to fall to as low as 0.3:1. Whereas other firms whose customers are largely credit based would be happier establishing their ratio close to 2:1 rather than 1:1.

Particular attention should also be paid to establishing the particular breakdown of current assets and current liabilities and in identifying the constituent parts of their stocks, work-in-progress, debtors and creditors. Specific reference to the nature and relative values of each of these items should be made. (For example, the age, condition and saleability of stocks; the nature and types of debtors; and the nature and payment factors relating to creditors and other obligations.)

Rather than simply calculating the absolute level of the ratio it is more important to monitor the changes in the level of the liquidity ratio over time. Careful monitoring of the CA:CL ratio will often provide an opportunity for the company to attempt to rectify the deteriorating condition.

Quick asset (or acid test) ratio   The current or working capital ratio contains items that cannot be readily converted into cash, in particular work-in-progress and stock. In many companies it can take a relatively long period of time to convert a firm's stock into cash. (The sales cycle is lengthy: i.e. a customer has to be found, then an order received; followed by the sending of an invoice; followed by a period awaiting payment by the debtor including the possibility of default etc.)

If stock is excluded from current assets in the above ratio, the quick asset (or acid test) ratio can be found (i.e. current assets − stock = quick assets).

Quick assets : Current liabilities
QA : CL

As with the current ratio, the quick ratio has no 'ideal' or standard answer.

Traditionally a ratio of 1 : 1 would have been considered highly desirable. In other words all current liabilities could be paid at least from the generation of cash from the quick assets. The ratio is influenced by a variety of factors including the type of business and the nature of the firm's debtors and creditors. Nowadays, operating on the premise that all of a company's current liabilities do not normally have to be paid immediately − a figure of 0.7 : 1 or even 0.6 : 1 will not normally cause undue alarm. In a predominantly cash-based business this ratio can fall even lower.

Category 3: efficiency ratios

The internal efficiency of a business's operations is extremely important. Efficiency ratios primarily examine how productively companies utilize stocks and debtors but they can also include creditors and other business aspects.

Efficiency ratios can be calculated from any financial information relating to the company. But it is crucial to remember that whatever efficiency ratios are calculated − they must be relevant and meaningful.

Stock turnover

The stock turnover ratio is important in the measuring of the length of time that the firm has, on average, stock in its warehouse. In the calculation of the ratio it is normal practice to use the *cost* price of sales (rather than selling price) since stocks are themselves shown at cost price.

The ratio can be expressed either in terms of a turnover rate or in days (or months):

$$\text{Stock turnover (rate)} = \frac{\text{Cost of sales}}{\text{Average stocks}}$$

or

$$\text{Stock turnover (days)} = \frac{\text{Average stocks}}{\text{Cost of sales}} \times 365 \text{ days}$$

Firms that carry too high stock levels are not utilizing their funds to optimal effect. Stocks need to be financed and excessive levels may utilize a substantial proportion of a firm's working capital. Stocks incur financing costs in the form of interest charges on loans and overdrafts, storage and insurance costs, and there is a possibility that some stocks may age quickly and become unusable. There is also an opportunity cost in that funds used in financing excessively high stock levels cannot be used elsewhere in the company.

On the other hand, if the firm has too low a level of stocks it may imply that there is a danger of a 'stock-out' – a situation that arises when the firm is unable to meet its sales orders because of insufficient stock levels of either raw materials or finished goods. A failure to meet orders can then mean a lost order and a loss of a substantial amount of customer goodwill. The stock turnover ratio has no standard answer but the management can utilize the ratio to highlight changes occurring in their firm and to compare turnover ratios in other companies. The management of each firm must determine the level of stocks to be held in the light of such factors as their own experience, rate of sales, reliability of suppliers and usage/wastage rates.

The ratio can vary enormously depending on the organizational structure of the firm to the nature of the goods being stocked. A well-run and efficient business with sound lines of communications between its suppliers can allow the ratio to be far lower than a firm having long delivery lead times and erratic delivery patterns in ordering their stocks. A firm stocking perishable commodities will also have a considerably lower ratio than a firm storing items with almost infinite lives.

Some companies attempt to keep stocks and stock-holding costs to a minimum by implementing a 'just-in-time' principle of stock control. In practice, such a policy means that a company will only replenish its stocks 'just-in-time' – or just before stock levels are extinguished. In fact some organizations that support 'just-in-time' practices have such low stock levels that their stock turnover ratio can be measured in hours (and not days or months).

Debtors' collection period

Most companies conduct their business on the basis of credit. Goods are sold to customers on credit, and at a future date the debtor is expected to pay for the goods. It is useful to calculate the average number of days that debtors take in paying for the goods. An excessively long period of time in waiting for a debtor to pay a company's invoice can result in substantial funds being tied-up in debts rather than receiving cash to pay into the company's bank account.

The key ratio is:

$$\text{Debtor turnover} \left(x \text{ days} \right) = \frac{\text{Average debtors}}{\text{Credit sales}} \times 365$$

(In some businesses in the retail sector whose customers predominantly pay cash for the goods, this ratio has only limited benefit.) In a similar manner it is possible to calculate the average time it takes for a company to pay creditors by use of the creditors' payment period.

$$\text{Creditors' payment (days)} = \frac{\text{Average creditors}}{\text{Credit purchases}} \times 365$$

(Note: in both the above formulae, the average debtors and average creditors can be found as a simple average, i.e. (opening balance + closing balance)/2. If the opening balance information is not available then the use of the closing balance only is permissible.)

Category 4: Financial/investment ratios

A company's profits or earnings are often regarded as one of the major indicators of its financial performance. However, because there are many ways by which a company's profit can be calculated (e.g. before or after tax, before or after debenture interest etc.) it is possible to standardize the definition by using a more precise definition of earnings. A company's earnings are based on its profit *after* deducting taxation, preference share dividends, dividends to minority groups and extraordinary items. In other words, earnings are the profits attributable to the ordinary shareholders of the company.

But the absolute level of earnings of a company means very little. To have meaning and relevance a company's earnings should be related to a 'yard-stick' or some basis of measurement. A common method is to use the number of shares. For example:

EXAMPLE 9.1

Both company A and company B have total earnings of £100.

Company A has 1,000 ordinary shares and company B has 2,000 ordinary shares. The EPS for company A is 10p (£100/1,000) and the EPS for company B is 5p (£100/2,000).

The fact that company A's EPS is twice that of company B's EPS does not necessarily mean or imply that company A has superior performance. It could simply mean that company A was formed with a far fewer number of shares.

The factor that is significant is the year-on-year rate of increase or decrease. If, in the previous year, company A had reported an EPS of 8p and company B reported an EPS of 3p, it would imply that A's EPS had increased by 25 per cent and B's increased by 67 per cent – giving company B superior earnings growth performance. These percentage changes form the basis of far more significant information on which to interpret the company's financial performance affairs.

(For a more detailed discussion on earnings share, refer to: FRS 3, *Reporting Financial Performance*.)

Price earning ratio

The EPS figure is also extremely important in the calculation of the price earning ratio (PER). The PER is a comparison of the market price of the company's share with its EPS.

For example, if the listed share price of company A is 80p and its EPS is 10p the PER would be 8 times (80p/10p) or more frequently just referred to as a PER of 8. In other words, at today's level of earnings (i.e. 10p) it would take 8 years for the aggregate earnings to be equal to today's share price. Effectively, the PER is a measure of the perceived degree of risk or perceived degree of confidence in the company. The higher the PER the greater the number of years that an investor is prepared to wait for the total earnings to be equal to the share price. So implicitly there is a higher measure of perceived confidence (and hence by implication lower risk) in the company. For example, if company A has a PER of 10 and company B has a PER of 25, *ceteris paribus*, investors will have a greater degree of confidence and lower perception of risk in company B than company A.

It must be emphasized that this ratio must be interpreted with great caution. It is possible that the reason that company A's PER is lower is because of a poorer earning performance – which is not fully or immediately reflected in its share price. Not only can a high PER indicate that a company is a leader in its industry but if the PER is significantly higher than the sector norm it can suggest that the share is 'overpriced' and is being valued on too high a multiple of earnings. Similarly, a low PER may suggest that a share is either undervalued or perhaps indicates that the market has little confidence in the company's prospects and is regarded as a poor investment.

As well as examining the PER based on the latest financial statements (the historical PER), it is also possible to calculate the prospective PER. Many analysts will attempt to estimate the future or prospective PER based upon the estimated or projected earnings for the coming year.

The major weakness in using prospective PERs is the degree of subjectivity and estimation involved and hence the degree of reliability and accuracy. The value of using PER comes from comparing PERs in the same markets or business sectors. For example, it is quite common to find that food supermarket chain stores have higher PERs than high technology computer hardware companies. The general perception of risk is far higher in computer technology than in food lines. Computer technology can change extremely rapidly and adversely affect the company's long-term prospects; whereas changes in food retailing products are considerably slower – resulting in lower perception of risk for these companies.

Gearing

The gearing (or sometimes referred to as leverage) ratio identifies the extent that a business is financed by outside sources of debt. In particular it compares the amount of loans and debentures (the firm's indebtedness) to the company's shareholders' funds (i.e. the equity plus reserves). A company that is financed by a higher proportion of debt is deemed to be more highly geared than a company that is financed predominantly by the shareholders' own funds.

The two normal sources of financing for a business are through equity and debt (loans and debentures). Since the gearing of a company is the relationship between these two funding sources (i.e. debt and equity) – gearing has an important effect on the long-term financial stability of a company.

The importance of this ratio can be viewed in the context of the practical and legal nature of these two sources of funding. The debt normally consists of a fixed return (the interest) to debenture and loan stock holders. The interest must normally be paid irrespective of the level of profitability that is obtained. In contrast, the return to equity holders is in the form of dividends. The level of these dividends can vary with the level of profit obtained and the amount of dividends that the directors decide to pay. As a result, in times of trading adversity, the debt holders must still be paid but there is no similar obligation to pay dividends to shareholders. In such circumstances a relatively low geared company will have the advantage of being in a better position to survive by cutting its (optional) dividends. In similarly difficult trading conditions, a high geared company will still have to attempt to meet its relatively high debt servicing obligations.

In times of trading prosperity, a higher geared company can achieve superior results. Since a large proportion of the business will usually be funded by fixed (or reasonably constant) interest debt (at say a rate of interest of 15 per cent) the available profits can be apportioned over a proportionally smaller amount of shareholders.

For example:

EXAMPLE TABLE 9.2
Two companies A and B both have earnings before interest of £20,000. Company A has equity of £100,000 (100,000 £1 ordinary shares) and debt of £10,000, i.e. A is 10% geared. Company B has £10,000 equity (10,000 £1 ordinary shares) and £100,000 debt, i.e. 1,000% geared. In both cases the debt servicing charges are 15%.
The results of each company are:

Company A	
Earnings	£20,000
Interest	(£1,500)
Available for distribution to shareholders	£18,500
Earnings per share 18.5p	

Company B	
Earnings	£20,000
Interest	(£15,000)
Available for distribution to shareholders	£5,000
Earnings per share 50p	

In times of trading difficulties, for example, if profits before interest fall below £15,000 company B will be unable to meet its interest commitments – with the possibility of the company facing failure. Because company A has a low gearing, a drop in earnings to £15,000 has little impact on the firm's ability to pay its £1,500 interest.

There are a number of commonly-used and acceptable definitions of gearing. A traditional method of calculation is termed accounting gearing.

In its simplest terms, a common definition is:

$$\frac{\text{Long-term loans}}{\text{Capital employed}} \times 100 = x \text{ \% gearing}$$

The above formula is frequently considered too simplistic and can be subject to a number of modifications. The other methods of calculating gearing can be calculated in a number of ways. A common alternative is to include preference share capital in the calculations. Preference shares normally have a dividend attached which must be paid before dividends to the ordinary shareholders. Effectively, this preference dividend commitment is similar, in practical terms (but not in legal terms), to the paying of interest. Accordingly preference dividends are treated in the same manner as loan and debenture interest in the gearing ratio. The company's reserves are also usually included in the denominator to identify the total amount of shareholders' funds. (In a legal sense the reserves belong to the company's shareholders.)

Hence,

1 Firstly, long-term debt and preference shares can be used in the numerator:

i.e.

$$\frac{\text{Debentures and long-term debt + preference shares}}{\text{Ordinary share capital + reserves}} \times 100 = x \text{ \% gearing}$$

or

2 All of the company's debt (both long- and short-term debt) can be included,

i.e.

$$\frac{\text{All types of debt}}{\text{Capital + reserves}} \times 100 = x \text{ \% gearing}$$

3 It is also possible to use the ratio on a net debt basis. In this method any cash balances in the company are offset against any indebtedness.

i.e.

$$\frac{\text{All types of debt minus cash/bank balances minus short-term investments}}{\text{Capital + reserves}} \times 100 = x \text{ \% gearing}$$

Note: some analysts add long-term liabilities back to capital and reserves.
(Whichever formula is selected, it must be used consistently.)

Dividend yield

The dividend yield ratio explains the gross dividend that an investor will receive in relation to the share valuation. The ratio is only concerned with the income (i.e. dividends) that results from ownership of a share.

It is defined as:

$$\frac{\text{Gross dividend}}{\text{Market price of share}} \times 100 = x\ \% \left(\text{dividend yield}\right)$$

The gross dividend is effectively the dividend before the basic rate of Advance Corporation Tax (ACT) (see chapter 10 Taxation and Foreign Currency in Financial Statements) is deducted.

For example:

If a company pays a net dividend of 20p and the ACT is 20%, the gross dividend will be (20p × 100/80) 25p.

Assuming a market share price of 400p, the dividend yield will be:

$$\frac{25p}{400p} \times 100 = 6.25\%$$

If an investor invests £1 in this company he will receive a return on this investment in income terms of 6.25p. For an investor that is only concerned with income, this 6.25% yield can then be compared with other companies and with other investments. (It must be stressed that this ratio is only concerned with dividend receipts and as such it ignores the possibility of any capital growth in the share price.)

Interest cover

This ratio is useful in providing an indication of the extent to which profits can fall before the payment of interest is placed at risk.

It is usually defined as:

$$\text{Interest cover (times)} = \frac{\text{Profit before tax and interest}}{\text{Gross interest payable}}$$

For example, a company with profits before tax and interest of £1,000 and gross interest payable of £500, has an interest cover ratio of two times – the firm can pay its interest twice over from its profits. Another way of examining its position is that the firm's profits can fall by a half (£1,000 to £500) before the payment of interest is threatened. There is no 'right' or 'wrong' ratio but the higher the ratio the greater the degree of interest cover safeguard (or safety margin) for the firm. Businesses that have high gearing and operate in rather volatile trading conditions will find greater financial comfort and security by having a higher rather than a lower figure. Firms in such situations would prefer to have a ratio of four or five times rather than once or twice.

Dividend cover

The dividend cover ratio examines the amount by which profits could fall before the payment of dividends is placed at risk.

$$\text{Dividend cover ratio (times)} = \frac{\text{Profits available for ordinary shareholders}}{\text{Ordinary dividends paid}}$$

For example, in company ABC, the profits available for distribution this year are £100 and the company proposes to distribute £40 in ordinary dividends. The dividend cover ratio is 2.5 times (£100/40).

The year's profits could fall from £100 to £40 before the payment of dividends (out of this year's profits) is placed in jeopardy. If the profits were £30 and the company still wishes to pay a £40 dividend the resulting dividend cover of 0.75 implies that the company cannot distribute a dividend from this year's profit. If the company is still determined about paying a £40 dividend the company will need to utilize the excess (i.e. £10) from its previously accumulated profits, i.e. its reserves.

Other ratios

It is frequently useful to calculate an assortment of other ratios and statistics. These other ratios can provide additional information *provided* that they are selected with care and are *relevant* for the user's purpose.

These ratios can include:

$$\text{Cash flow per share} = \frac{\text{Cash from operating activities}}{\text{Number of ordinary shares issued}}$$

This ratio examines the cash (as opposed to profit) that is generated for every share in the company. (See also chapter 8 on cash-flow.)

Value added ratios

In its simplest terms, a company's value added is the difference between the proceeds from the sale of goods and the cost of purchasing the raw materials and labour. By the addition of the company's skills, ingenuity and labour the company has converted raw materials into finished goods (i.e. this difference is termed the value added by the company). There are a number of value added ratios that can be calculated, with the most frequent being related to employees or capital employed:

e.g.

$$\text{Value added per employee} = \frac{\text{Value added}}{\text{Number of employees}}$$

This ratio will indicate the productivity of employees, highlighting, for example the effort of a particularly skilled workforce.

And,

$$\text{Value added per £1 of capital employed} = \frac{\text{Value added}}{\text{Capital employed}}$$

indicating the productivity of capital for every £1 invested in the company.

Finally, it is possible to calculate many other ratios and statistics. But it must be remembered that these ratios must be *meaningful* and *relevant*.

Limitations

It must be emphasized that ratios are merely an indication or pointer. They can highlight particularly favourable or adverse figures in a business. By themselves ratios are not definitive or absolute statements. Ratios form a basis for further investigation and research. They must not form the sole foundation or only criteria for decision-making. The ratios must be treated with a considerable degree of caution and apprehension. Nevertheless, provided the ratios are used with a discriminate application they can provide a useful analytical tool and act as a starting point to conduct further investigation into a business.

Since one of the major uses of ratios is to compare companies it is important that the limitations involved are strongly borne in mind. It should be stressed that whereas the user frequently requires forecast information that has predictive value, most information obtained from the financial statements is historical in nature. Also much of the information from financial statements is summarized and some types of information are regarded as confidential and not published. In many aspects the analysis of financial statements yields only the symptoms of and not the causes of the underlying situation.

Cross sectional analysis can be used (i.e. making comparisons with other businesses) but it will only have any real value if ratios are compared within the same type of business or market segment. It is no use comparing the ratios of a food supermarket with the ratios of a multi-national manufacturing company. It is feasible to compare ratios within the supermarket category or within the multi-national manufacturing company sector but cross comparison between food retailing and manufacturing companies has little benefit. Many different businesses have a different degree of product diversification and production policies. Also the financing arrangements and accounting policies can differ enormously. The nature and degree of financial and business risk can differ substantially between business segments making such cross comparison fraught with difficulties.

Additionally, in calculating the ratios, it must be remembered that accounting policies can differ dramatically between companies. For example, some companies will have adopted policies that revalue assets periodically whereas other companies will not necessarily have revalued land and buildings recently or even at all. In practice this will mean one company's assets will be stated at the original (usually lower) historical cost and other companies' assets might be stated at the (normally higher) current value. Since the asset valuation basis can vary greatly there will be implications for the calculation of ratios such as the return on capital employed and asset utilization.

Ratios to predict corporate failure

A large amount of research using quantitative data has been undertaken in attempting to predict the likelihood that a company is going to fail. By using a method termed multi-variate analysis, E. Altman linked a number of ratios together. In 1968 Altman analysed 22 accounting and non-accounting variables of USA companies and identified five key indicators. By weighting these five indicators Altman calculated a 'Z score' which he believed indicated whether a company was in a non-fail or fail situation.

Altman's model based the calculation of the 'Z score' upon the following formulae:

$$Z = 1.2x_1 + 1.4x_2 + 3.3x_3 + 0.6x_4 + 1.0x_5$$

where,

x_1 = working capital/total assets
x_2 = retained earnings/total assets
x_3 = profit before interest and tax/total assets
x_4 = market value of equity/book value of a company's debt
x_5 = sales/total assets

A Z score of three or above indicated a low probability of failure, while a score of 1.81 or less indicated a high probability of failure. (The intervening gap provided no specific guidance.)

Altman claimed that his model was able to predict with 95 per cent accuracy the failure of a company within one year prior to failure and with 72 per cent accuracy within a two year period prior to failure. In excess of two years, the degree of accuracy diminished substantially. Altman made a number of significant assumptions and his model is subject to a number of major limitations.

Other analysts have used different models and have used different variables. In the UK, Altman's model was adapted by R. Taffler who regarded five ratios as being indicative of failure, namely:

1   earnings before interest and tax/total assets;
2   total liabilities/net capital employed;
3   quick assets/total assets;
4   working capital/net worth;
5   cost of sales/stock.

(Readers interested in pursuing this area of study are advised to make reference to the Further Reading at the end of this part.)

Although these predictors of corporate failure have met with varying degrees of success they nevertheless can provide a broad approximation of the likelihood of failure. Although it must be emphasized that these models alone should not be the sole indicator in making a decision about the success (or otherwise) of a company.

Going concern in financial statements

The Auditing Practices Board (Statement of Auditing Standards 130, *The Going Concern Basis in Financial Statements*, November 1994) has issued a statement providing guidance for auditors in considering whether the going-concern concept for a company is applicable.

The Statement notes (para 31) that there may be a significant level of concern about a company's ability to continue as a going-concern if, for example, there are indications present such as:

- Financial indicators:
  - an excess of liabilities over assets;
  - net current liabilities;
  - necessary borrowing facilities have not been agreed;
  - default on terms of loan convenants and potential breaches of convenant;
  - significant liquidity or cash flow problems;
  - major losses or cash flow problems which have arisen since the balance sheet date and which threaten the entity's continued existence;
  - substantial sales of fixed assets not intended to be replaced;
  - major restructuring of debt;
  - denial of (or reduction in) normal terms of trade credit by suppliers;
  - major debt repayment falling due where refinancing is necessary to the entity's continued existence;
  - an inability to pay debts as they fall due.
- Operational factors:
  - fundamental changes in the market or technology to which the entity is unable to adapt adequately;

- externally forced reduction in operations (for example, as a result of legislation or regulatory action);
- loss of key management staff, labour difficulties or excessive dependence on a few product lines where the market is depressed;
- loss of key suppliers or customers or technical developments which render a key product obsolete.
- Other factors:
  - major litigation in which an adverse judgement would imperil the entity's continued existence;
  - issues which involve a range of possible outcomes so wide that an unfavourable result could affect the appropriateness of the going-concern basis.

Time series

Provided the process is conducted with due diligence and caution it can be useful to highlight a trend of financial information. Although there is a statutory requirement to show the corresponding and comparative figures for the previous financial year, companies listed on the London Stock Exchange are recommended to produce the major elements of their financial statements for at least the last five years and many companies extend this period to ten years (see below). Although the use of the previous year's comparative figures can yield some useful information, the provision of a five year summary is frequently of more interpretative value.

By using an analysis of a five or ten year time series it is possible to construct and evaluate trends (i.e. as in a time series) as regarding such key areas of sales, earnings, dividends and assets. The analyst must bear in mind the impact of inflation over a period of time. To appreciate a trend of data in real terms, the nominal figures (i.e. figures not adjusted for inflation) should be adjusted by a suitable index, such as the Retail Price Index. It is important to note that over time the company may have incorporated other adjustments to its accounting policies and assumptions. Additionally changes to a company's capital structure, such as the number of shares in issue, may affect and influence the use of time series analysis.

Five year summary

As a result of supportive comments in the mid-1960s by the Chairman of the London Stock Exchange, most listed companies now produce a summary of their financial details over at least the last five years. (In fact a number of companies produce a ten year summary and some companies even include a longer period of time.)

An example of a five year summary trend of Whitbread plc's profit and loss account is provided below:

EXAMPLE TABLE 9.3   WHITBREAD PLC (EXTRACT)

Profit and loss account (£m)	1990/91	1991/92	1992/93	1993/94	1994/95
Turnover	2,059.8	2,191.2	2,346.4	2,360.4	2,471.8
Operating profit before exceptional items	275.7	256.6	264.4	257.9	264.6
Operating profit before exceptional items (as % of turnover)	13.4%	11.7%	11.3%	10.9%	10.7%
Profit before exceptional items and tax	248.4	179.8	219.0	231.7	255.1
Profit before tax	161.5	118.6	177.0	234.0	275.4
Basic earnings per share (pence)*	21.48	13.05	22.73	34.88	42.76
Adjusted basic earnings per share (pence)*	37.36	31.40	31.54	34.39	38.52
Ordinary dividends per share (pence)	16.30	16.95	17.75	18.80	20.20
Interest cover (times covered)	10.1	5.5	5.8	9.8	27.9
Adjusted ordinary dividend cover (times covered)[#]	2.3	1.9	1.8	1.8	1.9
Average number of employees:					
Full-time	32,168	33,585	33,777	31,909	33,374
Part-time	33,480	30,168	30,716	30,480	31,864

Changes in accounting policies have, where material, been reflected in prior years.
* The number of shares used to calculate earnings per share includes the shares issued as a result of the equalization of the voting rights attaching to the 'A' and 'B' ordinary shares in 1993/94.
[#] Calculated by reference to adjusted basic earnings per share.

FURTHER READING

Altman, E., 'Financial ratios discriminant analysis and the prediction of corporate bankruptcy', *Journal of Finance*, September 1968.

Taffler, R. J., 'Forecasting company failure in the UK using discriminant analysis and financial data', *Journal of Royal Statistical Society*, 145, pp. 342–58, 1982.

PART 2

A structured approach

This part discusses the development of a practical and structured approach to analysing a limited company's financial statements.

Although there is no definitive or formal method involved in the analysis of a company's published financial statements it is possible to develop a workable and generally acceptable approach. In analysing a company's financial statements it is important to develop a structured approach that allows the analyst to extract the maximum information and draw the most meaningful and relevant inferences and conclusions.

Although the following stages of analysis are not exhaustive, they do allow the user to dissect a company's accounts to maximum effect and benefit.

Stage 1: background fact finding

As a starting point to analysing a company's financial statements it is advisable to seek any information of a general nature relating to the firm itself. This information might take the form of details obtained from newspapers, trade and professional journals, libraries and from other business sources that may contain relevant material concerning the company and the business in which it operates. The information does not necessarily have to be exclusively concerned with financial details. Information of a non-financial nature, especially concerning details of the industry or business can produce a valuable source of knowledge. For example, statistical business information from a number of trade associations and governmental statistical sources can be invaluable in identifying changes in business trends, growth patterns and market developments.

By using cross-sectional analysis (see part 1 of this chapter 9) the user can make comparisons with other companies in the same industrial or commercial or product grouping. Although comparisons with similar businesses can often be difficult it is nevertheless possible to obtain some useful details. Major differences in areas of sales, volatility of earnings and major asset changes should raise questions in the analyst's mind. For example, company A and company B are similar sized businesses with each manufacturing similar products. If in the previous financial year company A achieved a 25 per cent increase in sales but company B only obtained 10 per cent the user should certainly try to ascertain why these differences have arisen. In particular the user will want to know why the increase in company A's sales is so much higher than B's. In many instances the answers will not be immediately identifiable – but by continuing with a detailed analysis the answers should become more easily apparent. The same basic but crucial questioning approach should be applied when examining other accounting figures; and in particular, bear in mind the question – why has a specific figure changed in comparison with the previous year?

Stage 2: reading the financial statements

Once the latest set of financial statements of the company has been obtained it is important that the user does not randomly examine parts of this document. The statements need to be analysed in an ordered sequence with particular emphasis being placed on the more significant accounting areas. Some areas of the financial statements have only limited relevance and their content should not be given undue consideration. In some companies the Chairman frequently tends to pro- vide an overoptimistic approach to the company performance and its future prospects in the Chairman's Statement. This Statement is not audited and, as such, there is a temptation by some company chairs to paint an excessively vibrant and optimistic picture of the firm. At the other extreme some accounting statements are a highly valuable source of information and should be accorded the highest degree of significance. For example, a relevant and informative significant ac- counting statement is a company's cash flow statement. The cash flow statement is a vital component of the financial statements and should be accorded credence and respect. Cash is difficult to manipulate, relatively easy to understand and provides useful information on the company's cash flow movements. As regards the company's profit and loss account the analyst should also be cautious of placing undue reliance on the earnings figure. Earnings are more easy to manipu- late by accounting techniques and practices than are objective cash transactions. Caution should also be exercised in relation to the balance sheet – especially with regard to the valuation of fixed assets – notably land and buildings. Currently there is a variety of practice with the revaluation of land and buildings, with some companies revaluing periodically and others infrequently or not at all. All the accounting statements and notes should be read in their entirety – and not just selectively.

Most companies frequently perceive their financial statements as their 'shop window'. For many companies, the financial statements are the principal means of communication with their shareholders and other users and, as such, some firms have been known to 'overdress' their accounting windows with often irrelevant and less than useful information. Glossy photographs and colourful graphs and diagrams of the company, its activities and its directors should be treated with caution. Frequently these presentations add little to the analysis of the company and can distract the analyst from an objective assessment.

It should be ascertained whether the company has an unqualified or 'clean' auditors' opinion. The user should establish that the auditors have stated that, in their opinion, the financial statements provide a 'true and fair' view and comply with the 1985 Companies Act. If the auditors do not consider that the financial statements provide a 'true and fair' view, they will amend their opinion in their Report accordingly (i.e. their opinion is be qualified). A set of accounts with a qualified auditors' opinion should immediately place the user on the alert. Audit qualifications are one of the major danger signs of possible financial and/or trading difficulties both now and in the future. However, the user must not become complacent with the presence of an auditors' unqualified opinion. There have been a number of instances where listed companies have collapsed shortly after receiving an unqualified report. The auditors' report is only *an opinion* (albeit a significant opinion) and should certainly not be taken as an absolute assurance of financial soundness or propriety.

Stage 3: accounting policies

All financial statements will contain a section of the financial statements entitled 'Accounting Policies'. This section is usually contained within the supporting notes to the financial statements and it is normally found immediately after the company's final accounts.

These policies will describe and explain the accounting policies that the firm has adopted during the year. Users should be particularly vigilant about the following areas:

- Basis of accounting.
  This particular reference is important. The section will contain references to the basis on which the financial statements have been prepared, e.g. whether certain tangible fixed assets have been revalued. Since the 1989 Companies Act, it is a requirement that a statement is made stating whether (or not) the financial statements have been prepared in accordance with all applicable accounting standards.
- Depreciation.
- Stocks.
- Foreign currency.
- Research and development.
- Basis of consolidation.
- The inclusion and nature of intangible assets.

In particular the user should note whether any accounting policies have been changed during the year (this should be referred to in the notes) and the corresponding effect on the firm's profits. It is also important to not only examine the accounting policies of previous years but also to compare any changes in the light of policies in similar companies. If the firm has recently changed its accounting policy from that chosen in previous years or from that normally adopted by the rest of that type of industry the user should investigate further.

The UITF has issued Abstract 14 which requires the effects on earnings on any accounting changes to be noted and explained.

Stage 4: accounting analysis of final accounts

This stage will entail the actual analysis of the company's final accounts: i.e. the profit and loss account; the balance sheet; cash flow statement; and the statement of recognized gains and losses. All four statements should be examined in their entirety. No inferences or conclusions should be drawn from any one of these statements until all four have been examined. As well as generally appraising the information contained within these statements the user should be prepared to apply the ratio analysis tools discussed in part 1 of this chapter.

Initially a general and overall appraisal should be conducted looking for any items that are unusual, or different, or have particularly high/low figures, or have figures that have changed substantially from last year.

Subsequently the profit and loss account should be examined. The user should carefully analyse the sales and operating profit and compare changes with last year. Since FRS 3 now requires sales and profits to be split and identified as arising from sections of the business that have been acquired, discontinued and from continuing operations, the user can begin to draw a picture of the organization's financial and operational direction. FRS 3 allows areas of business expansion and contraction to be ascertained and dissected. Furthermore, the profits arising from the various activities can be compared with the corresponding turnover. For example, the profits on continuing activities can be compared with the sales from continuing activities and the resulting ratio can then be compared with profit margins on sales from acquired operations.

Additionally reference to the segmented information (that all public limited companies will produce under the requirements of SSAP 25, *Segmental Reporting*), will help the user to identify information based on class of business and geography concerning sales, profit and net assets by class of business and geographical segment. In particular information concerning amounts and possible growth potential of sales and profits can be noted and a business risk profile of products and geographical markets can be ascertained.

The user should then examine the remainder of the profit and loss account by examining the major profitability ratios. In particular emphasis should be placed on the return on capital employed, sales utilization and gross/net sales margins. The company's expenses should be carefully monitored with special reference being placed on the net debenture and loan interest paid. Although undue reliance should not be placed on the earnings per share of the company by itself: the EPS should be examined in the context of *all* the financial statements. FRS 3 has effectively required that all items that were previously classified as 'extraordinary' be taken 'above the line' and classified as 'exceptional' items. Therefore the user should examine the nature and amount of any exceptional items that have affected the EPS and perhaps consider eliminating the exceptional items from the EPS calculation when comparing this year's EPS with previous years and with other companies. The balance sheet must also be analysed extremely carefully. The user must establish the basis on which assets, notably fixed assets, are valued. A company that has not revalued its assets, but insists on using historical costs or only revaluing assets infrequently, will present a totally different picture to a company whose assets are periodically and frequently revalued. The nature, type and, if possible the current value of land and buildings should be ascertained. (In some cases obtaining the value of land and buildings from the financial statements may be difficult, if not practically impossible for some companies whose assets have not been periodically revalued.) Careful study of the current assets and current liabilities can assist in formulating a picture of the company's liquidity. The nature and extent of indebtedness and the level of gearing of the company should also be ascertained. The balance sheet and supporting notes will assist in identifying the type of debt and the date of redemption.

The cash flow statement is an extremely important accounting statement. As discussed earlier it is rather difficult to manipulate the cash flow position of the company. Either the firm has the cash or it does not. Many businesses fail not because of profitability problems but because of liquidity difficulties. The business simply runs out of cash to meet its day-to-day commitments. The user should pay special attention to the cash arising from operating activities. A company must obtain a healthy inflow of cash from its day-to-day core trading (operating) activities and decreasing operating cash flows should put the user on alert.

The returns on investment and servicing of finance will allow the user to identify the income measurement implications of company indebtedness. Debenture interest actually paid and received can be carefully monitored and, in conjunction with dividends paid and received, can be compared with previous years and with other companies. As far as investing activities are concerned, the user should carefully observe evidence of expansion and acquisitions undertaken and of any investments being sold. The financing activities section can help to identify new sources of capital and borrowings and any repayments.

The SORG can also provide helpful information by bringing together all the company's gains and losses – both realized and unrealized. Any unrealized revaluation deficits and currency translation transaction differences can be highlighted rather than being merely stated in the supporting balance sheet notes. Throughout the examination of the various financial statements the analyst should carefully apply the major ratios to help support the formation of an overall opinion. The application and interpretation of ratios should be performed in a structured fashion, preferably with ratios being classified under the following four major categories: profitability, liquidity, efficiency and financial/investment (see part 1 of this chapter 9).

Stage 5: identifying a trend

Provided due diligence and caution is used, it can often be useful to attempt to identify a trend or pattern of financial information. There is a statutory requirement to show the corresponding and comparative figures for the pervious financial year. Additionally, it is recommended that companies listed on the London Stock Exchange disclose (at least) the major elements of the financial statements for at least the last five years, with many companies extending this period to ten years. Although the use of the previous years' comparative figures can yield some valuable information it is frequently more desirable from a statistical standpoint to use time series analysis over a longer time period.

By using an analysis of a five or ten year time series it is possible to construct trends regarding such key areas as sales, earnings, dividends, assets and indebtedness. The analyst must bear in mind the impact of inflation over a period of time. To appreciate a trend of data in real terms, the nominal figures (i.e. figures not adjusted for inflation) should be adjusted by a suitable index – such as the retail price index (RPI). For example, an increase in sales of 5 per cent, given an increase in the RPI by 7 per cent, is a decrease in sales of 2 per cent in real terms.

It is important to appreciate that, over time, the company may have incorporated other adjustments to their accounting policies and assumptions. Also there may be changes to a company's capital structure, such as the number of shares in issue which may affect and influence the use of time series analysis.

Stage 6: other factors

The users should consider any other available information that might be considered useful or relevant in analysing the company. The extent of this information can encompass such areas as the business, political, social, technological and economic environment in which the company operates. Although it is not possible to be prescriptive, the user should be especially aware of any general developments in the company's business arena. Volatility in product nature and markets can be extremely pronounced in some sectors, such as consumer and fashion goods. Other fast changing areas include computer-based and bio-technology industries and there are increasing business challenges produced by industrially emerging countries anxious to gain a market position.

Additionally possible governmental and political changes that may affect or influence the demand for the company's products or services may have implications for the company's financial position. For example, changes in interest rates, taxation policies or governmental grants may have a considerable impact on the company's trading potential, its capital structure and investment opportunity.

Future

Ideally users require information or projections concerning the future. Although most companies will prepare budgeted information for the coming year(s), it is normally confidential to the company's management. Other external users have to be largely satisfied with historical information. Although the published financial statements are historical documents drafted for the previous financial year they nevertheless can produce some useful information. Historical information can be useful in so far as it forms a pattern or in constructing a trend line which can be extrapolated into the future. Significance can be attributed to events and business activities that happened in the previous financial year and their effects anticipated or projected into the future. Nevertheless financial statements are prepared on a historical basis – whilst the most useful investment information often concerns the future. This fundamental difference can, by implication, never be bridged. Historical centred information has many serious limitations – but frequently it is the only information that is publicly available.

Summary

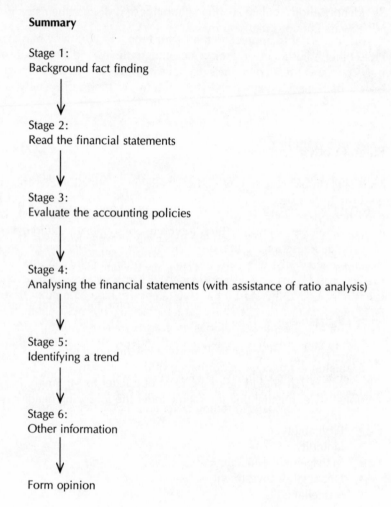

Stage 1:
Background fact finding

Stage 2:
Read the financial statements

Stage 3:
Evaluate the accounting policies

Stage 4:
Analysing the financial statements (with assistance of ratio analysis)

Stage 5:
Identifying a trend

Stage 6:
Other information

Form opinion

QUESTIONS

1 Carefully explain why the interpretation of financial statements is of crucial significance for all user-groups.
2 With specific reference to any *three* user-groups, discuss which key financial ratios are particularly relevant to these users' perceived needs.

3   Define what you understand by the term 'profitability'. How does profitability differ from liquidity?

4   *Calculation of Ratios:* Carefully examine the extract of the financial statements of Bass plc (in part 3 of this chapter 9).
    Bass is a company predominantly concerned with brewing, beverages and the retail drinks trade.
    Identify and calculate six financial ratios and discuss their significance. (State any assumptions that you make.)

PART 3

Case study analysis

You are acting as a financial advisor to a client, Mr Smith who has no financial knowledge.
    Mr Smith presents you with the annual report and accounts of Bass plc saying:

I have been advised by a friend that Bass plc is a sound investment. The problem is that I don't understand accounts at all – perhaps you could advise me whether, in your opinion, you believe that this company is worth investing in.

Required   You are required to carefully examine the extracts (below) from the financial statements of Bass plc.

1   With reference to your calculations of key financial ratios, you are required to evaluate the financial performance of this company.
    Your report should be in the form of a letter to Mr Smith, in good professional style, highlighting the ratios under the following headings:

- Profitability.
- Liquidity.
- Management efficiency.
- Financial or investment.
- Miscellaneous.

(You may wish to make reference to other information that is contained in the notes to the accounts).

2   Briefly discuss what other information you might require in the assessment of this company's performance but which is *not* contained within these financial statements.

3   Discuss the financial, business and other information that you might wish to obtain before recommending that your client invests in this company.

Note:

(a) Your letter and supporting information notes should not exceed 2,000 words.
(b) Assume the market share price of the company is 500p.
(c) State any assumptions that you make.

EXAMPLE TABLE 9.4 CASE STUDY EXTRACT FROM THE FINANCIAL STATEMENTS OF BASS PLC

Bass PLC

Annual Report
& Financial
Statements
1996

OPERATING AND FINANCIAL REVIEW

This operating and financial review discusses the performance of the Bass Group in the financial year ended 30 September 1996. It provides detailed information about the profitability, cash flow and capital investment of the Group and each of its five divisions. It also reviews financial issues including treasury management, taxation, and share price performance.

The glossary on page 56 explains some of the more technical or industry-specific terms used in this review and the financial statements.

GROUP SUMMARY

	1996 £m	1995 £m	change %
Turnover	5,109	4,541	+12.5
Operating profit	752	672	+11.9
Profit before tax	671	599	+12.0
Earnings per share	50.4p	43.4p	+16.1
Net capital expenditure	(568)	(353)	
Net trade loan repayment	25	31	
Operating cash flow	449	563	
Net cash flow	(148)	(120)	

There was a significant increase in Group turnover in 1996, up by 12.5% to £5,109m, resulting from both the impact of businesses included in 1996 results for the first time, and from organic growth.

The operating profit for the Group increased by 11.9% from £672m in 1995 to £752m in 1996. There was strong growth in operating profit in Holiday Inn Worldwide and

Bass Taverns (18.9% and 17.5% increases respectively) whilst, in a very competitive marketplace, Bass Brewers produced a strong 9.0% rise. Continued competition in bingo led to Bass Leisure recording a 10.8% lower operating profit. Britvic Soft Drinks' operating profit was 8.7% higher and included a full year's trading from the Robinsons' business.

Figure 1 shows an analysis of operating profit by division, with an increased proportion of Group profit being contributed by both Holiday Inn Worldwide (26%) and Bass Taverns (38%).

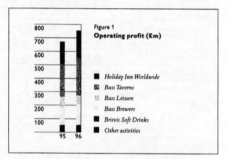

Figure 1
Operating profit (£m)

■ Holiday Inn Worldwide
▨ Bass Taverns
▨ Bass Leisure
  Bass Brewers
■ Britvic Soft Drinks
■ Other activities

The net interest charge was £78m, £5m higher than in 1995. This reflected both the impact of the £165m Harvester acquisition in September 1995 and the higher rate of interest payable on hedging international assets. Profit before tax was 12.0% higher at £671m.

At £215m, the taxation charge represents an effective rate of 32%, two percentage points lower than the previous year. As a result, earnings per share were 50.4 pence, a 16.1% rise on 1995. The final dividend recommended by the Board is 17.3 pence per share, which gives a total of 25.0 pence per share for the year; this level of dividend is covered 2.0 times by earnings.

The net cash flow for the Group was an outflow of £148m. Excluding the Carlsberg-Tetley acquisition (see Branded drinks – Bass Brewers, below), the normal cash flow was a £52m inflow against a £148m inflow in 1995, lower mainly as a result of higher capital expenditure.

OPERATING AND FINANCIAL REVIEW

HOTELS – HOLIDAY INN WORLDWIDE

	1996 £m	1995 £m	change %
Turnover	709	641	+10.6
Operating profit	195	164	+18.9
Net capital expenditure	(59)	(90)	
Operating cash flow	184	115	

	1996 $m	1995 $m	change %
Turnover	1,094	1,017	+7.6
Operating profit:			
Americas: CMH[1]	96	85	+12.9
franchise	143	129	+10.9
EMEA[2]	43	33	+30.3
Asia Pacific	9	8	+12.5
Total regions	291	255	+14.1
Other	9	5	+80.0
Total	300	260	+15.4

[1] Company managed hotels
[2] Europe, the Middle East and Africa

Holiday Inn Worldwide's turnover increased by 7.6% to $1,094m, with operating profit rising by 15.4% to $300m. The exchange rate averaged $1.54 to £1 compared with $1.59 to £1 in 1995, and this resulted in the division's reported sterling growth being higher than the underlying US dollar growth. In sterling terms, turnover and operating profit grew by 10.6% and 18.9% respectively. Over 47% of operating profit still came from the important Americas franchise business (see figure 2).

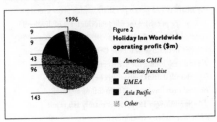

Figure 2
Holiday Inn Worldwide operating profit ($m)
■ Americas CMH
▨ Americas franchise
■ EMEA
■ Asia Pacific
▨ Other

In the **Americas**, revenue per available room (revpar) continued to improve, by 5.6% for the company managed hotels (CMH) and 5.9% for the franchised hotels. Average room rates were 4.2% higher for CMH and 6.4% for franchised hotels, whilst occupancy rates improved by 0.9 of a percentage point for CMH and declined by 0.3 of a percentage point for franchised hotels.

In the **CMH** business, the high operational gearing of company owned hotels meant that a significant proportion of the room revenue increases came through to operating profit. This was partly offset by increased depreciation charges resulting from the major refurbishment activity in the CMH estate over recent years. Primarily as a result of the strong growth in revpar, Americas CMH operating profit increased by $11m to $96m.

Growth in the number of hotels, gains in occupancy and average room rate, and a further improvement in the average royalty rate all contributed to **Americas franchise** operating profit increasing by 10.9% to $143m. The average royalty rate (4.13%, against 4.05% for 1995) should continue to increase as new franchises enter the system and as existing franchises are renewed at the present 5% rate. Americas franchise's results also received a boost from the high level of front-end fee income received (over $4m up), the result both of the active hotel property market with consequent change of ownership fees and the modernisation programme which led to early licence renewals. This high level of front-end fee income is not expected to be sustainable into the future.

Continued improving economic conditions, in the United Kingdom, Belgium and the Netherlands, benefited company managed hotels in those countries and contributed to Holiday Inn Worldwide's operations in **Europe, the Middle East and Africa (EMEA)** showing a 30% growth in operating profit. EMEA's strong owned and leased revpar growth of 8.5% continued to be led by firmer occupancy rates, up by 2.4 percentage points, but with an increasing contribution from improved average room rates (up 4.8%), with particularly strong growth coming from the United Kingdom and the Netherlands. With high operational gearing and tight cost control, company managed hotels were the major contributor to the region's operating profit, which improved to $43m.

OPERATING AND FINANCIAL REVIEW

In **Asia Pacific**, revpar improved by 0.3% with occupancy rates, on average, level with 1995, and average room rates increasing by 0.4%, reflecting a slowdown in economic growth in China in particular. Asia Pacific's results were also impacted by the loss of four hotels, and the refurbishment of three others. Combined with cost containment, the net effect was that Asia Pacific's operating profit grew by 12.5% to $9m.

Other income (including contract terminations and rebates) was relatively high at $9m, compared with $5m in 1995.

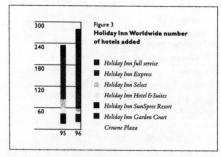

Figure 3
Holiday Inn Worldwide number of hotels added

- Holiday Inn full service
- Holiday Inn Express
- Holiday Inn Select
- Holiday Inn Hotel & Suites
- Holiday Inn SunSpree Resort
- Holiday Inn Garden Court
- Crowne Plaza

During the year, 280 hotels, representing some 34,000 rooms, joined the Holiday Inn system while 111 hotels, representing some 17,000 rooms, left. Of the hotels added, 172 were Holiday Inn Express (see figure 3), which are typically smaller in size and, hence, dilute the average hotel size in the system. At the end of the year, the system comprised some 2,249 hotels and 387,000 rooms. Of these, 2,071 were franchised, 87 were owned or leased, and 91 were management contracts or joint ventures. In addition, at 30 September 1996, there were franchise agreements for 559 hotels with approximately 59,000 rooms which, though formally approved, had yet to enter the system.

Holiday Inn Worldwide continued to be a strong cash generating business - operating cash flow of £184m for 1996 represents 41% of the Group's total. This operating cash inflow is £69m better than 1995, due to both improved profit and reduced net capital expenditure - the latter being £59m in 1996 compared with £90m in 1995.

LEISURE RETAILING - BASS TAVERNS

	1996 £m	1995 £m	change %
Turnover	1,278	1,121	+14.0
Operating profit:			
Managed	221	180	+22.8
Leased	61	60	+1.7
Total	282	240	+17.5
Net capital expenditure	(196)	(88)	
Operating cash flow	114	204	

Bass Taverns increased turnover by £157m to £1,278m and operating profit by £42m (17.5%) to £282m.

Within the **managed** estate, a total of 81 outlets were acquired, 46 of which traded as branded concepts. A further 137 existing outlets were converted to branded concepts. The total managed openings of 218 are analysed by brand in figure 4. At 30 September 1996, Bass Taverns owned and managed 2,778 outlets, including 118 Toby Restaurants, 102 Harvester restaurants, 75 Fork and Pitcher country inns, 69 O'Neill's 'Irish' bars and 15 All Bar One café bars.

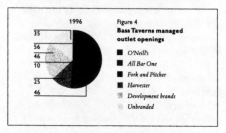

Figure 4
Bass Taverns managed outlet openings

- O'Neill's
- All Bar One
- Fork and Pitcher
- Harvester
- Development brands
- Unbranded

The average number of managed outlets increased by 3.8% to 2,681. Drinks sales per outlet increased by 6.6%, mainly through an improved mix of products sold and outlet quality, and also from price increases. Beer volumes grew by 2.4% in total due to the increased scale of operations, but fell by 1.3% on a per outlet basis as a result of the higher proportion of food-led outlets.

OPERATING AND FINANCIAL REVIEW

Company managed catering was expanded from 1,818 outlets at 30 September 1995, to 2,238 outlets at 30 September 1996. Food sales were up by 54% in total (see figure 5) and 12.4% on a per catering outlet basis, reflecting the full year impact of the Harvester acquisition.

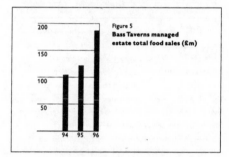

Figure 5
Bass Taverns managed estate total food sales (£m)

Amusement machines performance improved from the previous year's low point, with total income growing by 8.1%. Machine income benefited from the September 1995 Gaming Board review of stakes and prizes, allowing the roll-out of £4 cash/£8 token payout machines. It is, as yet, too early to assess the net impact of the further legislative changes introduced in June 1996 allowing the introduction of £10 all-cash machines in pubs whilst also permitting amusement machines to be sited in licensed betting offices for the first time.

Net operating margin increased from 18.1% in 1995 to 19.3% in 1996 as a result of the revenue growth referred to above and increased operating efficiencies. This improvement was restricted by the significant short-term cost increases associated with supporting the accelerated acquisition and brand conversion programme, and the one-off costs of opening outlets.

The **Bass Lease Company** operated an average of 1,443 leased outlets during the year. Wholesale turnover improved by 2.7% while beer volume fell by 0.7%, and rental income was flat as few rental agreements came up for review. After support and property costs, operating profit grew by £1m to £61m.

Bass Taverns remained a strong generator of cash with an operating cash inflow of £114m, despite the cost of the accelerated acquisition and brand conversion programme. Net capital expenditure of £196m included £77m on

acquiring and building new outlets, £50m on brand conversions and £62m on refurbishment of outlets.

Bass Taverns' outlet portfolio remained under constant review and, as a consequence, 16 outlets were sold.

LEISURE RETAILING – BASS LEISURE

	1996 £m	1995 £m	change %
Turnover	1,142	1,036	+10.2
Operating profit:			
Gala	31	36	–13.9
Coral	16	17	–5.9
Bass Leisure Entertainments	4	3	+33.3
Barcrest	8	11	–27.3
BLMS	7	7	–
Total	66	74	–10.8
Net capital expenditure	(127)	(102)	
Operating cash flow	(22)	19	

After showing a first half decline in operating profit of 16.7%, the second half profit fell by 3.1%. However, had it not been for the loss incurred by Coral on the last Saturday of the financial year (see below), the second half profit would have grown by 9.4%. Annual operating profit was down at £66m.

The bingo industry, in which **Gala** operates, continued to consolidate with the overall number of clubs diminishing. It is estimated that, during the year, 39 purpose-built clubs opened with approximately 75 'traditional' ex-cinema clubs closing. The market continued to move towards prime (including purpose-built) clubs, which are large, well-located, flat-floor clubs attracting a wide customer base.

During 1996, three prime clubs were acquired by Gala, eight purpose-built clubs were opened (two of which replaced traditional clubs), and one traditional club was sold, bringing Gala's total of UK prime clubs to 43 and the total UK estate to 135 (see figure 6). Gala remains the largest UK bingo operator, having operated on average 129 clubs during the year of which 35 were prime clubs. Gala plans to open 13 purpose-built clubs in the 1997 financial year.

OPERATING AND FINANCIAL REVIEW

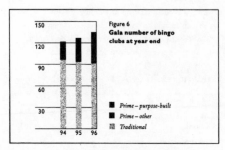

Figure 6
Gala number of bingo clubs at year end

■ *Prime – purpose-built*
■ *Prime – other*
▨ *Traditional*

Despite operating on average six more clubs, Gala's UK turnover was flat compared with 1995. Total UK admissions fell by 3.1% but the effect was mitigated by a 2.9% increase in average spend per head. Total admissions on a comparable club basis declined by 13.0%, though prime clubs fared better than the traditional estate.

In Spain, Gala continued its investment and, at 30 September 1996, operated five clubs.

Gala's operating profit was £31m compared with £36m reported in 1995.

Coral operated an average of 861 UK off-track betting shops during the year – up 16.8%, the increase coming from acquisitions in late 1995. These acquisitions were primarily responsible for Coral's UK turnover increasing by 11.4% in a market which has remained largely flat since the launch of the National Lottery. Turnover per shop, diluted by the acquisitions, fell by 4.5% but turnover in the acquired shops continued to grow under Coral management.

Coral's operating profit for 1996 was impacted by an estimated £4m loss on the last Saturday of the financial year as a result of jockey Frankie Dettori's winning all seven races in one day's racing at Ascot. Leaving aside this exceptional result, the net margin (after betting duty and levy) rose slightly, partly as a result of the 1% betting duty reduction introduced in March 1996.

Further deregulation saw amusement-with-prize (AWP) machines operating from June 1996 in all Coral's UK shops. Profit from the acquired businesses, together with the AWP contribution, the improved margins and

tight cost control, reduced the impact of the Ascot meeting, leaving operating profit only 5.9% down at £16m.

Bass Leisure Entertainments (BLE) increased operating profit by 33% to £4m on turnover which was 24% up. A further two prime bowls were opened, bringing the total to seven out of a total estate of 16. BLE also opened The Edge in Harrow, its first innovative youth entertainment centre which provides customers with varied electronic entertainment and access to the Internet.

Barcrest's exceptional export performance in 1995 was not repeated, with 28% fewer machines sold overseas. The UK AWP market was stimulated during 1996 by the review of stakes and prizes that took place in September 1995, and by the deregulation measures allowing the introduction of all-cash machines and their installation in betting shops, which occurred in June. Although Barcrest's UK AWP sales increased by 52%, the associated operational and development costs and the lower export volumes combined to depress operating profit to £8m.

BLMS acquired five small regional machine operators, substantially extending its presence in the south of England. The average number of machines sited rose by 18.4% due to the acquisitions and as a result of taking an initial near-50% share of the new licensed betting office market. Turnover increased by 15.3% but exceptionally high initial costs, resulting from the replacement of much of the estate following the review of stakes and prizes, and the introduction of all-cash machines, held operating profit level with 1995 at £7m.

Bass Leisure's total operating cash outflow was £22m compared with an inflow of £19m in 1995. This was principally the result of higher net capital expenditure. £53m was spent on the acquisition or construction of bingo clubs in the United Kingdom and Spain, and bowls, entertainment centres and betting shops in the United Kingdom. BLMS spent £36m on machine replacement and £6m on the acquisition of businesses. A further £19m was spent refurbishing existing Gala, BLE and Coral retail outlets.

OPERATING AND FINANCIAL REVIEW

BRANDED DRINKS - BASS BREWERS

	1996 £m	1995* £m	change %
Turnover	1,777	1,554	+14.4
Operating profit	157	144	+9.0
Net capital expenditure	(135)	(59)	
Trade loans	25	31	
Operating cash flow	139	160	

*1995 figures have been restated to include the trading activities of overseas brewing operations.

Bass Brewers recorded an operating profit of £157m, up by £13m (9.0%). However, restating 1995 to remove the profit from the gas business sold in that year, shows that growth in comparable operating profit was some 12.1%. The increase in turnover of 14.4% is primarily attributable to new products and the turnover from overseas operations consolidated for the first time in these results (see below).

The principal factor behind the growth in operating profit was the success of Hooper's Hooch. All three flavours had a strong market share position, with Hooper's Hooch being the leader in the alcoholic carbonates market with a full year volume of over 300,000 barrels.

Bass Brewers' domestic beer volume (excluding alcoholic carbonates) was up by 2.7%, with a flat performance in the on-trade being enhanced by a significant growth of 11.8% in the off-trade. The on-trade has recently begun to show signs of recovery.

Margins on a brand-by-brand basis generally showed continuing decline due to strong competitive pressures in

the marketplace. Overall, however, Bass Brewers' domestic wholesale margins per barrel remained flat in the on-trade, and increased by 8.3% in the off-trade. This was mainly due to the continuing shift towards higher margin premium products, including Caffrey's Irish Ale and Carling Premier. Figure 7 shows the increasing proportion of Bass Brewers' domestic volumes in the premium ale and premium lager sectors.

The higher volumes, as well as changes in product mix, resulted in a high level of contract packaging and some contract brewing – with an adverse effect on logistics costs. However, Bass Brewers continued to see savings in its core overheads as a result of programmes put in place in previous years.

Bass Brewers' domestic brands marketing expenditure was nearly 11% above 1995 levels, reflecting the continued commitment to the support of existing brands and to the development and launch of new brands.

Bass International Brewers continued to expand its interests by acquiring majority holdings in Vratislavice a.s. and Ostravar a.s., in addition to increasing its existing holding in Prague Breweries. The results of these businesses have been consolidated for the first time in the 1996 results.

Earnings growth in the Czech Republic was slower than planned as a result of difficulties in achieving price increases in a highly competitive market. The Bass Ginsber business in China, also consolidated in the Group's 1996 results, will, as expected, be slow in moving into profit.

Bass Beers Worldwide increased its turnover by over 32% on volumes which were 26% higher.

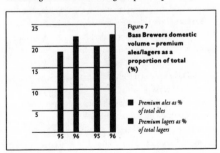

Figure 7
Bass Brewers domestic volume – premium ales/lagers as a proportion of total (%)

■ Premium ales as % of total ales
■ Premium lagers as % of total lagers

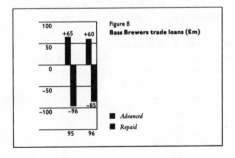

Figure 8
Bass Brewers trade loans (£m)

■ Advanced
■ Repaid

OPERATING AND FINANCIAL REVIEW

Bass Brewers continued to be characterised by its strength as a mature business, as reflected in the substantial operating cash flow of £139m. This inflow was slightly below 1995 despite a significant increase in net capital expenditure, including the cost of further investments in the Czech Republic. However, net trade loan investment fell as a result of the continuing reduction of the loan book (see figure 8).

In August 1996, the Group acquired a 50% share in Carlsberg-Tetley PLC (C-T). At the same time, agreement was reached with Carlsberg A/S, subject to regulatory approval, to merge C-T and part of Bass Brewers on a basis which will give Carlsberg a 20% share in the combined business. Further details concerning these arrangements are set out in notes 13 and 32 to the financial statements on pages 35 and 46 respectively.

BRANDED DRINKS –
BRITVIC SOFT DRINKS

	1996 £m	1995 £m	change %
Turnover	586	526	+11.4
Operating profit	50	46	+8.7
Net capital expenditure	(42)	(32)	
Operating cash flow	43	41	

Turnover for Britvic Soft Drinks increased to £586m in 1996 from £526m in 1995. Sales volumes rose by 5.6% compared with the 11.4% rise in turnover. This reflected price increases implemented in February following the significant increases in the cost of key raw materials during 1995. Operating profit improved by £4m to £50m, including the impact of a full year's trading from the Robinsons soft drinks business acquired in May 1995.

Temperatures were well below average for winter and spring and only average for the summer; this followed two well above average years and resulted in a reduction in the market volumes of carbonates of 3% (see figure 9).

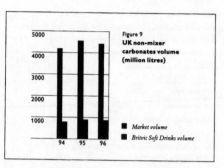

Figure 9
UK non-mixer
carbonates volume
(million litres)

■ Market volume
■ Britvic Soft Drinks volume

Britvic Soft Drinks' major competitor doubled its advertising and promotions expenditure, with particular impact in the spring, and Britvic Soft Drinks was able to maintain its market share only through significant increases in expenditure, including the packaging re-design for Pepsi and Tango. Pepsi's market share fell slightly, whilst Tango experienced a small increase. All brands showed some volume decline.

Britvic Soft Drinks also invested heavily in the new product introduction of Still Tango, Mountain Dew and Red Card, and withdrew from the Liptonice brand. In total, advertising and promotions expenditure increased by 24%.

Robinsons, acquired during 1995, performed well and in line with expectations, maintaining sales volume and achieving expected synergies. The full year contribution from Robinsons offset the impact of lower sales volumes, increased advertising and promotions expenditure, and the cost of new product investment on the existing Britvic Soft Drinks' business – the latter seeing a fall in operating profit in line with its major competitors in the United Kingdom.

The cost of key raw materials started to level out during 1996 with some costs starting to decline from their peak. However, gross profit margins did not fully recover due to the full year impact of the cost increases during 1995 and the continued trend in the marketplace towards sales of lower margin packs.

Operating cash flow for the division continued to be positive with a £43m inflow. Net capital expenditure amounted to £42m, of which £20m was invested in vending and dispense, to maintain and develop sales growth, and £12m in production facilities – in particular, to package single-serve plastic bottles.

OPERATING AND FINANCIAL REVIEW

OTHER ACTIVITIES

Other activities include overseas wine production, property development, and certain other investments. These businesses contributed an operating profit of £2m for 1996, against £4m in 1995.

INTEREST

The Group's net interest charge increased by £5m. This mainly reflected lower sterling interest receivable, which fell because of the reduction in deposits following acquisitions, principally of Harvester in August 1995 and C-T in August 1996. This reduction was partly mitigated by the receipt of interest relating to certificates of tax deposit and tax refunds.

The total interest payable rose slightly. This related mainly to the interest payable on debt taken out to finance and hedge assets acquired in high interest currencies such as Czech crowns. US dollar borrowing costs fell because of reductions in interest rates and borrowings. The impact of lower US dollar interest was, however, partially offset by the strengthening of that currency against sterling.

Overall, net debt was, on average, 28% higher than in 1995. However, interest cover continued to improve, rising to 9.6 times.

TAXATION

The tax charge represented an effective rate of 32% compared with 34% in 1995. This improvement arose principally from an increased benefit of tax depreciation, a reduction in tax adjustments and the settlement of prior year issues.

Excluding the prior year adjustment, the Group's effective tax rate was 33%, in line with the nominal UK rate. Whilst effective tax rates in excess of 33% applied to most of the Group's overseas operations, the UK effective rate was less than the nominal rate, as a result of tax depreciation.

EARNINGS AND DIVIDEND

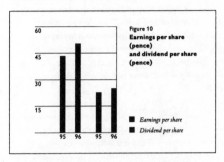

Figure 10
Earnings per share (pence) and dividend per share (pence)

■ Earnings per share
■ Dividend per share

Earnings increased to £444m, a 16.8% improvement on 1995. The weighted average number of shares rose to 881 million through shares being issued in respect of employee profit share, share saving and share option schemes, with the result that earnings per share increased by 16.1% to 50.4p (see figure 10).

The proposed final dividend is 17.3 pence per share; together with the interim dividend of 7.7p paid in July, this totals 25.0p, an increase of 10.1%. This level of dividend is covered 2.0 times by earnings (see figure 10).

CASH FLOW

	1996 £m	1995 £m
Operating activities	992	885
Net capital expenditure	(568)	(353)
Trade loans	25	31
Operating cash flow	449	563
Interest, dividends and tax	(397)	(415)
Normal cash flow	52	148
Major acquisitions	(200)	(268)
Net cash flow	(148)	(120)

Operating cash inflow was £449m, £114m down due to the increase in net capital expenditure of £215m exceeding the £107m increase in cash generated from operating activities.

OPERATING AND FINANCIAL REVIEW

Net capital expenditure is analysed by division below (see figure 11), and shows significant increases in Bass Taverns (£108m), Bass Leisure (£25m), and Bass Brewers (£76m) – the latter reflecting the acquisition activity in the Czech Republic.

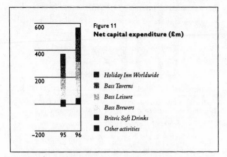

Figure 11
Net capital expenditure (£m)

■ Holiday Inn Worldwide
▨ Bass Taverns
▨ Bass Leisure
  Bass Brewers
■ Britvic Soft Drinks
■ Other activities

The net working capital movement was negligible, an outflow in stocks and debtors and an inflow in creditors reflecting the higher levels of trading. At the operating cash flow level, therefore, all divisions except Bass Leisure were generating inflows (see figure 12). This cash generated is used to fund tax, interest and dividend payments. Tax payments were £111m, £40m lower than in 1995, principally as a result of accelerated ACT recovery and tax refunds. Normal cash inflow was £52m, compared with £148m in 1995, reflecting the higher net capital expenditure. After the major acquisition cost of C-T of £200m, the net cash outflow was £148m compared with a £120m outflow in 1995.

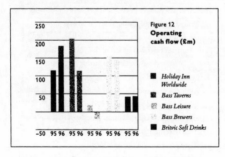

Figure 12
Operating cash flow (£m)

■ Holiday Inn Worldwide
▨ Bass Taverns
▨ Bass Leisure
  Bass Brewers
■ Britvic Soft Drinks

With an inflow from share issues of £28m, offset by the net debt acquired with business acquisitions of £43m and the effect of translating foreign currency denominated debt, net debt increased by £172m to £1,035m at 30 September 1996.

SHARE PRICE AND MARKET CAPITALISATION

The share price started the year at 640 pence, and never fell below that level. The high for 1996 was 843 pence, and the price closed at 779 pence on 30 September 1996 (see figure 13). This is a 22% increase on 30 September 1995, whilst the corresponding increase in the FTSE-100 index was 13%. Based on 779 pence, the historic price/earnings ratio was 15. At 30 September 1996, the market capitalisation of the Group was nearly £6,900m.

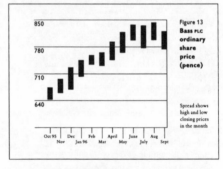

Figure 13
Bass PLC ordinary share price (pence)

Spread shows high and low closing prices in the month

TREASURY MANAGEMENT

Treasury policy is to manage financial risks through investment, borrowing and foreign exchange activities in relation only to underlying business needs. The activities of the Treasury function, which does not operate as a profit centre, are carried out in accordance with Board-approved policies and are subject to regular audit.

The Group's reported profits, net assets and gearing are all affected by movements in foreign exchange rates, particularly the US dollar. Under principles agreed by the Board, as far as is reasonably practical, the Group broadly matches the currencies of its borrowings with those of its

OPERATING AND FINANCIAL REVIEW

major overseas net assets. This had the effect that, during the year, the interest expense on US dollar borrowings hedged around 40% of Holiday Inn Worldwide and other US dollar profits. In 1996, the US dollar was, on average, 2.7% stronger than sterling compared with the year before, but, had it been identical, it is estimated that net interest payable would have been £2m lower, while operating profit would have been £5m lower.

Foreign exchange transaction exposure is managed by netting imports and exports where practical, with around 75% to 100% covered up to 12 months in advance through forward contracts or currency options. Most significant exposures of the Group are in currencies which are freely convertible.

Interest rate exposure is managed within parameters agreed by the Board, which stipulate that fixed rate borrowings should account for no less than 25% and no more than 75% of borrowings for each major currency. To achieve this, the Group enters into currency swaps, interest rate swaps, options and forward rate agreements. At 30 September 1996, 43% of borrowings were at fixed rates and 57% at variable rates. In broad terms, a 1% rise in US dollar interest rates would increase the net interest charge by £3m, whilst a change in sterling interest rates would have a broadly neutral effect on the net interest charge.

At 30 September 1996, gross debt amounted to £1,588m, comprising £876m of US dollar borrowings and £493m of sterling borrowings with the remainder in a variety of other currencies.

The Group continues to comply with all of its borrowing covenants, none of which represents a restriction on funding or investment policy in the forseeable future.

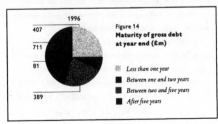

Figure 14
Maturity of gross debt at year end (£m)

1996

407
711
81
389

▨ Less than one year
■ Between one and two years
■ Between two and five years
■ After five years

Long-term financing requirements are met through sterling debentures and US dollar bonds. Short-term funding requirements are drawn under committed bank facilities or commercial paper programmes. At the year end, committed bank facilities amounted to £1,265m and uncommitted facilities to £233m. Of the total facilities, £391m was allocated to support the US dollar commercial paper programme. Approximately 74% of gross debt does not fall due for repayment before October 1997 (see figure 14).

The Group also held short-term deposits and investments of £553m. The policy on investment of funds restricts counterparties to those with an A credit rating or better. Limits are also set on the amount invested with individual counterparties and in individual countries. Most of the Group's funds are held in the United Kingdom, and there are no material funds where repatriation is restricted as a result of foreign exchange regulations.

Net debt at 30 September 1996 was £1,035m and, using the conventional measure of net debt expressed as a percentage of shareholders' funds, gearing was 26%; expressed in relation to market capitalisation, gearing was 15%.

The Group's current credit rating from Standard & Poor's and Moody's for long-term debt is A+ and A1 respectively and for short-term debt is A1 and P1 respectively.

ACCOUNTING POLICIES AND DISCLOSURE

A description of accounting policies appears on pages 26 and 27. There have been few regulatory changes in the United Kingdom during the year and the policies remain consistent with previous years. FRS8 (Related Party Transactions) was issued in the year but there were no material transactions requiring disclosure in the financial statements.

After the year end, the Accounting Standards Board published a revised version of FRS1 (Cash Flow Statements). Although adoption is not required for these financial statements, the cash flow statement and related notes are presented in the new format.

A summary financial statement has been produced for the first time this year. The information provided is more comprehensive than that required by the Companies Act.

DIRECTORS' REPORT

The directors of Bass PLC submit their Report for the financial year ended 30 September 1996.

Activities of the Group

The principal activities of the Group are in:–

- **Hotels,** through franchising, management or ownership;
- **Leisure retailing,** through ownership, management or leasing of public houses, restaurants, bingo clubs, betting shops, bowling and other amusement centres; through the manufacture, supply and operation of amusement and gaming machines; and
- **Branded drinks,** primarily through the production and distribution of beer and soft drinks.

Business Review and Future Developments

The Directors' Report should be read in conjunction with the Operating and Financial Review on pages 2 to 11, and the Chairman's Statement in the Annual Review and Summary Financial Statement which together include information about Group businesses, the financial performance during the year and likely developments.

Directors

The following were directors of the Company during the year:

Roger Carr (appointed – 18.9.96)   Sir Geoffrey Mulcahy
Kenneth Dixon (retired – 19.8.96)   Richard North
Bryan Langton   Sir Michael Perry
Robert C. Larson   Tony Portno
(appointed – 18.9.96)   Sir Ian Prosser
Sir Peter Middleton

Directors' details are set out on pages 24 and 25 of the Annual Review and Summary Financial Statement.

The Board is responsible to the shareholders for the good standing of the Company, the management of its assets for optimum performance and the strategy for its future development. There are eight regular Board meetings a year and other meetings as needed.

Kenneth Dixon, having reached the age of 67, retired from the Board on 19 August 1996 in accordance with the Company's Directors' Code. His position as Deputy Chairman was assumed by Sir Michael Perry.

On 18 September 1996, Roger Carr and Robert C. Larson and, on 1 December 1996, Tim Clarke and Iain Napier were appointed directors of the Company. In accordance with the Articles of Association, they will retire at the Annual General Meeting and offer themselves for re-appointment. The directors retiring by rotation are Sir Geoffrey Mulcahy and Sir Michael Perry who, being eligible, offer themselves for re-appointment. Of the directors seeking re-appointment, only Tim Clarke and Iain Napier have service contracts with the Company; these require two years' notice of termination, subject to retirement at 60.

Details of the directors' interests in the Company's shares are shown on pages 20 and 21.

No director was materially interested in any contract of significance to the Group's business, other than a service contract. Sir Ian Prosser, however, is a non-executive director of Lloyds TSB Group plc, which provides commercial banking and share registration services to the Company. Bryan Langton is a non-executive director of Wachovia Bank of Georgia NA, which provides lines of credit to Holiday Inns, Inc.

Corporate Governance

Directors' Responsibilities in relation to Financial Statements

The following statement, which should be read in conjunction with the Report of the Auditors set out on page 48, is made with a view to distinguishing for shareholders the respective responsibilities of the directors and of the auditors in relation to the financial statements.

The directors are required by the Companies Act 1985 to prepare financial statements for each financial year, which give a true and fair view of the state of affairs of the Company and the Group as at the end of the financial year and of the profit or loss for the financial year.

Following discussions with the auditors, the directors consider that, in preparing the financial statements on pages 22 to 47 inclusive, the Company has used appropriate accounting policies, applied in a consistent manner and supported by reasonable and prudent judgements and estimates, and that all applicable accounting standards have been followed.

The directors have responsibility for ensuring that the Company keeps accounting records which disclose with

DIRECTORS' REPORT

reasonable accuracy the financial position of the Company and which enable them to ensure that the financial statements comply with the Companies Act 1985.

The directors have general responsibility for taking such steps as are reasonably open to them to safeguard the assets of the Company and to prevent and detect fraud and other irregularities.

Compliance

The Board supports the principles of corporate governance outlined in the Code of Best Practice published by the Cadbury Committee on the Financial Aspects of Corporate Governance in December 1992 ("the Code"). The Board confirms that the Company complies with the requirements of the Code and has done so throughout the year. The Company also complies with the Listing Rules of the London Stock Exchange with respect to the Code. The auditors' report concerning such compliance appears on page 48.

In furtherance of the principles of good corporate governance, the Board has appointed the following committees, each with a formal constitution.

Executive Committee

The Executive Committee, which consists of the executive directors and the Company Secretary, meets approximately every two weeks to deal with all executive business of the Group not specifically reserved to the Board, or to any of the committees mentioned below. Among other matters, it reviews and, where relevant, authorises capital and revenue investment within limits agreed by the Board.

Audit Committee

The Audit Committee, chaired by Sir Michael Perry, consists of all the non-executive directors and meets at least three times a year. It assists the Board in observing its responsibility for ensuring that the Group's financial systems provide accurate and up-to-date information on its financial position and that the Group's published financial statements represent a true and fair reflection of this position. It also assists the Board in ensuring that appropriate accounting policies, internal financial controls

and compliance procedures are in place. The auditors attend its meetings as does the head of the Group's internal audit function, who has direct access to the Chairman of the Committee.

Remuneration Committee

The Remuneration Committee, chaired by Sir Michael Perry, consists of all the non-executive directors and meets, on average, four times a year. It is responsible for advising on remuneration policy for senior executives and for determining the remuneration packages of the executive directors. The report of the Remuneration Committee is set out on pages 16 to 21.

Nomination Committee

The Nomination Committee comprises the Chairman, Deputy Chairman and at least one other non-executive director. It is responsible for nominating, for the approval of the Board, candidates for appointment to the Board.

Routine Business Committee

The Routine Business Committee comprises any two executive directors or any one executive director together with a senior officer from an agreed and restricted list of senior executives: it is, however, always chaired by a director. It attends to business of a routine nature and to the administration of matters, the principles of which have been agreed previously by the Board or the Executive Committee.

Non-executive directors

Bass complies with the Code for those companies where the Chairman is also the Chief Executive in having experienced non-executive directors, who represent a source of strong independent advice and judgement. There are five such directors, each of whom has significant commercial experience and responsibilities outside Bass. Their understanding of the Group's operations is enhanced by regular divisional presentations outside Board meetings and by visits to the divisions.

Internal financial control

The Board is responsible for the Group's system of internal financial control. In order to discharge that responsibility in

DIRECTORS' REPORT

a manner which ensures compliance with laws and regulations and promotes effective and efficient operations, the directors have established clear operating procedures, lines of responsibility and delegated authority. In particular there are procedures for:–

- capital investment, with detailed appraisal, authorisation and post-investment review;
- financial reporting, within a comprehensive financial planning and accounting framework; and
- monitoring of business risks, with key risks identified and reported to the Board and Audit Committee.

There are also procedures for monitoring the system of internal financial control. This is an annual process, which involves:–

- certificated reports from relevant senior executives and divisional directors concerning the operation of those elements of the system for which they are responsible, and a report from the Head of Group Internal Audit concerning the operation of the system as a whole;
- reports from the Head of Group Internal Audit on the work carried out under the annual internal audit plan; and
- reports from the external auditors.

The Board has reviewed the effectiveness of the system of internal financial control in operation during the financial year through the monitoring process set out in the above paragraph. It must be recognised that such a system can provide only reasonable and not absolute assurance and, in that context, the review revealed nothing which, in the opinion of the Board, indicated that the system was inappropriate or unsatisfactory.

Going Concern

The financial statements, which appear on pages 22 to 47 have been prepared on a going concern basis as, after making appropriate enquiries, the directors have a reasonable expectation that the Group has adequate resources to continue in operational existence for the forseeable future.

Donations

The Company continues to support community initiatives and charitable causes and in 1996 donated £1.1 million (1995 £1.1 million). The Company made no payments for political purposes.

The Environment

Bass is committed to a policy that recognises that every company in the Group is part of a wider community of employees, shareholders, customers, suppliers and others, who all have a responsibility to act in a way that respects the environment. Bass therefore takes account of developments in environmental research and its manufacturing divisions have regular site environmental audits and retail sites have energy and waste management systems. Rigorous checks are carried out to achieve improvement in fuel economy and a reduction of atmospheric emissions.

Holiday Inn environmental conservation programmes let guests play their part to help the environment. Since mid-1994, Holiday Inn Worldwide has managed a programme called "Conserving for Tomorrow" combining a change in operational procedures with guest action to lower water and energy usage and reduce the amount of detergent introduced into the environment. In Bass Taverns, CFC-free cellar cooling units have been installed. The Group is actively involved in the United Kingdom in promoting and supporting a responsible plan for the recovery of packaging waste.

Share and Loan Capital

In the year to 30 September 1996, the issued share capital of the Company increased by 4,846,720 ordinary shares to 883,261,747 ordinary shares as a result of shares issued under the Employee Shares Schemes. Details are given in note 21 on page 41.

On 30 September 1996, the following listed securities of the Company were redeemed at par:
£1,452,853 10.65% Debenture Stock 1996/99, and
£14,977,191 7¾% Unsecured Loan Stock 1992/97.

Employee Share Schemes

Bass encourages employee participation in the Company's success through share ownership. The Bass Employee Profit Share Scheme, adopted in 1980, made an

DIRECTORS' REPORT

appropriation of shares in February 1996 out of profits allocated to it by the Board. At 30 September 1996, 6,485,301 ordinary shares were held by the Trustees on behalf of 25,893 participants.

The Bass Employee Savings Share Scheme (1992) granted options in June 1996 over 2,485,488 shares at £6.54 per share to a total of 5,541 employees. Under this scheme and its predecessor, 9,351 option holders hold options over 11,415,833 shares.

There are 284 participants in the Bass Executive Share Option Schemes, holding options over 6,934,429 ordinary shares.

Options under the Bass Executive Share Option Scheme (1995) were granted during the year to 267 participants over 2,525,900 shares. Options under this scheme are exerciseable only if a performance condition is met and for options granted in 1996, the condition established by the Remuneration Committee was that the Company's adjusted earnings per share over a three year period shall increase by at least six percentage points over the increase in the Retail Price Index over the same period. The performance condition applying to 1997 will be reported in the 1997 Annual Report.

No awards have been made under the Long Term Incentive Plan, which is described on page 16, as the first performance period is not completed until 30 September 1998.

During the year, the Company's Employee Share Ownership Plan trust acquired 80,000 Bass PLC ordinary shares at 796p per share with a view to using such shares towards satisfying future entitlements under the Long Term Incentive Plan or other employee share schemes.

Dividends
An interim dividend of 7.7p per ordinary share was paid on 29 July 1996. The directors recommend a final dividend of 17.3p per ordinary share to be paid on 10 February 1997 to shareholders on the Register at the close of business on 24 December 1996; this makes a total dividend for the year of 25p per share, which will absorb £221m.

Substantial Shareholding
The Company has been notified by The Prudential Corporation Group of Companies of its interest in 3.6 per cent of the Company's ordinary share capital.

CREST
On 3 December 1996, the Directors passed a resolution to enable the Company's ordinary shares to join and be transferred via the CREST settlement system. The shares are expected to enter the system on 13 January 1997.

A resolution to amend the Company's Articles of Association to make them consistent with the inclusion of securities in CREST will be proposed at the forthcoming Annual General Meeting.

Policy on Payment of Suppliers
The Company agrees payment terms with each of its major suppliers and abides by these terms, subject to satisfactory performance by the supplier. Amounts owed to other suppliers are settled on or before the end of the month following receipt of a valid invoice.

Annual General Meeting
The Notice convening the Annual General Meeting to be held at 12.00 noon on Thursday 6 February 1997 is contained in a circular sent to shareholders with this Report.

Auditors
Ernst & Young have expressed their willingness to continue in office as auditors of the Company and their re-appointment will be put to members at the Annual General Meeting.

By order of the Board

F S Wigley
Secretary
3 December 1996

GROUP PROFIT AND LOSS ACCOUNT

For the year ended 30 September 1996	Note	1996 £m	1995 £m
Turnover – continuing operations	1	**5,109**	4,541
Costs and overheads, less other income	5	**(4,357)**	(3,869)
Operating profit – continuing operations	2	**752**	672
(Loss)/surplus on disposal of fixed assets		**(3)**	5
Loss on disposal of operations		**–**	(5)
Profit on ordinary activities before interest	2	**749**	672
Interest receivable		**50**	54
Interest payable and similar charges	8	**(128)**	(127)
Profit on ordinary activities before taxation		**671**	599
Tax on profit on ordinary activities	9	**(215)**	(203)
Profit on ordinary activities after taxation		**456**	396
Minority equity interests		**(12)**	(16)
Earnings available for ordinary shareholders		**444**	380
Ordinary dividends	10	**(221)**	(199)
Retained for reinvestment in the business	22	**223**	181
Earnings per ordinary share	11	**50.4p**	43.4p

Notes on pages 28 to 47 form an integral part of these financial statements.

STATEMENT OF TOTAL RECOGNISED GROUP GAINS AND LOSSES

For the year ended 30 September 1996	1996 £m	1995 £m
Profit attributable to ordinary shareholders	444	380
Revaluations	1	(16)
Currency translation differences*		
Goodwill	16	(4)
Other assets and liabilities	(16)	10
Other recognised gains/(losses)	1	(10)
Total recognised gains	445	370

NOTE OF HISTORICAL COST GROUP PROFITS AND LOSSES

For the year ended 30 September 1996	1996 £m	1995 £m
Reported profit on ordinary activities before taxation	671	599
Realisation of property revaluation gains/(losses) of previous periods	2	(17)
Difference between historical cost depreciation charge and actual depreciation charge	1	1
Historical cost profit on ordinary activities before taxation	674	583
Historical cost profit retained after taxation, minority equity interests and dividends	226	165

RECONCILIATION OF MOVEMENT IN SHAREHOLDERS' FUNDS

For the year ended 30 September 1996	1996 £m	1995 £m
Profit attributable to ordinary shareholders	444	380
Ordinary dividends	(221)	(199)
	223	181
Other recognised gains/(losses)	1	(10)
Issue of ordinary shares	28	27
Movement in goodwill*		
Acquisitions	(22)	(87)
Currency translation differences	(16)	4
Net addition to shareholders' funds	214	115
Opening shareholders' funds	3,697	3,582
Closing shareholders' funds	3,911	3,697

*Foreign currency denominated net assets, including purchased goodwill eliminated against Group reserves, and related foreign currency borrowings are translated at each balance sheet date giving rise to exchange differences which are taken to Group reserves as recognised gains and losses during the period.

Notes on pages 28 to 47 form an integral part of these financial statements.

BALANCE SHEETS

30 September 1996	Note	Group 1996 £m	Group 1995 £m	Company 1996 £m	Company 1995 £m
Fixed assets					
Tangible assets	12	4,838	4,416	14	17
Investments	13	708	594	4,648	4,200
		5,546	5,010	4,662	4,217
Current assets					
Stocks	14	234	199	–	–
Debtors	15	631	611	750	548
Investments		481	684	326	561
Cash at bank and in hand		72	69	–	1
		1,418	1,563	1,076	1,110
Creditors: amounts falling due within one year	16	(1,624)	(1,531)	(1,636)	(1,284)
Net current (liabilities)/assets		(206)	32	(560)	(174)
Total assets less current liabilities		5,340	5,042	4,102	4,043
Creditors: amounts falling due after one year	17	(1,261)	(1,269)	(1,527)	(1,476)
Provisions for liabilities and charges	18	(51)	(12)	–	–
Minority equity interests		(117)	(64)	–	–
Net assets	20	3,911	3,697	2,575	2,567
Capital and reserves – equity interests					
Called up share capital	21	221	220	221	220
Share premium account	22	591	564	591	564
Revaluation reserve	22	1,006	1,009	–	–
Capital reserve	22	–	–	241	241
Profit and loss account	22	2,093	1,904	1,522	1,542
Shareholders' funds		3,911	3,697	2,575	2,567

Signed on behalf of the Board

Sir Ian Prosser
R C North

3 December 1996

Notes on pages 28 to 47 form an integral part of these financial statements.

GROUP CASH FLOW STATEMENT

For the year ended 30 September 1996	Note	1996 £m	1996 £m	1995 £m	1995 £m
Operating activities	25		992		885
Interest paid		(127)		(128)	
Dividends paid to minority shareholders		(5)		(4)	
Interest received		51		57	
Returns on investments and servicing of finance			(81)		(75)
UK corporation tax paid		(92)		(112)	
Overseas corporate tax paid		(19)		(39)	
Taxation			(111)		(151)
Tangible fixed assets		(547)		(372)	
Trade loans		(60)		(65)	
Other fixed asset investments		(56)		(68)	
Paid		(663)		(505)	
Tangible fixed assets		24		97	
Trade loans		85		96	
Other fixed asset investments		45		28	
Received		154		221	
Capital expenditure and financial investment			(509)		(284)
Consideration for acquisitions	24	(246)		(306)	
Cash and overdrafts acquired		12		–	
Acquisitions			(234)		(306)
Equity dividends			(205)		(189)
Net cash flow	25		(148)		(120)
Management of liquid resources and financing	26		154		123
Movement in cash and overdrafts			6		3

Notes on pages 28 to 47 form an integral part of these financial statements.

ACCOUNTING POLICIES

Basis of accounting
The financial statements are prepared under the historical cost convention as modified by the revaluation of certain tangible fixed assets. They have been drawn up to comply with applicable accounting standards. A summary of the significant accounting policies is set out below.

Consolidation
i) Basis of consolidation
The Group financial statements comprise the financial statements of the parent company and its subsidiary undertakings. The results of those businesses acquired or disposed of during the year are included for the period during which they were within the Group's control.

No profit and loss account is presented for Bass PLC as permitted by Section 230 of the Companies Act 1985.

ii) Goodwill
Any difference between the purchase consideration of an acquired business and the fair value attributed to its tangible assets and liabilities represents discount or goodwill. Goodwill is eliminated against reserves. To the extent that goodwill denominated in foreign currencies continues to have value, it is translated into sterling at each balance sheet date and any movements are accounted for as set out under 'Foreign currencies' below. On disposal of a business, any goodwill previously eliminated on acquisition is included in determining the surplus or loss on disposal.

iii) Associated undertakings
Those undertakings, not being subsidiary undertakings, in which the Group owns not less than 20 per cent of either the allotted share capital or the total capital and over which it exercises significant influence are treated as associated undertakings. The Group does not account for its attributable share of the results of these undertakings as it is not material to the Group's results.

Foreign currencies
Transactions in foreign currencies are recorded at the exchange rates ruling on the dates of the transactions adjusted for the effects of any hedging arrangements. Assets and liabilities denominated in foreign currencies are translated into sterling at the relevant rates of exchange ruling at the balance sheet date.

The results of overseas operations are translated into sterling at weighted average rates of exchange for the period. Exchange differences arising from the retranslation of opening net assets (including goodwill) denominated in foreign currencies are taken direct to reserves, net of exchange differences arising from foreign currency borrowings used to hedge against those investments. All other exchange differences are taken to the profit and loss account.

Treasury instruments
Interest rate agreements are treated as hedges, the profit and loss account reflecting only the net interest receivable or payable under such agreements.

Currency swap agreements are valued on the basis of exchange rates ruling at the balance sheet date with net gains or losses being included in current asset investments or borrowings respectively. Interest payable or receivable arising from a swap is charged or credited to the profit and loss account on a gross basis over the term of the swap agreement.

Gains or losses arising on forward exchange contracts are taken to the profit and loss account in line with the underlying transactions they are hedging.

Fixed assets and depreciation
i) Intangible assets
No value is attributed to trademarks, concessions, patents and similar rights and assets, including hotel franchises and management contracts.

ii) Tangible assets
Freehold and leasehold properties including related licences are stated at cost or valuation less depreciation where relevant. All other fixed assets are stated at cost.

iii) Interest
Interest paid in respect of certain major projects is capitalised to the extent that it relates to the period prior to the project becoming operational.

iv) Revaluation reserve
Surpluses and deficits, to the extent that any deficit is regarded as temporary, arising from the professional valuations of properties are taken direct to the revaluation reserve. Where a permanent diminution in value of an individual property is identified, the deficit is eliminated first against any revaluation reserve in respect of that property with any excess being charged to the profit and loss account. Valuation surpluses or deficits realised on sale are transferred from the revaluation reserve to the profit and loss account reserve.

ACCOUNTING POLICIES

v) Depreciation

Freehold land and licences are not depreciated.

Hotels and public houses held as freehold or with a leasehold interest in excess of 50 years are maintained, as a matter of policy, by a programme of repair and refurbishment such that their residual values are at least equal to book values. Having regard to this, it is the opinion of the directors that depreciation on any such property, as required by the Companies Act 1985 and accounting standards, would not be material.

Leasehold hotels and public houses are amortised over the unexpired term of the lease when less than 50 years.

Other freehold and leasehold properties are written off over 50 years, with the exception of breweries and maltings which are written off over 25 years, from the later of the date of acquisition and latest valuation.

Other tangible fixed assets are depreciated over their estimated useful lives, namely:

Plant and machinery	4-20 years
Information technology equipment	3-5 years
Equipment in retail outlets	3-10 years
Vehicles	3-10 years

vi) Investments

Fixed asset investments are stated individually at cost less any provision for permanent diminution in value.

Deferred taxation

i) Deferred taxation is provided using the liability method on all timing differences which are expected to reverse in the foreseeable future. Where this policy gives rise to a balance which will be offset against future taxation liabilities, this balance is carried forward as a debtor.

ii) Advance corporation tax on dividends paid or proposed which is expected to be recovered in the future is incorporated in the deferred taxation balance.

iii) No liability is considered to arise for deferred taxation in respect of UK industrial buildings allowances as the properties are expected to be used in the business for periods longer than that for which the allowances could be reclaimed on disposal. Similarly, no liability is considered to exist for taxation deferred by UK roll-over relief due to the level of continuing capital investment.

iv) UK deferred taxation is provided in respect of liabilities expected to arise on the distribution of profits from overseas subsidiary undertakings to the extent such distributions are required to be made. UK deferred taxation is not provided in respect of liabilities which might arise on the distribution of other unappropriated profits of overseas subsidiary undertakings as there is currently no intention to remit such profits.

Leases

Operating lease rentals are charged to the profit and loss account on a straight line basis over the term of the lease.

Pensions

The regular cost of providing pensions to current employees is charged to the profit and loss account over the average expected service lives of those employees. Variations in regular pension cost are amortised over the average expected service lives of current employees.

Differences between the amount charged in the profit and loss account and the payments made to the pension plans are treated as either provisions or prepayments in the balance sheet.

Research and development

Expenditure on research and development is charged to the profit and loss account as incurred.

Stocks

Stocks are stated at the lower of cost, including an appropriate element of production overhead cost, and net realisable value.

Turnover

Turnover represents sales (excluding VAT and similar taxes) of goods and services, net of discounts, provided in the normal course of business.

Cash flow presentation

The cash flow statement and related notes are stated in accordance with FRS1 (Revised); comparative figures have been restated accordingly.

Glossary

Additional information concerning terms used in these financial statements can be found in the glossary on page 56.

NOTES TO THE FINANCIAL STATEMENTS

1 Turnover – continuing operations		1996			1995		
		External £m	Inter divisional £m	Total £m	External £m	Inter divisional £m	Total £m
By division							
Hotels:	Holiday Inn Worldwide	709	–	709	641	–	641
Leisure retailing:	Bass Taverns	1,278	–	1,278	1,121	–	1,121
	Bass Leisure	1,119	23	1,142	1,016	20	1,036
Branded drinks:	Bass Brewers	1,435	342	1,777	1,251	303	1,554
	Britvic Soft Drinks	548	38	586	497	29	526
Other activities		20	2	22	15	6	21
		5,109	405	5,514	4,541	358	4,899

	By origin £m	By destination £m		By origin £m	By destination £m
By geographic region					
United Kingdom	4,301	4,252		3,861	3,823
Rest of Europe, the Middle East and Africa	267	312		192	232
United States	435	435		414	410
Rest of Americas	77	78		56	57
Asia Pacific	29	32		18	19
	5,109	5,109		4,541	4,541

2 Profit – continuing operations		Operating profit £m	Non-operating exceptional items £m	Profit on ordinary activities before interest £m	Operating profit £m	Non-operating exceptional items £m	Profit on ordinary activities before interest £m
By division							
Hotels:	Holiday Inn Worldwide	195	(5)	190	164	–	164
Leisure retailing:	Bass Taverns	282	2	284	240	–	240
	Bass Leisure	66	(2)	64	74	(1)	73
Branded drinks:	Bass Brewers	157	2	159	144	(6)	138
	Britvic Soft Drinks	50	(1)	49	46	–	46
Other activities		2	1	3	4	7	11
		752	(3)	749	672	–	672
By geographic region							
United Kingdom		564	–	564	509	–	509
Rest of Europe, the Middle East and Africa		27	1	28	15	–	15
United States		147	–	147	128	–	128
Rest of Americas		12	–	12	15	–	15
Asia Pacific		2	(4)	(2)	5	–	5
		752	(3)	749	672	–	672

Non-operating exceptional items comprise surplus/(loss) on disposal of fixed assets and operations.

NOTES TO THE FINANCIAL STATEMENTS

3 Continuing operations

Details of acquisitions in the year are set out in note 24. None of the acquisitions had a material effect on turnover or operating profit of the Group.

There were no material disposals or terminations of businesses during the current year or 1995.

4 Exchange rates

The results of overseas operations have been translated into sterling at weighted average rates of exchange for the year. In the case of the US dollar, the translation rate is £1 = $1.54 (1995 £1 = $1.59).

Foreign currency denominated assets and liabilities have been translated into sterling at the rate of exchange on 30 September 1996. In the case of the US dollar, the translation rate is £1 = $1.56 (1995 £1 = $1.58).

5 Costs and overheads, less other income	1996 £m	1995 £m
Raw materials and consumables	1,678	1,509
Staff costs (note 6)	848	807
Excise duty on own products	600	543
Depreciation of tangible fixed assets	229	206
Maintenance and repairs	89	84
Changes in stocks of finished goods and work in progress	(16)	(8)
Advertising costs	54	43
Other external charges	875	685
	4,357	3,869
The following amounts are included above:		
Hire of plant and machinery	34	34
Property rentals	71	65
Income from fixed asset investments	(17)	(16)
Auditors' remuneration – audit services	1	1
– non-audit services	1	–

6 Staff	1996 £m	1995 £m
a Costs		
Wages and salaries	756	716
Employee profit share scheme	15	15
Social security costs	59	55
Pensions (note 6c)	18	21
	848	807

NOTES TO THE FINANCIAL STATEMENTS

6 Staff (continued)		1996	1995
b Average number of persons employed including part time employees			
Hotels:	Holiday Inn Worldwide	**13,974**	13,791
Leisure retailing:	Bass Taverns	**44,121**	39,294
	Bass Leisure	**15,048**	13,551
Branded drinks:	Bass Brewers	**8,292**	6,023
	Britvic Soft Drinks	**3,137**	3,083
Other activities		**300**	327
		84,872	76,069

c   **Pensions**

Retirement and death benefits are provided for eligible Group employees in the United Kingdom principally by the Bass Employees' Security Plan which covers approximately 16,388 (1995 17,500) employees and the Bass Executive Pension Plan which covers approximately 672 (1995 590) employees. Members of these plans are contracted out of the State Earnings Related Pension Scheme. The assets of these plans are held in self-administered trust funds separate from the Group's assets. There are no significant pension plans operated by the Group outside the United Kingdom.

The pension costs related to the two principal plans are assessed in accordance with the advice of independent qualified actuaries using the projected unit method. The latest actuarial valuations of the plans were made at 31 March 1994. The significant assumptions in these valuations were that wages and salaries increase on average by 5.5% per annum, the long term return on assets is 8.0% per annum, the rate of growth of equity dividends is 4.0% per annum and pensions increase by 4.0% per annum. The average expected remaining service life of current employees is 14 years. At 31 March 1994, the market value of the combined assets of the plans was £1,315m and the actuarial value of the assets was sufficient to cover 116% of the benefits that had accrued to members after allowing for expected future increases in earnings.

The regular pension cost for the year of the two principal plans amounted to £39m (1995 £41m) with contributions to those plans being £16m (1995 £16m). The variation from regular cost amounting to £22m (1995 £22m) arises from spreading the surplus in the two principal plans on a straight line basis over the average expected remaining service life of current employees.

The movement in pension prepayment arises as follows:

	1996 £m	1995 £m
At 30 September 1995	**36**	36
Contributions	**16**	16
Regular cost	**(39)**	(41)
Variation from regular cost	**22**	22
Notional interest on balance	**3**	3
At 30 September 1996	**38**	36

The Group has no significant exposure to any other post-retirement benefit obligations.

NOTES TO THE FINANCIAL STATEMENTS

7   Directors' emoluments

Aggregate emoluments of the directors of the Company were as follows:

	1996 £000	1995 £000
Basic salaries	1,365	1,352
Fees	126	126
Benefits	75	69
Annual bonuses	526	565
Pension contributions	250	309
	2,342	2,421

More detailed information concerning the emoluments, shareholdings, options and Long Term Incentive Plan interests is shown in the Report of the Remuneration Committee on pages 16 to 21.

8 Interest payable and similar charges	1996 £m	1995 £m
Bank loans and overdrafts	26	15
Other loans	102	112
	128	127

9 Tax on profit on ordinary activities	1996 £m	1995 £m
UK corporation tax	152	170
UK deferred tax	14	12
	166	182
Overseas corporate tax	26	30
Overseas deferred tax	23	(9)
	215	203

UK tax has been calculated on taxable profits at 33% (1995 33%). The charge for the current year has been increased by £4m (1995 reduced by £14m) for timing differences and reduced by £5m (1995 increased by £2m) in respect of adjustments relating to prior years. There is no tax relating to the loss on disposal of fixed assets (1995 £nil).

	1996 pence per share	1995 pence per share	1996 £m	1995 £m
10 Ordinary dividends				
Interim	7.7	7.1	68	62
Proposed final	17.3	15.6	153	137
	25.0	22.7	221	199

11 Earnings per ordinary share

Earnings per ordinary share have been calculated by dividing the earnings available for ordinary shareholders of £444m (1995 £380m) by 881m (1995 875m) being the weighted average number of ordinary shares in issue during the year.

NOTES TO THE FINANCIAL STATEMENTS

12 Tangible fixed assets

By division	Holiday Inn Worldwide £m	Bass Taverns £m	Bass Leisure £m	Bass Brewers £m	Britvic Soft Drinks £m	Other activities £m	Total £m
Cost or valuation:							
At 30 September 1995	1,015	2,392	703	756	326	40	5,232
Exchange and other adjustments	(6)	–	(3)	(2)	–	–	(11)
Assets of acquired businesses	27	–	22	92	1	–	142
Additions	76	210	110	114	40	1	551
Disposals	(23)	(9)	(31)	(14)	(11)	(1)	(89)
At 30 September 1996	**1,089**	**2,593**	**801**	**946**	**356**	**40**	**5,825**
Depreciation:							
At 30 September 1995	119	189	123	282	87	16	816
Exchange and other adjustments	–	–	(3)	(1)	–	–	(4)
Provided in the year	42	38	43	75	28	3	229
On disposals	(12)	(3)	(23)	(9)	(7)	–	(54)
At 30 September 1996	**149**	**224**	**140**	**347**	**108**	**19**	**987**
Net book value:							
At 30 September 1996	**940**	**2,369**	**661**	**599**	**248**	**21**	**4,838**
At 30 September 1995	896	2,203	580	474	239	24	4,416

Properties

The directors carried out a valuation of the Group's properties at 30 September 1992 in conjunction with the Group's own professionally qualified staff and Chesterton International Property Consultants. The valuation which was incorporated in the financial statements for that year was on an open market basis for existing use in respect of all properties other than breweries and maltings which were reviewed by reference to depreciated replacement cost.

	1996 £m	1995 £m
Historical cost		
The comparable amounts under the historical cost convention for properties which have been revalued would be:		
Group		
Cost	2,823	2,552
Depreciation	(137)	(126)
Net book value	2,686	2,426
Company		
Net book value	9	9

NOTES TO THE FINANCIAL STATEMENTS

12 Tangible fixed assets (continued)

By category	Properties £m	Plant and machinery £m	Fixtures, fittings, tools and equipment £m	Group total £m	Company total £m
Cost or valuation:					
At 30 September 1995	3,472	476	1,284	5,232	31
Exchange and other adjustments	(5)	(2)	(4)	(11)	–
Assets of acquired businesses	76	58	8	142	–
Additions	220	74	257	551	1
Disposals	(22)	(9)	(58)	(89)	(1)
At 30 September 1996	**3,741**	**597**	**1,487**	**5,825**	**31**
Depreciation:					
At 30 September 1995	44	217	555	816	14
Exchange and other adjustments	(4)	–	–	(4)	–
Provided in the year	18	44	167	229	3
On disposals	(3)	(6)	(45)	(54)	–
At 30 September 1996	**55**	**255**	**677**	**987**	**17**
Net book value:					
At 30 September 1996	**3,686**	**342**	**810**	**4,838**	**14**
At 30 September 1995	3,428	259	729	4,416	17
Depreciable assets at 30 September 1996					
The cost or valuation of depreciable assets* included above is:	2,849	622	1,490	4,961	31

Properties	Cost or valuation £m	Depreciation £m	Group total £m	Company total £m
Freehold	3,090	(23)	3,067	6
Leasehold: unexpired term over 50 years	401	(2)	399	1
unexpired term under 50 years	250	(30)	220	2
	3,741	(55)	3,686	9

Cost or valuation of properties comprises:	
1992 and subsequent valuations	2,941
At cost since	800
	3,741

*Including assets in respect of which depreciation is not charged because it is immaterial.

NOTES TO THE FINANCIAL STATEMENTS

13 Fixed asset investments	Shares in associated undertakings £m	Loans to associated undertakings £m	Trade loans £m	Other investments and advances £m	Total £m
Group					
Cost:					
At 30 September 1995	58	16	430	139	643
Exchange and other adjustments	(1)	–	–	1	–
Consideration for acquisitions (note 24)	(19)	–	–	(27)	(46)
Revaluation	–	–	–	1	1
Additions and advances	201	10	60	40	311
Disposals and repayments	(3)	(11)	(85)	(39)	(138)
Investments written off	–	–	(11)	–	(11)
At 30 September 1996	**236**	**15**	**394**	**115**	**760**
Provision for diminution in value:					
At 30 September 1995	15	1	29	4	49
Investments written off	–	–	(11)	–	(11)
Provided in the year	2	–	12	–	14
At 30 September 1996	**17**	**1**	**30**	**4**	**52**
Net book value:					
At 30 September 1996	**219**	**14**	**364**	**111**	**708**
At 30 September 1995	43	15	401	135	594

	Shares in Group undertakings £m	Loans to Group undertakings £m	Total £m
Company			
Cost:			
At 30 September 1995	2,689	1,514	4,203
Additions	64	1,678	1,742
Disposals and repayments	–	(1,294)	(1,294)
At 30 September 1996	**2,753**	**1,898**	**4,651**
Provision for diminution in value:			
At 30 September 1995	3	–	3
At 30 September 1996	**3**	**–**	**3**
Net book value:			
At 30 September 1996	**2,750**	**1,898**	**4,648**
At 30 September 1995	2,686	1,514	4,200

NOTES TO THE FINANCIAL STATEMENTS

	1996		1995	
13 Fixed asset investments (continued)	**Cost less amount written off £m**	**Replacement cost £m**	Cost less amount written off £m	Replacement cost £m
Group				
Listed investments:				
Associated undertakings	–	–	15	15
Other	24	24	26	26
	24	24	41	41
Unlisted investments:				
Associated undertakings*	219		28	
Other	36		44	
	255		72	
	279		113	

All listed investments are listed on a recognised investment exchange, and their market value is at least equal to the replacement cost stated above. In the opinion of the directors, the market value of unlisted investments is at least equal to the amount stated above.

*On 25 August 1996, the Group acquired a 50% share in Carlsberg-Tetley PLC (C-T). At the same time, agreement was reached with Carlsberg A/S (Carlsberg), subject to regulatory approval, to merge C-T and Bass Brewers Limited on a basis which will give Carlsberg a 20% share in the combined business. The merger will proceed only in the event that regulatory approval is obtained on terms satisfactory to the Group. In the meantime, C-T is being managed by Carlsberg but the Group will receive 50% of all profit earned by C-T from the date of acquisition to the date of the merger taking place or the Group disposing of its holding. The Group's investment in C-T is included in associated undertakings at cost as the Group's share of profit in the year to 30 September 1996 is not material. Goodwill has not been recognised at this point given the uncertainty surrounding completion and since the amount is not material to shareholders' funds.

14 Stocks	1996 £m	1995 £m
Raw materials	55	43
Work in progress	25	30
Finished stocks	115	94
Consumable stores	39	32
	234	199

The replacement cost of stocks approximates to the value stated above.

NOTES TO THE FINANCIAL STATEMENTS

	Group		Company	
15 Debtors	**1996** £m	1995 £m	**1996** £m	1995 £m
Trade debtors	**416**	398	–	–
Amounts owed by subsidiary undertakings	–	–	**663**	473
Other debtors	**58**	54	**4**	1
Corporate taxation	**22**	29	**28**	21
Certificates of tax deposit	**10**	19	**10**	15
Pension prepayment (note 6)	**38**	36	**4**	4
Other prepayments	**87**	75	**3**	2
ACT recoverable (note 18)	–	–	**38**	32
	631	611	**750**	548

Included in trade debtors is £nil (1995 £2m), in other debtors £8m (1995 £8m) and in other prepayments £17m (1995 £18m) falling due after more than one year. Pension prepayment and ACT recoverable shown above are wholly due after more than one year.

	Group		Company	
16 Creditors: amounts falling due within one year	**1996** £m	1995 £m	**1996** £m	1995 £m
Borrowings (note 19)	**407**	439	**56**	49
Trade creditors	**221**	177	**2**	2
Corporate taxation	**304**	261	**41**	37
Other taxation and social security	**126**	134	**2**	3
Accrued charges	**226**	205	**1**	1
Proposed dividend	**153**	137	**153**	137
Amounts owed to Group undertakings	–	–	**1,364**	1,043
Other creditors	**187**	178	**17**	12
	1,624	1,531	**1,636**	1,284

	Group		Company	
17 Creditors: amounts falling due after one year	**1996** £m	1995 £m	**1996** £m	1995 £m
Borrowings (note 19)	**1,181**	1,177	**403**	381
Amounts owed to Group undertakings	–	–	**1,124**	1,095
Other creditors and deferred income	**80**	92	–	–
	1,261	1,269	**1,527**	1,476

NOTES TO THE FINANCIAL STATEMENTS

	Group			Company
	Provisions	Deferred taxation	Total	Deferred taxation
18 Provisions for liabilities and charges	£m	£m	£m	£m
At 30 September 1995	11	1	12	–
Net transfer to debtors (note 15)	–	–	–	6
Profit and loss account	–	37	37	(2)
Expenditure	(4)	–	(4)	–
ACT transfers to corporation tax	–	34	34	34
ACT recoverable	–	(38)	(38)	(38)
Exchange and other adjustments	–	10	10	–
At 30 September 1996	**7**	**44**	**51**	**–**

Deferred taxation

Deferred taxation has been provided to the extent that the directors have concluded on the basis of reasonable assumptions that it is probable that the liability will crystallise in the foreseeable future.

	Group		Company	
	1996	1995	1996	1995
	£m	£m	£m	£m
Provided				
Timing differences related to:				
short-term items	17	30	–	2
long-term items	118	57	–	–
Tax effect of losses carried forward	(53)	(52)	–	–
ACT recoverable	(38)	(34)	(38)	(34)
	44	1	(38)	(32)
Not provided				
Excess of tax allowances over book depreciation of fixed assets	304	279	–	–
Other timing differences	(7)	(3)	1	1
	297	276	1	1

NOTES TO THE FINANCIAL STATEMENTS

| 19 Borrowings | Group 1996 | | Company 1996 | | | |
	Within one year £m	After one year £m	Within one year £m	After one year £m	Group 1995 £m	Company 1995 £m
Bank loans and overdrafts						
Secured:						
Overseas loans	31	27	–	–	32	–
Other bank loans	2	30	–	–	27	–
	33	57	–	–	59	–
Unsecured:						
Bank loans	22	294	1	153	260	109
Overdrafts	44	–	50	–	47	49
	66	294	51	153	307	158
Total bank loans and overdrafts	99	351	51	153	366	158
Other borrowings						
Secured:						
2016 debenture stock 10.38%	–	250	–	250	250	250
Other debenture stock and loans	7	4	–	–	16	2
	7	254	–	250	266	252
Unsecured:						
2003 Guaranteed Notes 6.625% ($300m)	–	191	–	–	188	–
2002 Guaranteed Notes 8.125% ($350m)	–	223	–	–	220	–
1999 Guaranteed Notes 6.75% ($250m)	–	159	–	–	157	–
US dollar commercial paper	296	–	–	–	376	–
Other loan stock	5	3	5	–	43	20
	301	576	5	–	984	20
Total other borrowings	308	830	5	250	1,250	272
Total borrowings	407	1,181	56	403	1,616	430

The 2016 debenture stock is secured by a first floating charge on the undertakings and the assets of the Company and certain of its UK subsidiary undertakings and by cross guarantees given by these undertakings. The other secured borrowings are secured on the individual assets purchased from the proceeds of advances. The terms, rates of interest and currencies of these borrowings vary.

The US dollar commercial paper is repayable within one year but is supported by committed medium-term facilities. It is the Group's intention to refinance the borrowings on a continuing basis.

Facilities committed by banks amounted to £1,265m (1995 £1,215m) of which £353m (1995 £258m) was utilised at 30 September 1996 and £391m (1995 £376m) was in support of the outstanding US dollar commercial paper.

Interest on the loan stock is at a fixed rate of 4.50%. Interest on other borrowings is at variable rates unless otherwise stated. Interest on the unsecured bank loans drawn at 30 September 1996 is at rates between 3.26% and 13.57%. All borrowings are redeemable at par.

NOTES TO THE FINANCIAL STATEMENTS

	Group 1996					
	Bank loans and overdrafts	Other borrowings	Total	Company 1996	Group 1995	Company 1995
19 **Borrowings** (continued)	£m	£m	£m	£m	£m	£m
Analysis by year of repayment						
Due within one year (note 16)	99	308	407	56	439	49
Due: between one and two years	77	4	81	–	83	48
between two and five years	230	159	389	153	370	83
after five years	44	667	711	250	724	250
Due after more than one year (note 17)	351	830	1,181	403	1,177	381
Total borrowings	450	1,138	1,588	459	1,616	430
Amounts repayable by instalments, part of which falls due after five years	140	1	141	–	144	–

Interest rate agreements

In order to manage interest rate risk, the Group enters into interest rate swap agreements, interest rate collars and forward rate agreements. At 30 September 1996, notional principal balances under interest rate agreements were:

	Fixed payable			Fixed receivable		
	Termination dates	1996 millions	1995 millions	Termination dates	1996 millions	1995 millions
Interest rate swaps						
US dollar	1998-2001	345	365	1997-2003	520	550
Sterling				1999-2003	150	150
Deutsche mark	1998	30	–			
Canadian dollar	1999	20	–			
Forward rate agreements						
US dollar		40	485		40	95
Sterling		–	25		100	175
Interest rate collars – US dollar	1998	45	45			

The US$345m interest rate swaps, paying fixed at an average rate of 7.84%, hedge floating rate US dollar borrowings. The US$520m fixed interest rate swaps, which were originally taken out at the time of the US bond issues in 1992 and 1993, reduce the proportion of US dollar debt which is at fixed rates. The weighted average interest rate on these swaps is 6.56%. The £150m interest rate swaps provide sterling interest receivable at a weighted average rate of 8.02%.

The notional principal balances indicate the extent of use of these instruments, but exposure is limited to the interest rate differentials on the balances and, accordingly, the risk at the year end was immaterial.

The Group is exposed to loss in the event of non-performance by the counterparties to these agreements but such non-performance is not expected.

Currency swap agreements

As part of the strategy to provide a currency hedge against currency net assets, the Group enters into currency swap agreements. A currency swap agreement has the effect of depositing cash, surplus to immediate requirements (e.g. sterling) and borrowing currencies which are required (e.g. US dollar). At 30 September 1996, the Group had swapped £50m for US$78m (at 30 September 1995, no currency swap agreements were outstanding).

Forward exchange contracts

At 30 September 1996, the Group had contracted to exchange the equivalent of £57m (1995 £47m).

NOTES TO THE FINANCIAL STATEMENTS

	1996 Total £m	1996 Net operating £m	1995 Total £m	1995 Net operating £m
20 Assets – continuing operations				
By division				
Hotels: Holiday Inn Worldwide	1,241	914	1,192	896
Leisure retailing: Bass Taverns	2,431	2,290	2,258	2,119
Bass Leisure	735	646	643	558
Branded drinks: Bass Brewers*	1,386	1,125	1,282	1,062
Britvic Soft Drinks	386	297	393	293
Other activities*	785	70	805	66
	6,964	**5,342**	6,573	4,994
Non-operating assets				
Investment in Carlsberg-Tetley PLC		200		–
Current asset investments		481		684
Cash at bank and in hand		72		69
Corporate taxation		22		29
Non-operating liabilities				
Borrowings		(1,588)		(1,616)
Proposed dividend		(153)		(137)
Corporate taxation		(304)		(261)
Deferred taxation		(44)		(1)
Minority equity interests		(117)		(64)
	6,964	**3,911**	6,573	3,697
By geographic region				
United Kingdom	5,687	4,414	5,431	4,155
Rest of Europe, the Middle East and Africa	415	314	307	256
United States	677	467	710	480
Rest of Americas	117	89	102	88
Asia Pacific	68	58	23	15
	6,964	**5,342**	6,573	4,994
Net non-operating liabilities	–	(1,431)	–	(1,297)
	6,964	**3,911**	6,573	3,697

*Figures for 1995 have been restated to include in Bass Brewers gross assets and net operating assets related to its overseas brewing operations which were previously included in other activities; this restatement amounts to £44m and £40m respectively.

NOTES TO THE FINANCIAL STATEMENTS

21 Called up share capital	Authorised millions	£m	Allotted and fully paid millions	£m
Ordinary shares of 25p each				
At 30 September 1995	1,160	290	878	220
Issued: Employee Profit Share Scheme			2	–
Option schemes			3	1
At 30 September 1996	**1,160**	**290**	**883**	**221**

Aggregate consideration in respect of shares issued during the year was £28m (1995 £27m).

At 30 September 1996 options were outstanding to subscribe for ordinary shares of 25 pence each as follows:

	Bass Employee Savings Share Schemes millions	Bass Executive Share Option Schemes millions	Total millions
At 30 September 1995	12.4	6.0	18.4
Granted	2.5	2.5	5.0
Exercised	(1.4)	(1.5)	(2.9)
Expired	(2.1)	(0.1)	(2.2)
At 30 September 1996	**11.4**	**6.9**	**18.3**
Option exercise price per ordinary share (pence)	367-654	385-812	
Final exercise date	28 Feb 2004	3 Sept 2006	

NOTES TO THE FINANCIAL STATEMENTS

22 Reserves – equity interests	Share premium account £m	Revaluation reserve £m	Capital reserve £m	Profit and loss account £m	Total £m
Group					
At 30 September 1995	564	1,009	–	1,904	3,477
Premium on allotment of ordinary shares	27	–	–	–	27
Retained earnings for the year	–	–	–	223	223
Goodwill eliminated (see below)	–	–	–	(38)	(38)
Revaluation surplus on investments	–	1	–	–	1
Revaluation surplus realised	–	(2)	–	2	–
Revaluation element in depreciation charge	–	(1)	–	1	–
Exchange adjustments on: assets	–	(1)	–	9	8
borrowings	–	–	–	(8)	(8)
At 30 September 1996	**591**	**1,006**	**–**	**2,093**	**3,690**
Company					
At 30 September 1995	564	–	241	1,542	2,347
Premium on allotment of ordinary shares	27	–	–	–	27
Retained earnings for the year	–	–	–	(20)	(20)
At 30 September 1996	**591**	**–**	**241**	**1,522**	**2,354**

The capital reserve of the Company is distributable other than £70m which represents the share premium on allotment of shares issued as part of the consideration for the acquisition of the Holiday Inn Business in North America, in respect of which merger relief under Section 131 of the Companies Act 1985 was applied.

	Group		
Goodwill	Cost of goodwill eliminated £m	Exchange adjustment £m	Total £m
Eliminated to 30 September 1995	1,476	89	1,565
Acquisitions (note 24)	22	–	22
Exchange adjustments	–	16	16
Eliminated to 30 September 1996	**1,498**	**105**	**1,603**

23 Parent company profit

Profit on ordinary activities after taxation dealt with in the financial statements of the Company amounted to £201m (1995 £330m).

NOTES TO THE FINANCIAL STATEMENTS

24 Acquisitions

With effect from 1 October 1995, the Group increased its holdings in Prague Breweries a.s., Vratislavice a.s., Ostravar a.s. and Bass Ginsber Beer Company Limited.

Other acquisitions during the year include a majority stake in a UK hotel joint venture, three bingo club operations in Spain and a number of machine supply businesses.

	Book value Overseas brewing operations £m	Accounting alignments Overseas brewing operations £m	Fair value adjustments Overseas brewing operations £m	Fair value to the Group Overseas brewing operations £m	Other £m	Total £m
Tangible fixed assets	79	13	1	93	49	142
Current assets	38	2	(3)	37	2	39
Total assets	117	15	(2)	130	51	181
Liabilities	(40)	(3)	(4)	(47)	(19)	(66)
Net assets	77	12	(6)	83	32	115
Minority share of net assets acquired				(37)	(8)	(45)
Bass share of net assets acquired				46	24	70
Fair value of consideration						
Net cash				22	24	46
Fixed asset investments				42	4	46
Goodwill on acquisition				18	4	22

Cash, net of overdrafts acquired, was £12m.

Goodwill of £22m analysed above has been eliminated against reserves in the year. Neither post-acquisition results nor the prior year results of the acquired businesses were material to the Group.

The consideration for acquisitions shown in the cash flow statement comprises:

	£m
Net cash in respect of acquisitions above	46
Investment in Carlsberg-Tetley PLC	200
	246

NOTES TO THE FINANCIAL STATEMENTS

25 Net cash flow	1996 £m	1995 £m
Profit on ordinary activities before interest	749	672
Depreciation	229	206
Loss/(surplus) on disposal of fixed assets	3	(5)
Loss on disposal of operations	–	5
Increase in stocks	(24)	(1)
Increase in debtors	(5)	(62)
Increase in creditors	28	74
Amortisation of and provisions against investments	16	8
Provisions expended*	(4)	(12)
Operating activities	992	885
Net capital expenditure** (note 27)	(568)	(353)
Trade loans	25	31
Operating cash flow (note 28)	449	563
Net interest paid	(76)	(71)
Dividends paid	(210)	(193)
Tax paid	(111)	(151)
Normal cash flow	52	148
Major acquisitions	(200)	(268)
Net cash flow	(148)	(120)

*Cash flow related to provisions created on acquisition or charged as exceptional or extraordinary items in prior years.
**Net capital expenditure comprises amounts paid less received for tangible fixed assets and fixed asset investments, together with expenditure on non-major acquisitions (1996 £34m, 1995 £38m).

26 Management of liquid resources and financing	1996 £m	1995 £m
New borrowings	854	932
Net commercial paper repaid	(84)	(60)
Other borrowings repaid	(846)	(894)
	(76)	(22)
Ordinary shares issued	28	27
Financing	(48)	5
Liquid resources*	202	118
Total financing and liquid resources	154	123

*Liquid resources primarily comprise short-term deposits of less than one year and short-term investments in commercial paper.

NOTES TO THE FINANCIAL STATEMENTS

27 Net capital expenditure		1996 £m	1995 £m
Hotels:	Holiday Inn Worldwide	59	90
Leisure retailing:	Bass Taverns	196	88
	Bass Leisure	127	102
Branded drinks:	Bass Brewers	135	59
	Britvic Soft Drinks	42	32
Other activities		9	(18)
		568	353

28 Operating cash flow		1996 £m	1995 £m
Hotels:	Holiday Inn Worldwide	184	115
Leisure retailing:	Bass Taverns	114	204
	Bass Leisure	(22)	19
Branded drinks:	Bass Brewers*	139	160
	Britvic Soft Drinks	43	41
Other activities*		(9)	24
		449	563

*Figures for 1995 have been restated to include in Bass Brewers operating cash flow related to its overseas brewing operations which was previously included in other activities; this restatement amounts to £28m outflow.

	Cash and overdrafts			Other borrowings			
29 Net debt 30 September 1996	Cash at bank and in hand £m	Overdrafts £m	Total £m	Current asset investments £m	Due within one year £m	Due after one year £m	Total £m
At 30 September 1995	69	(47)	22	684	(392)	(1,177)	(863)
Net cash flow (note 25)	(151)	3	(148)	–	–	–	(148)
Financing and liquid resources movement	154	–	154	(202)	69	7	28
Other borrowings acquired	–	–	–	–	(36)	(7)	(43)
Exchange adjustments	–	–	–	(1)	(4)	(4)	(9)
At 30 September 1996	**72**	**(44)**	**28**	**481**	**(363)**	**(1,181)**	**(1,035)**
30 September 1995							
At 30 September 1994	49	(30)	19	802	(444)	(1,199)	(822)
Net cash flow (note 25)	(103)	(17)	(120)	–	–	–	(120)
Financing and liquid resources movement	123	–	123	(118)	52	(30)	27
Other borrowings acquired	–	–	–	–	–	(2)	(2)
Minority shareholders' loans capitalised	–	–	–	–	–	58	58
Exchange adjustments	–	–	–	–	–	(4)	(4)
At 30 September 1995	69	(47)	22	684	(392)	(1,177)	(863)

NOTES TO THE FINANCIAL STATEMENTS

30 Financial commitments

The Group had annual commitments under operating leases at 30 September 1996 which expire as follows:

	Properties		Other	
	1996 £m	1995 £m	1996 £m	1995 £m
Within one year	2	3	7	3
Between one and five years	17	10	13	15
After five years	47	48	–	–
	66	61	20	18

31 Contracts for expenditure on fixed assets

	Group	
	1996 £m	1995 £m
Contracts placed for expenditure on fixed assets not provided for in the financial statements	79	45

32 Contingencies

	Group		Company	
	1996 £m	1995 £m	1996 £m	1995 £m
There are contingent liabilities not provided for in the financial statements relating to:				
Guarantees – liabilities of subsidiary undertakings	–	–	1,385	1,385
– other	113	114	3	4
Other	16	17	–	–
	129	131	1,388	1,389

The Group has given warranties in respect of the disposal of certain of its subsidiary undertakings. It is the view of the directors that, other than to the extent that known liabilities have been provided for in these financial statements, such warranties are not expected to result in financial loss to the Group.

Due to the substantial number of properties owned by the Group, it is not practicable to quantify the provision for taxation of chargeable gains which might arise in the event of properties being sold at their revalued amounts. Compliance with the DTI Orders is not expected to have given rise to material unprovided taxation liabilities for chargeable gains.

In addition to the contingencies shown above, the Group will suffer a loss of £60m, reduced by 50% of the profits of Carlsberg-Tetley PLC in the period from acquisition to disposal and increased by any related costs if, because of regulatory constraints, it decides not to proceed with the proposed merger of Carlsberg-Tetley PLC and Bass Brewers Limited and disposes of its holding. If the merger proceeds, the Group has given warranties in respect of Bass Brewers Limited; such warranties are not expected to result in financial loss to the Group.

NOTES TO THE FINANCIAL STATEMENTS

33 Principal operating subsidiary undertakings

Bass PLC is the beneficial owner of all (unless specified) of the equity share capital, either itself or through subsidiary undertakings, of the following companies:

Corporate activities

Bass America Inc. (incorporated and operates in the United States)
Bass Holdings Limited
Bass International Holdings NV (incorporated and operates in the Netherlands)
Bass Investments PLC (a) (b)
Bass Overseas Holdings Limited (a)

Holiday Inn Worldwide

Holiday Corporation (incorporated and operates principally in the United States)
Holiday Inns Franchising Inc. (incorporated and operates principally in the United States)
Holiday Inns, Inc. (incorporated and operates principally in the United States)

Bass Taverns

Bass Taverns Limited
The Bass Lease Company Limited
Toby Restaurants Limited

Bass Leisure

Barcrest Limited
Bass Leisure Activities Limited
Bass Leisure Entertainments Limited
Bass Leisure Group Limited (a)
Bass Leisure Limited
BLMS Limited
Coral Racing Limited
Gala Leisure Limited

Bass Brewers

Bass Beers Worldwide Limited (a)
Bass Brewers Limited
Bass Brewers 1996 Limited (d)
Bass Ginsber Beer Company Limited (incorporated and operates in China) (55%)
Bass Ireland Limited
Prague Breweries a.s. (incorporated and operates in the Czech Republic) (51%)

Britvic Soft Drinks

Britannia Soft Drinks Limited (50% Bass PLC, 25% Whitbread and Company PLC, 25% Allied-Domecq PLC) (a) (c)
Britvic Soft Drinks Limited (90% Britannia Soft Drinks Limited, 10% Pepsico Holdings Limited)
Robinsons Soft Drinks Limited (100% Britannia Soft Drinks Limited)

Other activities

Bass Developments Limited (a)
Société Viticole de Château Lascombes SA (incorporated and operates in France) (97.5%)
White Shield Insurance Company Limited (incorporated and operates in Gibraltar) (a)

(a) Shares held directly by Bass PLC.
(b) Bass PLC owns all the 5% and 7% Cumulative Preference shares of Bass Investments PLC.
(c) Bass PLC holds a majority of voting rights in Britannia Soft Drinks Limited (50% plus one ordinary share) which is accordingly treated as a subsidiary undertaking and consolidated in the Group's financial statements.
(d) This company owns the Group's investment in Carlsberg-Tetley PLC (see note 13), being all of the deferred ordinary shares of £1 each and all the ordinary shares of US$0.01 each, and representing 50% of the total issued share capital of £90m.
(e) Unless stated otherwise, companies are incorporated in Great Britain, registered in England and Wales and operate principally within the United Kingdom.
(f) The companies listed above include all those which principally affect the amount of profit and assets of the Group. A full list of subsidiary and associated undertakings at 30 September 1996 will be annexed to the next annual return of Bass PLC to be delivered to the Registrar of Companies.

REPORT OF THE AUDITORS

Report of the auditors to the members of Bass PLC on the financial statements

We have audited the financial statements on pages 22 to 47, including the more detailed information set out in the Report of the Remuneration Committee on pages 16 to 21 as detailed in note 7 to the financial statements, which have been prepared under the historical cost convention as modified by the revaluation of certain fixed assets and on the basis of the accounting policies set out on pages 26 and 27.

Respective responsibilities of directors and auditors

As described on pages 12 and 13, the Company's directors are solely responsible for the preparation of the financial statements including the selection of suitable accounting policies. It is our responsibility to form an independent opinion, based on our audit, on those financial statements and to report our opinion to you.

Basis of opinion

We conducted our audit in accordance with Auditing Standards issued by the Auditing Practices Board. An audit includes examination, on a test basis, of evidence relevant to the amounts and disclosures in the financial statements. It also includes an assessment of the significant estimates and judgements made by the directors in the preparation of the financial statements, and of whether the accounting policies are appropriate to the Company's circumstances, consistently applied and adequately disclosed.

We planned and performed our audit so as to obtain all the information and explanations which we considered necessary in order to provide us with sufficient evidence to give reasonable assurance that the financial statements are free from material misstatement, whether caused by fraud or other irregularity or error. In forming our opinion we also evaluated the overall adequacy of the presentation of information in the financial statements.

Opinion

In our opinion the financial statements give a true and fair view of the state of affairs of the Company and the Group as at 30 September 1996 and of the Group's profit for the year then ended and have been properly prepared in accordance with the Companies Act 1985.

Corporate governance matters

In addition to our audit of the financial statements, we have reviewed the directors' statements on pages 12 and 13 on the Company's compliance with the paragraphs of the Code of Best Practice specified for our review by the London Stock Exchange. The objective of our review is to draw attention to any non-compliance with those paragraphs of the Code which is not disclosed. We carried out our review in accordance with Bulletin 1995/1 'Disclosures relating to corporate governance' issued by the Auditing Practices Board.

As we have reviewed only such financial controls as we considered necessary for the purpose of expressing our audit opinion on the financial statements, and as we are not required to, we do not express any opinion on the effectiveness of the Group's system of internal financial control or corporate governance procedures as such. Similarly, while we have considered the going concern concept in the context of our audit as a whole, we are not required to carry out a special review, and accordingly we do not express any separate opinion on the Group's ability to continue in operational existence. However, we have assessed whether the statements on going concern and internal financial control are consistent with the information of which we are aware from our audit.

Opinion

With respect to the directors' statements on going concern on page 14, and internal financial control on pages 13 to 14 (other than their opinion concerning effectiveness which is outside the scope of our report), in our opinion the directors have provided the disclosures required by paragraphs 4.5 and 4.6 of the Code (as supplemented by the related guidance for directors) and such statements are consistent with the information of which we are aware from our audit work on the financial statements.

Based on enquiry of certain directors and officers of the Company, and examination of the relevant documents, in our opinion the directors' statement on pages 12 and 13 appropriately reflects the Company's compliance with the other paragraphs of the Code specified for our review.

Ernst & Young,
Chartered Accountants, Registered Auditor, London.
3 December 1996

10 | Taxation and Foreign Currency in Financial Statements

This chapter examines:

- nature and significance of taxation in company accounts;
- accounting for foreign currency.

TAXATION

Virtually all company financial statements will show taxation in varying forms in their financial statements. The calculation of taxation in company accounts is an extremely complex area – this chapter does not attempt to calculate the taxation computations but merely to draw the reader's attention to key terminology and its significance. Readers requiring more information are advised to consult a taxation textbook. The most frequently noticeable types of UK taxation that the user will come across in financial statements are corporation tax and deferred tax.

Corporation tax

Corporation tax is a tax based upon the accounting trading profits of a company. The amount of taxation that a company actually pays to the taxation authorities is not always directly related to the amount of accounting profit shown in the profit and loss account.

The 'profit' used to assess taxation is often a 'different' profit from that used for accounting purposes and disclosed in the profit and loss account. This difference arises because a number of items that are shown in the profit and loss account are not always used for taxation purposes. For example, a company will include depreciation of fixed assets as an expense in the profit and loss account. Since the taxation authorities recognize that the amount of depreciation to be included is often rather subjective, the legislation has standardized the amount of depreciation against which the tax charge can be set. Accordingly the taxation authorities disallow depreciation as a taxation deductible expense and instead allow all companies to claim standardized depreciation allowances – termed capital allowances.

The system of company taxation is further complicated by the payment of dividends. The UK has adopted a system of company taxation that is termed the *imputation system*. Under this system, when a company distributes dividends to its shareholders, it is legally obliged to account to the taxation authorities for a special tax charge known as Advance Corporation Tax (ACT). This ACT charge is a way of deducting a basic rate tax charge on the dividends on behalf on the shareholders. To indicate that the company has, in effect paid the basic rate tax charge on the shareholder's behalf, the shareholder is provided with evidence in the form of a 'tax credit' and will not be taxed on this amount in the future (i.e. the shareholders receive their dividends net of the basic rate of tax). As far as the company is concerned, a dividend paid by a company is a distribution of part of its taxed income. Consequently, the amount of dividends (both paid and proposed) that is shown in a company's financial statements will be on a net basis, i.e. the actual cash amount that has or will be paid to shareholders.

The net amount of corporation tax (after offsetting ACT) is termed mainstream corporation tax.

For example:

ABC plc distributes a total net dividend of £1,000.

If the basic rate of tax is 20%, the ACT will be:

$$20 \div 80 \left(\text{i.e. } 20\% \div (100 - 20\%) \right) \times £1,000 = £250$$

i.e. the gross dividend is £1,250 $(1,000 + 250)$

In the shareholders' hands no further tax would be levied – provided the tax payer was a basic rate tax payer (because the company has already paid ACT). A tax payer subject to higher rate tax levels would have to pay the additional amount of the difference between the higher rate and basic rate taxation.

The treatment of taxation of a company is subject to SSAP 8, *The Treatment of Taxation Under the Imputation System*. ACT is accounted and paid to the tax authority on a quarterly basis. ACT can be offset against mainstream corporation tax – but is restricted to the ACT tax rate on the company's profits that are being subject to corporation tax.

If a dividend payment is greater than the chargeable profits then it is not possible for ACT to be recovered immediately. The tax authorities permit unrelieved ACT to be carried back against corporation tax payments (within certain time limits) and carried forward indefinitely to be set against future liabilities. Any unrecovered ACT will be shown in a company's balance sheet as an asset. If the company believes that the ACT will be recoverable at a future date then the ACT will be specifically shown as a deferred asset. If the company considers that there will be insufficient tax liabilities in the future to offset the ACT – then the ACT should be written-off as irrecoverable.

Income   If a UK company receives a dividend from another UK company a tax credit will be attached to any dividend paid.

According to the imputation system there is no further taxation liability because such dividends are not liable for corporation tax.

It is important to note however that in a company's profit and loss account the dividends received are shown gross (i.e. by adding back the tax credit to the net dividend). The tax element part of the gross dividend (i.e. the tax credit) is then shown separately in the tax charge in the profit and loss account.

Also note that it is possible for companies to offset ACT (paid on dividends paid by the company) against any ACT on dividends that the company receives.

Franked investment income   Some companies will have an entry in the profit and loss account entitled 'franked investment income'. This is income that has already suffered corporation tax – such as dividends received from another UK company. Franked income is not normally subjected to corporation tax again. (For further details see SSAP 8.)

Deferred tax

As referred to above, the profit on which taxation is calculated may be different from the profit shown in the profit and loss account. The reasons for using different profit figures are based on two types of differences:

1   Permanent differences:
    These are differences that will always cause the 'accounting profit' to differ from the 'taxable profit'. For example entertaining customers of a company is *permanently disallowed* by legislation as a deduction against taxation.
2   Timing differences:
    SSAP 15, *Accounting for Deferred Tax* defines timing differences as 'the differences between profits and losses as computed for tax purposes and results as stated in financial statements, which arise from the inclusion of items of income and expenditure in tax computations in periods different from those in which they are included in financial statements. Timing differences originate in one period and are capable of reversal in one or more subsequent periods' (para 18).

For example, ABC plc purchases a machine for £1,000 and depreciates it over five years using the straight-line method. The taxation authorities allow (say) a 25% capital allowance on a reducing balance method. In the profit and loss account the company will show £200 depreciation each year (£1,000/5). However for tax purposes, the taxation authorities will allow: in year 1, £250 (25% of £1,000; year 2, £187 (25% of £750) etc. Since the short-term timing differences between depreciation and the capital allowances will 'reverse' as the years progress, deferred tax is calculated to 'smooth-out' the resulting differences between the accountant's calculations of profit and the calculation of profit for tax purposes. In essence, deferred taxation attempts to remove the effect of the timing differences from the profit and loss account. Companies will transfer an amount to the deferred tax account that is equal to the difference between corporation tax payable on trading profits and the taxation that would have been payable if the company's capital allowances had equalled the depreciation charge.

Since deferred taxation is the tax relating to these timing differences, SSAP 15 requires that tax deferred because of the effect of timing differences 'should not be accounted for to the extent that it is probable that a liability or asset will not crystallise' (SSAP 15, para 26).

In deciding whether deferred tax is going to crystallize companies must take into account all relevant information and make a number of assumptions. For example, in deciding whether deferred tax is going to crystallize companies must assess whether it is expected to have sufficient capital allowances in the future to offset against potentially taxable profit. This decision will be based on an assessment on whether a company will have sufficient capital investment to generate capital allowances in the forthcoming years. SSAP 15 suggests the company's 'financial plans or projections covering a period of years [should be] examined . . . to enable an assessment to be made of the likely pattern of future liabilities'.

Disclosure

1   Deferred tax relating to the ordinary activities of the company should be *shown separately* as part of the tax on profit or loss on ordinary activities – either on the face of the profit and loss account or in a note.
2   The amount of any *unprovided* deferred tax should be declared in the balance sheet itself or in supporting notes.
4   Disclosure of transfers to or from deferred tax.
5   Total of any unprovided deferred tax should be noted.

For further information refer to SSAP 15.

Value added tax

The accounting of VAT is discussed in SSAP 5, *Accounting for Value Added Tax*. The main essence of this standard for the user of company reports is that companies are only, in effect acting as a collection agent of the taxation authorities. The financial statements of most large companies should normally only include accounting figures *net* of VAT. In the vast majority of cases when a company pays VAT on purchases it can offset this charge against VAT it charges on sales and only pay the net figure to the Government. If a company is not registered for VAT (or is exempt) then any VAT that is paid on inputs (purchases and express) is not reclaimable. Therefore the total amount of net purchases plus VAT is shown in the profit and loss account.

FOREIGN CURRENCY

Many large companies nowadays trade in many different countries around the world. Many of the transactions with customers and suppliers are conducted in a variety of different currencies. Some of these currencies can fluctuate considerably against each other and, in turn, these fluctuations can cause a number of accounting difficulties.

The major accounting problem is the rate of foreign currency exchange to be used in translating the financial statements of foreign subsidiaries – which are denominated in a different currency from that of the parent company.

SSAP 20, *Foreign Currency Translation* examines the problem of foreign currency from two angles:

1 The individual company basis – where the company enters directly into a business transaction that is undertaken in a foreign currency.
2 In the case of groups of companies where the parent company undertakes its business activity through subsidiaries or branches whose operations are denominated in a currency that is different from that of the parent company.

Individual companies

During an accounting period, a company may enter into transactions which are denominated in a foreign currency. SSAP 20 normally requires the result of each transaction to be translated into the company's local currency using the exchange rate in operation on the *date on which the transaction occurred*; if the rates do not fluctuate significantly, an average rate may be used as an approximation.

In practice this is interpreted as:

1 Non-monetary assets (e.g. buildings, plant and vehicles etc.) will have been translated at date of acquisition.
2 Monetary assets and liabilities, that are denominated in a foreign currency should be shown at the closing rate (i.e. rate of exchange at the balance sheet date).

Any exchange differences should be accounted for and taken to the firm's profit and loss account.

Groups of companies

SSAP 20 normally requires that a company that has foreign subsidiaries or branches should use the so-called closing rate/net investment method. (This method examines the impact of currency movements on the parent company's share of the subsidiary's shareholders' funds, i.e. its equity and reserves.)

If the parent company accounts are denominated in pounds (sterling) and a subsidiary is shown in dollars, the accounts of the subsidiary must be translated into pounds (sterling) before the group accounts can be determined.

The adoption of the closing rate/net investment method normally requires, in practice, that for:

1 *Profit and loss account:* Items should be consistently translated in the parent company's profit and loss account at the average or the closing rate. (SSAP 20 notes that the use of the closing rate is more likely to achieve the objective of reflecting the financial statements prior to translation.) A case can be argued that the average rate more fairly reflects the profit, losses and cash flow as they arise throughout an accounting period. The use of either method is permitted provided the chosen method is used consistently.
2 *Balance sheet:* Items should be translated into the parent company's balance sheet at the closing rate (i.e. balance sheet date). Any differences between the current year's closing rate and last year's closing rate that cause differences in retranslating the opening net investment at the current closing rate should be taken directly to reserves.

There is an exception to the use of the closing rate/net investment method. This exception is where the affairs of the foreign company are 'so closely inter-linked with those of the investing company . . . that its results may be regarded as being more dependent on the economic environment of the investing company's currency than on that of its own reporting currency' (SSAP 20, para 22).

Examples include, where the foreign subsidiary:

1 acts as a selling agent of the parent – receiving stocks of goods from the investing company and remitting the proceeds back to the company;
2 produces a raw material or manufactures parts or sub-assemblies which are then shipped to the investing company for inclusion in its own products;
3 is located overseas for tax, exchange control or similar reasons.

(In such cases, the temporal method (whose mechanics are identical to the preparation of the accounts of an individual company) is used.)

Hyper-inflation

SSAP 20 notes that where a company operates in a country where there is a very high rate of inflation, it may not be possible to produce meaningful historical cost accounts by the application of a simple translation process. In these circumstances (SSAP 20, para 26) it is suggested that the financial statements stated in the local currency should be firstly adjusted (if possible) to reflect the price levels, before the translation process is undertaken.

Disclosure provisions

SSAP 20 requires the methods used in the translation of the financial statements of foreign enterprises and the treatment of exchange differences to be disclosed in the financial statements. Additionally, companies should also disclose (*inter alia*) the net amount of exchange gains and losses on foreign currency borrowings and identify separately:

1 the amount offset to reserves;
2 the net amount charged and credited to profit and loss account (also the net movement on reserves arising from exchange differences should be noted).

The user should attempt to determine the extent of any exposure to transactions denominated in a foreign currency. In particular the user should determine any reference to the supporting notes to the accounts and ascertain from the Statement of Recognized Gains and Losses any foreign currency gains and losses taken directly to reserves in the balance sheet. In accordance with the requirements of SSAP 20, companies using the closing rate will take gains and losses direct to reserves. It is important that the user is vigilant in identifying any substantial foreign currency losses that might be debited to reserves.

(Since the introduction of FRS 3, currency gains/losses that are taken to reserves will also now be highlighted in the Statement of Recognized Gains and Losses.) For further information see SSAP 20, *Foreign Currency Translation*.

QUESTIONS

1 What is deferred tax?
   What are timing differences?
2 Explain what you understand by (1) corporation tax, and (2) ACT.
3 With reference to SSAP 20, explain the two methods of accounting for foreign currency transactions.
4 Discuss specific aspects of foreign currency transactions that users should examine when analysing financial statements.

11 | Group Accounts

This chapter examines:

- nature of group accounts;
- definition of a subsidiary;
- acquisition and merger accounting;
- consolidated accounts.

For an array of complex and interwoven reasons, a considerable number of companies frequently conduct their business operations through the formation and ownership of additional companies. In its simplest form, a group of companies exists where one company, termed the parent or holding company, controls another company, termed the subsidiary.

Most companies have subsidiaries because of a mixture of economic, operational, organizational, political and practical reasons. Some companies obtain subsidiaries by acquisitions and mergers whilst other companies establish separate subsidiary companies as being the most effective or most practical reason by which they prefer to conduct their trading activities.

Once a group of companies, under the ownership or control of a parent has been established, it is necessary to produce group accounts to assist in obtaining an overall picture of the entire group of companies. The most common method of producing group accounts is by the production of consolidated accounts.

GROUP STRUCTURES

Company A plc owns and controls the ordinary shares of company B Ltd. A plc and B Ltd will not only have to prepare their own accounts but, because company A owns and controls B, A will be required to produce another set of accounts that incorporates both A's and B's accounts together. These combined sets of accounts are termed *group accounts*.

There are both legal and accounting regulations governing the circumstances when group accounts need to be prepared and the contents of the accounting information. Thus,

A plc
will produce its *own* profit and loss
account* and its *own* balance sheet

(*Individual profit and loss account
of A plc is not a legal requirement if
A produces group accounts and
discloses its own individual profit.)

A plc
will also produce a group profit and
loss account and a group balance
sheet

B plc
will produce its *own* profit and
loss account and its *own* balance sheet

DEFINITION OF A SUBSIDIARY

The definition of a subsidiary has been legally written in very wide-ranging terms. The extensive nature of the definition has been implemented to prohibit some companies, who in the past, avoided the previous definition of subsidiary and thereby did not produce consolidated accounts. The present definition of a subsidiary (Companies Act 1985, amended by Companies Act 1989, Sec 258–260) is shown below:

Company S will be a subsidiary undertaking of company H:

IF:

1) H holds a majority of the *voting* rights on all or substantially all matters or has the right to direct its overall policy or to alter its constitution, OR
2) H is a member of S, and has the right to appoint or remove directors holding a majority of the voting rights at meetings of the Board, OR
3) H can exercise a dominant influence over S by virtue of:
   a)   provisions in S's memorandum or articles of Association OR
   b)   a written control contract, OR
4) H is a member of S and controls alone, pursuant to an agreement with other members, a majority of the voting rights in S, OR
5) H has a participating interest in S and:
   a)   H actually exercises a dominant influence over S, OR
   b)   H and S are managed on a unified basis, OR
6) H is a parent of any undertaking which is S's parent.

(Companies Act 1989, S21)

An undertaking is defined as a body corporate (wherever incorporated) or partnership or an un-incorporated association carrying on a trade or business with or without a view to profit.

Definition of above terms

- A participating interest is an interest held by an undertaking in the shares of another undertaking which it holds on a long-term basis for the purpose of securing a contribution to its activities by the exercise of control or influence arising from or related to that interest. A holding of 20 per cent or more shall be presumed to be a participating interest unless the contrary is shown.
- Control is defined 'as the ability . . . to direct the financial and operating policies of another undertaking with a view to gaining economic benefits from its activities'.
- Dominant influence is 'influence that can be exercised to achieve the operating and financial policies desired by the holder'.
- Managed on a unified basis is where two or more undertakings are managed on a unified basis if the whole of the operations of the undertakings are integrated and they are managed as a single unit.

Exemptions

FRS 2, *Accounting for Subsidiary Undertakings*, requires a subsidiary to be excluded from consolidation if:

1 severe long-term restrictions hinder the parent company's rights over the subsidiary's assets or management;
2 the group's interest in the subsidiary is held exclusively with a view to subsequent resale and the subsidiary has not previously been consolidated;
3 the subsidiary's activities are so different from those of other undertakings that consolidation of the accounts would be incompatible with the obligation to give a 'true and fair' view. (The Companies Act permits (rather than requires) exclusion in 1 and 2 above.)

If a company is not consolidated:

1 because of long-term restrictions – then treat as a fixed asset investment in the financial statements;
2 because the company is held exclusively for resale and has not been previously consolidated – show as a current asset at the lower of cost or net realizable value;
3 because of different activities – use the equity method (i.e. as a percentage of post-acquisition profits).

Although the detailed preparation of consolidated accounts is outside the remit of this book it is nevertheless useful, primarily for analytical purposes, to understand the principles by which a consolidated balance sheet is prepared.

EXAMPLE 11.1 EXAMPLE OF A CONSOLIDATED BALANCE SHEET

A plc acquired 75% (7,500 £1 ordinary shares) of the shares in B Ltd on 1 January 1990 for £20,000 cash.

B Ltd's revenue reserves on that date were £10,000. The balance sheets at 31 December 1996 are as follows:

Balance sheets as at 31 December 1996	A plc (£)	B Ltd (£)
Sundry net assets	20,000	50,000
Investment in B Ltd		
(7,500 shares of £1 each)	20,000	–
	£40,000	£50,000
Represented by:		
Share capital (£1)	20,000	10,000
Revenue reserves	20,000	40,000
	£40,000	£50,000

Required

Prepare the consolidated balance sheet of A Ltd as at 31 December 1996.

Step 1: calculate the goodwill arising upon consolidation

Firstly the goodwill arising on consolidation must be determined. This goodwill is calculated by comparing the consideration (i.e. the acquisition cost) against the fair value of the net assets acquired at the date of acquisition. (In the above example, the fair value of net assets is equivalent to the shareholders' funds (i.e. ordinary shares plus reserves).

The consideration is £20,000 for 75% of the shares of B's 7,500 ordinary share. (Note that the shares have a £1 par or nominal value – but total consideration for these shares is £20,000 – as indicated in A's balance sheet by the description 'Investment in B Ltd'.)

In return for the consideration, A receives 75% of B's ordinary shares (75% of £10,000) which is £7,500 and 75% of B's reserves at the date of the acquisition which is £7,500 (i.e. 75% of £10,000).

So for an outlay of £20,000 cash, A receives, in return, a total of £15,000 of ordinary shares and reserves. It is often more convenient to show the above calculations in a specific account – termed a cost of control account:

Cost of control			
Consideration:		75% of ordinary shares	
		(75% × £10,000) = £7,500	
Cash	£20,000		
		75% of reserves	
		(at date of acquisition)	
		(75% × £10,000) = £7,500	
		Goodwill	£5,000
		(balancing figure)	
	£20,000		£20,000

Step 2: determine the minority interests

Since A owns 75% of B's ordinary shares, the remainder (25%) must belong to other 'external' (to the group) shareholders – termed minority interests.

Minority interests

		25% of B's ordinary shares (i.e. 25% × £10,000) = £2,500
Balancing figure (to consolidated balance sheet)	£12,500	
		25% of reserves (£40,000) (i.e. 25% × £40,000) = £10,000
	£12,500	£12,500

Step 3: calculation of the subsidiary's post-acquisition reserves

The post-acquisition reserves of B are totalled with all of the reserves of A. This is achieved by taking the pre-acquisition reserves, shown in the cost of control account (i.e. £7,500), from the total reserves in the reserves account.

Since there is a 25% minority interest stake in B, then 25% of the reserves (£10,000) also belong to the minority interests (i.e. 25% of £40,000 – see minority interest account).

This means, in total, subtracting £7,500 and £10,000 from £60,000 (£20,000 + £40,000) to give a balance of £42,500.

(Note: it is important to remember that only the post-acquisition reserves of the subsidiary are shown in the consolidated balance sheet.)

Revenue reserves

Cost of control	£7,500	A's reserves	£20,000
Minority interests	£10,000	B's reserves	£40,000
Balance to consolidated balance sheet	£42,500		
	£60,000		£60,000

Step 4: preparation of consolidated balance sheet as at 31 December 1996

	(£)
Intangible assets:	
Goodwill arising on consolidation	5,000
Tangible assets:	
Sundry net assets (£20,000 + £50,000)	70,000
	75,000
Financed by:	
Ordinary shares	£20,000
Reserves	42,500
Minority interests	12,500
	75,000

Note: for illustration purposes, the goodwill arising on consolidation, (£5,000) is shown in the balance sheet – without adjustment. In practice the provisions of SSAP 22 would apply and, under the current provisions, goodwill will need to be written-off immediately to reserves in the balance sheet or amortized to the profit and loss account over its useful economic life.

The preparation of the consolidated profit and loss account is relatively straightforward. The sales, profits and expenses are totalled with a significant adjustment. All intra-group transactions (i.e. where companies in the same group trade with each other) must be eliminated. These transactions are not 'genuine' trading activities and only transactions external to the group should be included.

ACQUISITION AND MERGER ACCOUNTING

There are two major methods of producing consolidated accounting: the acquisition accounting method and the merger accounting method.

FRS 6, *Acquisitions and Mergers* establishes out the circumstances in which the two methods of accounting for a business combination are to be used. Acquisition accounting regards the business combination as the acquisition of one company by another.

Acquisition accounting has the following accounting features:

1 Any difference between the consideration paid for a business and the fair value of the net assets obtained is accounted for as goodwill.
2 The identifiable assets and liabilities acquired are included in the consolidated balance sheet at their fair value at the date of acquisition.
3 The earnings of the acquired company are included in the group profit and loss account from the date of acquisition.
4 If a company issues shares to obtain another company, any excess (of the market value of the share price above the par value) must be transferred to a share premium account.

Merger accounting

Merger accounting treats two or more parties that are combining on a equal footing. In essence, this method assumes that the companies have, in effect always been combined since their formation (i.e. 'since the cradle' as it is commonly termed). Merger accounting is usually implemented without the restatement of net assets to fair value. The earnings for an accounting period are not time-apportioned but will include the whole of an accounting period in the consolidated profit and loss account.

No goodwill is normally reported since all shares issued by the acquirer to purchase a company are deemed to be issued at par value. Accordingly, since the shares that form the consideration purchase price are deemed to have been issued at par value, no share premium is recorded.

FRS 6 restricts the use of merger accounting for 'those business combinations where the use of acquisition accounting would not properly reflect the true nature of the combination' (FRS 6, para (e)). A merger is a business combination in which, rather than one party acquiring control of another, the parties come together to share in the future risks and benefits of the combined entity.

FRS 6 *requires* that a business combination should be accounted for by using merger accounting *if*:

1   the use of merger accounting for the combination is not prohibited by legislation, and;
2   the combination meets all the criteria set out below:
    (a)   No party to the combination is portrayed as either the acquirer or acquired.
    (b)   All parties to the combination, as represented by the boards of directors or their appointees, participate in establishing the management structure for the combined entity and in selecting management personnel, and such decisions are made on the basis of a consensus between the parties to the combination rather than purely by exercise of voting rights.
    (c)   The relative sizes of the combining entities are not so disparate that one party dominates the combined entity by virtue of its relative size.
    (d)   Under the terms of the combination or related arrangements, the consideration received by the equity shareholders of each party to the combination comprises primarily of equity shares in the combined entity. Any non-equity consideration represents an immaterial proportion of the fair value of the consideration received by the equity shareholders of that party. (Where one of the combining entities has, within the preceding two year period, acquired equity shares in another of the combining entities then this consideration should be taken into account in determining whether the criteria have been met.)
    (e)   No equity shareholders of any of the combining entities retain any material interest in the future performance of only part of the combined entity.

UK LEGAL REQUIREMENTS

Companies Act 1985, Schedule 4A (para 10) lays down the conditions that must be met if a business combination is to be accounted for as a merger. The conditions are:

1   at least 90 per cent of the nominal value of the relevant shares in the undertaking acquired is held by both or on behalf of the parent company and its subsidiary undertaking;

2 the proportion referred to in 1 was attained pursuant to an arrangement;
3 the fair value of any consideration (other than the issue of equity shares) did not exceed 10 per cent of the nominal value of the equity shares issued;
4 the adoption of the merger method of accounting accords with generally accepted accounting principles or practice.

FAIR VALUES IN ACQUISITION ACCOUNTING

FRS 7, *Fair Values in Acquisition Accounting* establishes the principles to be followed when accounting for a business combination under the acquisition method of accounting. Prior to the introduction of FRS 7, a number of companies using acquisition accounting to record their combinations were tempted to distort the fair values of the subsidiaries they were about to acquire.

For example:

EXAMPLE 11.2

A plc is to acquire B plc for £100 consideration. A 'realistic' value of the net assets of B is £80, giving the difference £20 as being goodwill.

This £20 goodwill, in accordance with the options expounded in SSAP 22, is to be written-off to the reserves of the group's balance sheet. However, there was a temptation for some companies to understate the fair value of some of the assets that were being acquired. In many cases this understatement was conducted by overstating the costs of future re-organization and restructuring costs that were estimated as being necessary after the acquisition. In the above example, in B's case, it is estimated that, after acquisition, the costs that A would incur in restructuring B will be £20.

By entering this £20 provision against the value of the net assets of B, the fair values of B's net assets will now be £60 (£80 – £20) which means the goodwill is now recalculated to £40 (£100 – £60) which again is written-off to the reserves and not against earnings in the profit and loss account. In other words, a future profit and loss account expense is effectively written-off to reserves at the time of the acquisition. After the acquisition, some companies subsequently write-down the excessively high provision of £20 to more realistic levels. If the provision is written down to £12, it means that the difference, £8 (£20 – £12) can be written back to the post-acquisition profits.

The companies legislation and FRS 7, *Fair Values in Acquisition Accounting* requires the identifiable assets and liabilities of the acquired entity to be included in the consolidated financial statements of the acquirer at their *fair values* at the date of acquisition. Essentially, the fair values are the values at which the transaction would take place between independent parties on an 'arm's length' (i.e. independent) basis. In particular FRS 7 provides specific guidance on the valuation of individual asset items. FRS 7 specifically prohibits the liabilities of the acquired entity from including provisions for future operating losses.

The basic requirements of FRS 7 are that:

• Tangible fixed assets should have their fair values based on market value. Stocks and work-in-progress should be shown at the lower of net realizable value and replacement cost.

- Monetary assets and liabilities should take into account the amounts expected to be received or paid and the timing of these receipts and payments. The timing factor should be incorporated into the calculation by using discounted cash flow techniques.

The assets and liabilities that are recognized in determining the fair values should be those of the acquired entity that existed at the *date of acquisition*. In practice this means that the inclusion of possible liabilities must be restricted to those obligations that existed at the time of the acquisition and should not include any future provisions (such as for future operating losses, restructuring or redundancy costs) which may or may not materialize.

Changes in the assets and liabilities resulting from the acquirer's intentions or from events after the acquisition should be dealt with as *post-acquisition* items.

QUESTIONS

1   What do you understand by the term: group accounts? What advantages exist for companies that prepare consolidated accounts?
2   Define a subsidiary.
3   In the preparation of consolidated accounts, explain the differences in the consolidated accounts between the use of acquisition accounting method and the merger accounting method.
4   Explain the circumstances when FRS 6, *Acquisitions and Mergers* requires the use of the merger method of accounting.
5   Rose Ltd acquired 80 per cent of the ordinary share capital and 30 per cent of the preference share capital of Crown Ltd on 31 December 1996. At this date the profit and loss account of Crown Ltd was £25,000. The following balance sheets were prepared at 31 December 1996:

	Rose Ltd (£)	(£)	Crown Ltd (£)	(£)
Shares in Crown Ltd				
(6,000 preference shares	5,000			
8,000 ordinary shares of £1 each)	35,000	40,000		—
Net assets		160,000		70,000
		£200,000		£70,000
Represented by:				
Share capital:				
Preference shares (of £1 each)		100,000		20,000
		20,000		10,000
Ordinary shares (of £1 each)		120,000		30,000
Profit and loss account		80,000		40,000
		£200,000		£70,000

Required:

(a) You are required to prepare the consolidated balance sheet of Rose Ltd as at 31 December 1996.
(b) State the circumstances when Rose Ltd could use merger accounting to account for its merger with Crown Ltd.
(c) Discuss your reactions as a shareholder in Rose Ltd to the use of merger accounting.

12 | Statement of Principles

This chapter examines:

- the meaning and significance of a conceptual framework of accounting;
- the UK's Statement of Principles.

The Accounting Standards Board is currently engaged upon a complex and challenging project – the formulation of a so-called Statement of Principles. It is attempting to develop a conceptual framework that will underlie accounting and financial reporting.

A conceptual framework is, in essence a statement of generally accepted theoretical principles that form a framework of reference. It can be argued that it is neither feasible nor logical for an accountant, auditor or financial manager to make a rational choice of accounting procedure without some form of framework of principle or accounting constitution. In short, a conceptual framework is a definitive and written theory of accounting against which practical problems can be objectively and comprehensively tested.

The development of a conceptual framework can be traced back primarily to the USA, when in the 1970s, the Financial Accounting Standards Board (FASB) initiated a detailed research project into the construction of a constitutional framework. At the time of the origination of the project, a conceptual framework was defined by the FASB as 'a constitution, a coherent set of interrelated objectives and fundamentals that can lead to consistent standards and that prescribes the nature, function and limits of financial statements and financial accounting'. Macve visualizes a conceptual framework as providing a structure for 'thinking about what is "better" accounting and financial reporting. It is a theoretical endeavour with the practical aim of clarifying the objectives of financial reporting, and how alternative practices are likely to help achieve those objectives'. He defines a conceptual framework as 'a basic structure for organising one's thinking about what one is trying to do and how to go about it'. It involves 'asking basic questions of the kind: For whom and by whom are accounts to be prepared? For what purposes are they wanted? What kind of accounting reports are suitable for these purposes? . . . and how could accounting practices be improved to make them more suitable?'

In addition to the USA, work was undertaken in Australia and Canada – all with varying degrees of success. The International Accounting Standards Committee has also issued its own version of conceptual framework entitled 'Framework for the Preparation and Presentation of Financial Statements' from which parts of the Statement of Principles have been developed.

Over the last decade there has been an increasing demand for the construction of a conceptual framework in the UK. This pressure has particularly resulted from growing criticism in the UK of the way that accounting standards have been formulated and developed over recent years. Solomons stated that 'accounting standards, where they exist all, have everywhere developed in a rather haphazard manner. "Fire fighting" is the description usually applied to the process'. If standard-setting organizations had produced accounting standards within the context of an explicitly stated conceptual framework, then previously issued standards could have been more logically constructed and more rigorously applied. Instead, there are many instances where standards have been urgently issued in response to a pressing problem rather than being issued in a considered, pre-emptive and proactive manner. Under a conceptual framework inconsistency, ambiguity and disputes should be significantly minimized.

Over the last few years the Accounting Standards Board (ASB) has commenced this conceptual developmental process by producing what it has termed a Statement of Principles. By drawing upon the more worthwhile and relevant parts of a conceptual framework that have already been developed in the international arena, the ASB believes that it will eventually be feasible to produce a reasonably comprehensive, potentially worthwhile and practicably workable constitutional framework for accounting. At the time of writing, the chapters comprising the Statement of Principles are currently in draft form – either as an exposure draft or as a discussion draft. It is expected that all chapters will receive formal authorization in due course.

OBJECTIVES OF THE STATEMENT OF PRINCIPLES

The ASB believes that a Statement of Principles will set out the concepts that underlie the preparation and presentation of financial statements for external users.

The ASB considers that there are a number of purposes of a conceptual framework. The main objectives being to:

- Assist the ASB in the development of future financial statements and in its review of existing statements.
- Help to reduce the number of alternative accounting treatments.
- Assist the preparers and auditors of financial statements.
- Assist the users in interpreting the information contained in financial statements.

CHAPTERS IN THE STATEMENT OF PRINCIPLES

1 Objective of financial statements.
2 Qualitative characteristics of financial information.
3 Elements of financial statements.
4 Recognition.
5 Measurement.
6 Presentation.
7 Principles underlying consolidation procedures.

The Statement of Principles is not an accounting standard and its contents do not override any specific accounting standard. However the ASB will be 'guided' by the Statement of Principles in its preparation and revision of standards. Eventually it is envisaged that the number of cases of conflict between the statement and accounting standards will diminish. The ASB has made it explicitly clear that the Statement of Principles is to apply to the financial statements of all commercial and industrial organizations in both the private and public sector.

Chapter 1: the objective of financial statements

Chapter 1 defines the objective of financial statements as providing information about 'the financial position, performance and financial adaptability of an enterprise that is useful to a wide range of users in making economic decisions'. The chapter stresses that financial statements do not provide all the information that users may need to make economic decisions, primarily because financial statements are predominantly backward-looking as opposed to being futuristic in content and construction. The chapter notes that financial statements show the result of stewardship of management – in other words, provide accountability for management of the assets with which the directors have been entrusted. The chapter emphasizes that to evaluate economic decisions, users will require an assessment of the ability of a firm to generate cash – both in terms of timing and certainty of generation. Users are more effectively able to evaluate the cash flow position of a firm by the provision of a cash flow statement. Information is needed about the performance of an enterprise, in particular concerning its profitability and also about the enterprise's financial position. These requirements will be mainly provided by the profit statement and by the balance sheet – with a supporting statement of movements in reserves. The chapter concludes by emphasizing that the component parts of the financial statements are closely interrelated and no one financial statement is likely to provide all the information necessary to serve the needs of any one user. All the financial statements should be examined together and in their entirety.

Chapter 2: the qualitative characteristics of financial information

The chapter splits the characteristics of financial information into two categories: primary and secondary.

Primary characteristics To be of value to most users, information must be of *relevance* to the decision takers. The chapter defines relevance as information that influences decisions. In particular, information that is both predictive and confirmatory will enhance its value.

Reliability To be useful information must be reliable. Reliability is regarded in terms of being free from material error and bias. It can be depended upon to faithfully represent, in terms of a valid description, the information to which it refers. To faithfully represent transactions, the information should not only show their legal form but also their substance and economic reality. The information must be neutral (free from bias) and prepared on a prudent and complete basis.

Secondary characteristics The secondary characteristics are centred upon *comparability* and *understandability*. Information lacking these qualities would be of limited value to users – irrespective of its relevance or reliability.

Comparability is important in allowing users to compare financial statements over time. A key feature of comparability is centred upon consistency. The measurement display of the financial effects of transactions must be carried out in a consistent way with users being informed of any changes. Information should be presented in such a way that it is readily understandable by users. For their purpose, users are assumed to have reasonable knowledge of business, economic activities and accounting, and possess a willingness to study the information with a reasonable degree of diligence.

Chapter 3: the elements of financial statements

This chapter discusses the definitions of the elements of financial statements. It identifies the essential features that each of these elements should possess. Any item that does not fall within the definition of an element in this section should *not* be included in the financial statements. (It does not follow that because an item falls within these definitions it will necessarily be recognized in the financial statements, as it must additionally meet the recognition criteria explained in the sub-section on chapter 4 below.)

The elements are:

- assets;
- liabilities;
- equity;
- gains and losses;
- contributions from and distributions to owners.

Assets and liabilities Assets are defined as 'rights or other access to future economic benefits controlled by an entity as a result of past transactions or events'. Future economic benefits are viewed in terms of the ability to enjoy and consume goods or services and are evidenced by the prospective receipt of cash. Liabilities are defined 'as an entity's obligations to transfer economic benefits as a result of past transactions or events'.

Equity Equity is the 'ownership interest in the entity: it is the residual amount found by deducting all the liabilities of the entity from all the entity's assets'.

Gains and losses Gains are seen as 'increases in equity, other than those relating to contributions from owners; whereas losses are decreases in equity, other than those relating to distributions to owners'.

Contributions Contributions from owners are defined as 'increases in equity resulting from investments made by owners in their capacity as owners'; whereas 'distributions to owners are decreases in equity resulting from transfers made to owners in their capacity as owners'.

Chapter 4: recognition

This chapter defines the process of incorporating an item into the primary financial statements. It involves depiction of the items in words, by a monetary amount and the inclusion of that amount in the financial statements.

This chapter insists that an item should be recognized in the financial statements *if*:

1 the item meets the definition of an element appearing in the financial statements *and*;
2 there is sufficient evidence that the change in assets or liabilities inherent in the item has occurred *and*;
3 the item can be measured at a monetary amount with sufficient reliability.

The recognition process Recognition is triggered where a past event indicates that there has been a measurable change in assets or liabilities of the entity and the event that triggers recognition must have occurred prior to the balance sheet date.

Chapter 5: measurement in financial statements

This chapter examines the principles underlying the measurement of the elements of the balance sheet and of the components of the statements of financial performance of a reporting entity.

The chapter begins with the premise that:

$$\text{Assets} - \text{liabilities} = \text{equity (capital)}$$

The owners of the equity have a residual claim on the net worth of the business, but this claim has important implications for the balance sheet and the statements of financial performance. The chapter stresses that the method of measuring assets and liabilities will determine the amount at which capital is measured. Chapter 5 states that the capital does not measure the economic wealth of an entity because, in practice, the goodwill inherent in the equity is not fully reflected in the balance sheet and assets are not shown at current economic value.

The chapter is predominantly concerned with the method of valuation of assets. It examines the use of historical cost in financial reporting and contrasts these methods with current value systems. It regards current values as being generally more relevant (although in practice often more subjective than historical costs). It defines historical cost as the actual cost of acquiring an asset and thus it emerges naturally from the recording of assets. Historical cost has the advantage of being widely practised over a long period of time. It is familiar and understandable to most users and preparers of financial statements and is also an administratively cheap valuation method. It is relatively objective and provides a dependable and verifiable method of accounting. The major disadvantage of the historical cost method is that 'it records values at the date of acquisition of the specific assets and, accordingly, historical costs are typically established at dates earlier than that of financial statements'. In times of changing prices historical costs lack the property of comparability.

The chapter refers to three major methods of current values:

1   Entry value accounting – based on the cost of acquiring an asset in current market conditions.
2   Exit values – based largely upon on net realizable values.
3   Values in use – that is predominantly the present value of the net future cash flows that can be obtained by retaining the asset in the business.

In general terms, although current values are probably perceived to be less reliable than historical cost, they have the major advantage of relevance. The chapter accepts that it would be expensive and confusing to provide information based on all these different methods of current value. It suggests a more practical solution might be to use the 'value to the business' principle. This rule values assets at the lower of their replacement cost or recoverable amount.

In its conclusion the chapter presents three possible options:

1   return to historical cost accounting;
2   introducing a full current value system;
3   reducing some of the anomalies that currently exist in historical cost accounting.

The ASB, without being too prescriptive, believes that a voluntary approach based upon 3 above would be the preferred approach.

Chapter 5 was supported by the ASB's Discussion Paper 'The Role of Valuation in Financial Reporting'. The Discussion Paper stresses the defects of current accounting practice under which assets are stated in companies' balance sheets 'as a hybrid mixture of historical cost and unsystematic and illogical modifications of it'. Commenting on this Discussion Paper, David Tweedie, Chairman of the ASB indicated that he could not find the existence of any logic in British balance sheets: 'Any statement which adds together assets at original cost with assets at a range of revaluations made at a range of times must be seriously flawed. The time has come to move to a more credible system'. (For a more detailed discussion on this topic, students are recommended to read this Discussion Paper.)

Chapter 6: presentation of financial information

This chapter analyses the way in which information should be presented in the financial statements. Accounting information should be presented in the form of a structured set of financial statements with supporting notes. The chapter stresses that the 'form of presentation to be adopted in a particular case involves consideration of the appropriate prominence and detail of disclosure in the primary statements themselves, in the notes and, in some cases, in supplementary information'.

Aggregation The contents of financial statements by their very voluminous nature frequently result in the need for such data to be structured, and condensed by being aggregated. The decision as to the degree of aggregation will depend on the extent to which the benefits of disclosing greater detail is offset by the cost of preparing and using more detailed information. An excessive degree of detail can distract many users from utilizing the financial statements to optimal effect.

Structure and articulation The chapter highlights the separate features of classification and articulation in financial statements. Classification of items in financial statements by their nature or function assists in the analytical process. In addition, there is discussion on the merits of further classifying items into reasonably homogeneous groups to assist analysis, e.g. classifying items with similar characteristics.

Financial statements should also articulate (or interrelate) because they reflect aspects of the same transaction or event. In other words, the primary financial statements should be built upon the same foundations, apply the same judgements and the same methods of calculations.

Other areas in this chapter refer to the need to disclose, by *notes*, the accounting polices adopted; stating any significant assumptions and identifying any changes. The notes to the financial statements should 'amplify or explain the items in the primary statements' but reliance must not be placed upon the notes to correct a misrepresentation in the primary statements.

The chapter examines the structure, content and presentation of the *primary accounting statements*, i.e. the statements of financial performance; the profit and loss account and the statement of recognized gains and losses; and the balance sheet and the cash flow statement. In particular the chapter emphasizes the term 'financial adaptability', which is defined as 'the ability of an organization to take effective action to alter the amounts and timing of cash flows so that it can respond to unexpected needs or opportunities'. It notes that the various primary financial statements can help in assessing the financial adaptability of an organization.

Chapter 7: the reporting entity

This chapter predominantly expounds the general principles underlying the consolidation procedures in group accounting. The chapter discusses the differing types of investments that a company can have. In particular it examines investments in subsidiaries, associated undertakings and joint ventures. The methods of accounting for subsidiary and associate undertakings in the consolidated accounts are discussed. This includes features of and the respective use of acquisition, merger and equity accounting.

CONCLUSION

In countries around the world the formulation of a conceptual framework of accounting has caused a number of significant challenges and problems. Many critics of a conceptual framework argue that it is too theoretical, too academic and too abstract to be of meaningful and practical use. As the FASB discovered in the USA, many of the difficulties of formulation are centred more on politics rather than accounting. However, these particular difficulties should not deter the ASB in its quest for a UK framework. The statement is long overdue and, ultimately the longer-term benefits for accounting and the accounting standards setters should outweigh any criticism. When the ASB finally completes its work on the Statement of Principles it should provide a welcome and useful contribution to accounting.

QUESTIONS

1   What do you understand by the term 'a conceptual framework of accounting'?
2   Do you believe accounting will benefit or suffer from the introduction of a conceptual framework of accounting?
3   What is the Statement of Principles?
    What do you consider to be its strengths and weaknesses?
4   What are the salient features of each chapter of the Statement of Principles?
5   Discuss to what extent you believe that the Statement of Principles is too abstract, too theoretical and of little relevance to practical accounting.

FURTHER READING

Accounting Standards Board, *Statement of Principles*, 1991.

Accounting Standards Board, *Discussion Paper: The Role of Valuation in Financial Reporting*, 1993.

FASB – definition of conceptual framework from its USA conceptual framework programme, 1976.

Macve, R., *Conceptual Framework of Accounting and Reporting: The Possibilities of an Agreed Structure*, ICAEW, 1981.

Solomons, David, *Guidelines for Financial Reporting Standards*, ICAEW, 1989.

13 | International Influences on Company Reporting

This chapter examines:

- differences in international accounting practices;
- classification and harmonization of accounting systems.

Since the 1980s a particularly noticeable influence on many companies has been the internationalization of business activity. An increasing number of businesses are operating in a global trading environment. Many companies' customers are increasingly becoming located in other countries. Their supply of raw materials, labour and capital is frequently accessed and obtained in the international arena. Many companies are operating and competing in global markets either directly as a trading outlet or indirectly through the use of subsidiary undertakings. There are numerous and significant practical and conceptual accounting differences that provide a potential source of difficulties in analysing and commenting upon the financial statements of companies operating in different countries throughout the world.

These difficulties are caused by a number of differences that are based on legal, historic, cultural and organizational reasons. These accounting differences between companies in different countries can be extremely significant and unless the nature and basis of these differences are understood, the value of the information that can be extracted from these financial statements produced in different countries will be extremely limited. The analyst must always bear in mind the socio-economic and legal differences that exist in each country before commenting upon any company reporting information.

CLASSIFICATION OF ACCOUNTING SYSTEMS

There are a number of complex and interwoven factors that have been significant in influencing and determining accounting practices in European countries over the centuries. The major influencing factors are predominantly based upon:

- The nature of each country's legal system.
- The major types of businesses, shareholders, and the providers of corporate finance.
- The influence of taxation systems.
- The impact of the accounting profession in each country.
- Miscellaneous factors.

Legal systems

A significant determinant and influence in corporate reporting practice is the prevailing legal system in each country. Most of Europe's legal structures can be broadly classified into those systems based either on Common Law or the more highly codified Roman Law. Countries that have a Common Law system have only strictly limited amounts of codified law. In countries such as the UK and Ireland the prevailing legal influence is that of the Common Law. Subsequently, the Common Law is interpreted by the Courts to produce the body of case law which has affected the amount of accounting regulation that is contained within company law. Common Law systems have tended to be adopted around the world where England has had historically a large degree of political and economic influence. For example the common law system is adopted, in varying degrees, by such countries as Australia, India, many Far Eastern countries, parts of the USA and Canada. From a legal perspective and in general terms, countries that follow a case law basis have traditionally had a legal system that has neither been too specific, nor too precise nor overburdensome as to the legal regulation of accounting practices and procedures.

In contrast, the legal systems of many other countries such as France, Germany, Spain, Italy and, to a certain extent, Japan are predominantly based upon the more codified, highly structured and formalized principles of Roman Law. Accordingly, a considerable amount of company law and accounting practice has been prescribed by Statute as opposed to being heavily influenced by the accounting profession. This approach has led some countries to develop and legally establish national accounting plans within their legislative framework. For example, France and Spain have both established national accounting plans, whose content has been largely defined, implemented and controlled by the State.

Business type

Another factor influencing accounting systems is the nature of the prevailing types of businesses operating in each country. These differences are also compounded by the nature of the providers of corporate finance. In countries where there is a predominance of relatively small family-dominated companies, such as in France and Italy, the need for comprehensive and publicly available accounting statements is considerably reduced – as 'external' pressure from independent shareholders is lacking.

Usually shareholders in these small family-based companies tend to be involved in a managerial and operational capacity and therefore have access to virtually all the accounting dominated information that they need.

In Germany a substantial proportion of companies' equity is owned, either directly or indirectly by banking and similar-type lending institutions. In Germany over 60 per cent of the equity of listed companies is held in various forms by banking institutions. In a similar manner to small family-dominated companies, these investing institutions (by virtue of their privileged Boardroom position that a large shareholding usually permits) can relatively easily obtain access to company information which would otherwise have been denied to them. In contrast, in countries such as the UK and Ireland, the ownership of publicly listed companies is considerably more diverse and extensive. Accordingly, investors have relatively smaller shareholdings and have traditionally required detailed accounting statements that have been verified by independent auditors. In general terms, there is tendency for companies in countries that have a widespread dispersion of shareholdings, not to allow access to 'privileged' or 'inside' information. The emphasis in these countries is to produce accounts that are more orientated at providing comprehensive and extensive disclosure of company information. In turn, this information will be increasingly subjected to more onerous audit-driven pressure to provide a 'true and fair' audit opinion to assist in meeting external shareholder pressure.

There are also some countries that are historically associated with more active equity markets. The UK, Ireland and, to a lesser extent, the Netherlands produce financial statements that are predominantly orientated at providing an unbiased view of the company's financial position and which are aimed particularly at the external shareholders. Countries such as France, Germany, Spain and Italy have, in relative terms, rather limited external shareholder involvement. In these latter instances the accounting emphasis tends to be centred upon the protection of the interests of creditors in preference to those of the company's shareholders. In accounting terms, the practical outcome has led to concise financial statements and less comprehensive disclosure provisions. This creditor emphasis has also led to the production of accounting statements that tend to be extremely conservative in nature and in countries such as Germany, the legal interests of creditors are deemed paramount.

Taxation

In Germany, France, Italy and Spain the financial statements tend to be used far more explicitly for taxation computations than, for example, companies in the UK or USA. In general terms, in most of continental Europe, an expense that is to be tax-deductible must also appear in the financial statements. The close relationship between the 'taxable' profit and the accounting profit is particularly emphasized in France, Germany and Italy. However in the UK and USA, a company's tax computations are usually based on adjusted earnings figures that will be substantially different from the earnings figures (based on financial accounting techniques) appearing in the profit and loss account. Although companies in the UK have considerable freedom in choosing the method of depreciation in their own accounts, the taxation authorities have established strict rules on the amount of depreciation (in the form of capital allowances) that may be offset against taxation. The practical effect is that many companies in continental Europe will be tempted to minimize their tax liabilities by, for example overproviding for depreciation in the profit and loss account. The overall result can provide a relatively overconservative corporate profit figure.

Accounting profession

In most continental European countries (that follow Roman Law principles), the outlook of the accounting profession in general, and that of auditors in particular, is to provide financial statements that are largely constructed with the sole purpose of being 'legalistically correct'. In these circumstances the auditors will not necessarily concern themselves with the strict reporting upon the truth and fairness or commercial significance of the accounts. The Statutory Code in each of these countries normally expects that the primary responsibility of the external auditors will be to ensure that the management's accounting figures are accurate to the extent that they are mathematically plausible and conform legalistically. With legal systems that are based upon Common Law principles, there is less legal exposition and regulation in respect of accounting requirements and more emphasis on the individual accountant's personal judgement. Although in countries such as the UK and the USA, auditors must ensure that companies comply with company legislation, their responsibilities and judgements are considerably deeper and wider. In countries based upon Common Law, auditors usually have a duty to report upon the existence of 'truth and fairness' in the financial statements. In ascertaining the existence of a 'true and fair view' the auditors will usually be expected to ensure that the financial statements conform to generally accepted accounting principles and standards. The concept of 'truth and fairness' in financial statements, by virtue of the EU Eighth Directive, has gradually filtered into most European countries' legislation. In many countries the concept of 'truth and fairness' is still frequently interpreted as largely observing compliance with Statute. Since these countries lack a detailed and extensive legal framework for accounting statements, the professional accounting bodies have traditionally tended to play a significant role in the formulation, implementation and monitoring of accounting standards and practice. Traditionally in the UK, the accounting profession has been strong and relatively powerful. This strength has led the UK accountancy bodies to play a significant role in developing accounting regulation. In many other countries the accounting profession is much smaller, weaker and consequently their role has been superseded by statutorily imposed requirements.

Miscellaneous influences

There are political and economic factors that can influence reporting practice. Nobes and Parker (see their book *Comparative International Accounting* for further information) classify a number of these factors as being accidents of history (p. 20). For example, the USA has established Securities and Exchange Acts following the economic and stock market turmoil of the 1920s and 1930s. These Acts implemented greater statutory disclosure provisions and monitoring of accounting standards. Parts of the Japanese commercial code also reflect Germanic influence as a result of the effects of war with Prussia in the early part of the twentieth century. And parts of the French legislative based accounting plan was influenced by German occupation during the Second World War.

OTHER CLASSIFICATIONS

In 1967 Mueller (and Choi and Mueller, 1984) classified international accounting systems into four major categories:

1 *The macroeconomic influence of accounting:* Under this category accounting is regarded as an integral component of national economic policies. Countries with a high degree of State dominated economic control would be included – such as Sweden.
2 *Microeconomic approach:* A microeconomic approach is more prevalent where countries have a high proportion of small privately-dominated or family-led businesses. Frequently the 'economic rules' have led to the development of detailed and quite complex accounting models and rules (such as in the Netherlands).
3 *Accounting as independent discipline:* In countries such as the UK, Ireland and USA accounting has historically been perceived as a discipline that is separate from the State. Accounting regulation, rules and practices have been largely in the hands of the accounting profession. As a generalization, the State has tended to delegate its powers concerning accounting regulation to accountants.
4 *Uniform accounting systems:* Uniform accounting systems have developed where countries have maintained a high degree of control and direction of business activity. A uniform system is usually typified by the State imposing comprehensive business and accounting plans. Frequently the State requires the adoption of detailed and highly structured national accounting plans such as in France or Spain.

HARMONIZATION

In 1973 the International Accounting Standards Committee was formed by representatives of the world's accountancy profession. Its major objective was to implement more commonly acceptable accounting standards and to achieve greater compatibility of financial statements on a world-wide basis. Since its formation it has issued over 30 International Accounting Standards (IASs).

From the original ten country members in 1973, the Committee has now grown to over 100 members. Although the IASC has no specific legal or accounting authority, it attempts to gain respect and acceptance by working with the professional accounting bodies in each of the member countries. Many of the professional accounting bodies in each country will frequently ensure that their own accounting standards and regulations encompass (or at least ensure that they do not conflict with) the pronouncements of the IASC.

Since the IASC pronouncements are issued on a world-wide applicability basis the content and extent of its IASs is usually extremely wide ranging and often allows a considerable variety of accounting practice. In fact, the wide ranging nature of the IASs is frequently perceived as a serious shortcoming of the IASC's work. The acute difficulties of applying specific and restrictive accounting regulation on a global basis are obvious – there are simply too many differences in countries' legal, economic, social and cultural constructs. To have any realistic chance of at least some national recognition the IASs need to be formulated in a rather generalized and far-reaching manner.

In some instances the IASC pronouncements are adopted by industrially/ commercially developing countries who have not yet formulated their own comprehensive accounting regulatory framework.

From a European perspective, the European Union has an explicit and strongly-supported objective of attempting to obtain a 'unified business environment' throughout Europe. The European Union has always believed that to achieve greater compatibility, the degree of variation permissible in the accounting practice of Member States must be limited by implementing a detailed and prescriptive approach. To help to accomplish its policy, the EU has issued a number of directives concerning specific accounting issues that Member States must adopt into their own legislation. In particular, the Fourth Directive has attempted to standardize the format and content of company financial statements throughout Europe. The Seventh Directive was introduced to regulate the methods and procedures involved in the consolidation of accounting statements.

ANALYTICAL PERSPECTIVE

A user of financial statements must carefully bear in mind the nature of international differences in accounting practices and policies.

When companies are being compared in different countries, it is of crucial importance that differences between countries especially as regards their cultural, economic, legal, social and historical influences must be understood. For example, there is little value in comparing a UK company's balance sheet with a German company's balance sheet. UK companies can periodically revalue their fixed assets to current value – whereas Germans companies are legally prohibited from revaluing fixed assets and must show these assets at their historical cost. Also there can be a substantial difference in earnings when a USA-based company is compared to a UK company as regards topics such as deferred taxation and goodwill (e.g. the UK currently insists on a partial provision method of deferred tax whereas in the USA the more extensive comprehensive method is used; in the USA the immediate write-off method of goodwill is not acceptable).

There are many other major differences and readers wishing to gain a deeper understanding of international differences are advised to consult the Further Reading listed at the end of this chapter.

UK/USA COMPANIES

The differences between UK and USA accounting policies are evident in the case of UK companies who wish their shares to be listed on USA stock exchanges. UK companies must prepare a Reconciliation Statement which explains accounting differences between the two countries.

An example of this reconciliation is given in example table 13.1.

EXAMPLE TABLE 13.1   EXTRACT FROM CABLE AND WIRELESS PLC
RECONCILIATION STATEMENT

	1996 US$m	1996 £m	1995 Restated £m
Net income as reported under UK GAAP	931	607	252
US GAAP adjustments:			
Amortisation of goodwill	(31)	(20)	(17)
Goodwill written off in respect of sale of subsidiary undertakings	5	3	21
Capitalisation of interest	3	2	1
Deferred tax – full provision	(47)	(31)	(86)
– tax effect of other US GAAP reconciling items	11	7	(4)
Pension costs	(10)	(7)	13
Restructuring costs	(33)	(21)	22
Other	5	3	(4)
Minority interests	5	3	10
Net income under US GAAP	839	546	208
Earnings per share under US GAAP	$0.37	24.2p	9.4p
Earnings per ADR* under US GAAP	$1.11	72.6p	28.2p

The effect on shareholders' equity of the differences between UK GAAP and
US GAAP is as follows:

	1996 US$m	1996 £m	1995 Restated £m
Shareholders' equity as reported under UK GAAP	5,003	3,259	3,339
US GAAP adjustments:			
Goodwill	1,477	962	409
Capitalisation of interest	310	202	200
Deferred tax – full provision	(1,210)	(788)	(755)
– tax effect of other US GAAP reconciling items	(165)	(108)	(86)
Proposed final dividend	237	154	137
Pension costs	(32)	(21)	(15)
Restructuring costs	7	5	22
Unrealised gains on equity securities	81	53	39
Other	(28)	(18)	(15)
Minority interest	176	115	92
Shareholders' equity under US GAAP	5,856	3,815	3,367

An exchange rate of US$ 1.5348 has been used to translate £ to US$. Such translations are for convenience only and should not be construed as representations that the £ amounts have been converted into US$ at that or any other rate.
* Computed on the basis that one American Depositary Receipt (ADR) represents three ordinary shares.

**ADDITIONAL INFORMATION FOR
US INVESTORS**

US listing

The Company's ordinary shares are listed on the New York Stock Exchange in the form of American Depositary Receipts (ADRs) and traded under the symbol CWP. Each ADR represents three ordinary shares. The ADR programme is administered on behalf of the Company by The Bank of New York and enquiries relating to the ADRs and dividend payments should be addressed to The Bank of New York, American Depositary Receipts, 22nd Floor West, 101 Barclay Street, New York, NY 10286, USA (Telephone 212-815-2204, Fax 212-571-3050, Telex 62763).

Other enquiries regarding the Company should be addressed to T E McDonnell, Vice President Investor Relations, 35th Floor, 777 Third Avenue, New York, NY 10017, USA.

The Company is subject to the regulations of the Securities and Exchange Commission as they apply to foreign companies and will file its annual report on Form 20-F and other information as required on or before 30 September 1996. When filed, a copy of the Form 20-F may be obtained from T E McDonnell, Vice President Investor Relations, at the address above.

Dividends to ADR holders

Payment of the dividend to ADR holders will be made by The Bank of New York, on 13 September 1996 to holders of record on 11 June 1996. The ADRs are expected to trade ex dividend on the New York Stock Exchange from 7 June 1996.

The current income tax convention between the UK and the US includes provisions which entitle qualifying US resident ADR holders to a refund of the UK tax credit attaching to the dividend. On payment of such dividend a 15% withholding tax is deducted from the total of the dividend and the related tax credit. This withholding tax will normally be eligible for credit against US Federal income taxes by filing Form 116 'Computation of Foreign Tax Credit' with the Federal income tax return. For ADR holders who benefit from these arrangements, the recommended final dividend of 6.92 pence per ordinary share becomes 22.06 pence per ADR. This makes a total dividend for the year of 31.88 pence per ADR.

The actual rate of exchange used in determining the dollar payment to ADR holders will be the exchange rate on 2 September 1996.

Basis of preparation

The Group prepares its consolidated accounts in accordance with generally accepted accounting principles (GAAP) in the United Kingdom which differ in certain material respects from US GAAP. The significant differences relate principally to the following items and the adjustments necessary to restate net income and shareholders' equity in accordance with US GAAP are shown below.

a) Goodwill

Under UK GAAP goodwill arising on acquisition is eliminated directly against reserves. Amounts are transferred from reserves and charged through the profit and loss account when the related investments are sold or written down as a result of permanent diminutions in value. Under US GAAP goodwill is capitalised and amortised by charges against income over the period, not to exceed 40 years, over which the benefit arises. For US GAAP goodwill has been amortised by the Group over periods varying between 5 and 40 years.

Under UK GAAP the profit or loss on the disposal of all or part of a previously acquired business is calculated after taking account of the gross amount of any goodwill previously eliminated directly against reserves. Under US GAAP an adjustment to profit or loss on disposal is required in respect of goodwill previously amortised.

b) Capitalisation of interest

Under UK GAAP the capitalisation of interest is not required, but the Group does capitalise interest, net of tax, incurred in relation to separately identifiable major capital projects. US GAAP requires that gross interest cost should be capitalised on all qualifying assets during the time required to prepare them for their intended use.

c) Deferred tax

Under UK GAAP provision is made for deferred taxation only when there is a reasonable probability that the liability will arise in the foreseeable future. US GAAP requires full provision for deferred income taxes under the liability method on all temporary differences and, if required, a valuation allowance is established to reduce gross deferred tax assets to the amount which is more likely than not to be realised.

d) Marketable securities

Under UK GAAP investments in marketable securities are recorded at historic cost less provision for permanent diminutions in value. Under US GAAP investments classified as available for sale are reported at fair value, with unrealised gains or losses reported as a separate component of shareholders' equity.

e) Pension costs

Under UK GAAP the expected cost of pensions is charged to the profit and loss account so as to spread the cost of pensions over the expected service lives of employees. Surpluses arising from actuarial valuations are similarly spread. Under US GAAP costs and surpluses are similarly spread but based on prescribed actuarial assumptions, which differ in certain respects from those used for UK GAAP.

f) Restructuring costs

Under UK GAAP restructuring costs shown as exceptional items are charged to the profit and loss account in full irrespective of whether they have been agreed or incurred. Under US GAAP certain of these costs are only charged to the profit and loss account when certain specific criteria have been met.

g) Ordinary dividends

Under UK GAAP dividends proposed after the end of an accounting period in respect of that accounting period are deducted in arriving at retained earnings for that period. Under US GAAP such dividends are not deducted until formally approved.

h) Earnings per ordinary share

Under UK GAAP earnings per share are based on profit for the financial year and computed using the weighted average number of ordinary shares in issue during the year. Under US GAAP earnings per share are based on net income, and computed using the weighted average number of ordinary shares in issue and ordinary share equivalents outstanding during each year.

QUESTIONS

1 Discuss the major factors that have influenced international company reporting practices.
2 Explain why the analyst needs to be aware of international differences in company financial statements.
3 Discuss the four categories that Mueller identifies in classifying financial statements.
4 Do you believe that European countries in particular should attempt to standardize or harmonize their financial statements?
5 'Legal, cultural, economic, and historical accounting differences are simply too great to allow any meaningful analytical comparisons between countries'. Discuss to what extent you agree with this statement.

FURTHER READING

Comparative International Accounting, Nobes, C. and Parker, R. 1996, Prentice Hall.
International Accounting, Choi, D. S. and Mueller, G., 1992, Prentice Hall.

14 | Conclusion

The analysis of company financial statements must not be perceived as an exact science. An enormous amount of the information contained within a set of financial statements must be interpreted with a great deal of caution and an open and critical frame of mind.

It is important to appreciate that the financial statements are not, as many people believe, a precise, definite and totally objective portrait of the company's performance and affairs. In the preparation of the financial statements the accountant has to undertake a considerable number of value judgements and exercise a considerable degree of discretion on a number of accounting policies and practices. The accounting standards, legislation and the professional accounting techniques, ethics and practices will direct and guide the accountant (quite considerably in some areas) but in other instances judgement and discretion are needed.

The non-accountant must be able to realize the direction that the accountant has taken but he or she does not always have to follow along the same accounting path. At all times the user of financial statements must have an open, cautious and independent frame of mind. In many instances the reader wants additional or supporting information – but frequently published financial statements are too limited, too generalized and too often fail to portray, what many people would recognize, as some reasonable form of financial reality. The financial statements can be compared to that of a painting – perhaps a Van Gogh impressionist scene. The accountant – acting as the painter – reflects his/her own perceptions of reality and encapsulates these perceptions of the company's performance and affairs in the eventual form of the published financial statements. The accountant using experience, training and professional knowledge can paint a picture of a company's affairs that can quite easily be understood or interpreted in a different light by others. Although financial statements can reflect the nature, extent and intentions of accounting standards and legislation, there can be sizeable differences of opinion over interpretation as to whether the financial statements do in fact portray reality – in the eyes of the reader. But most certainly published financial statements are not to be perceived as a John Constable 'photographic' painting, i.e. financial statements are certainly neither precise nor definitive and offer considerable scope for a variety of interpretations.

Vigilance, caution and scepticism are the watch words for successful analysis of company financial statements.

Index